North-East Identities and Scottish Schooling

The Elphinstone Institute

Occasional Publications 4

General Editor – Ian Russell

Elphinstone Institute Occasional Publications
is a peer-reviewed series of scholarly works in ethnology and folklore.
The Elphinstone Institute at the University of Aberdeen was established in 1995
to study, conserve, and promote the culture of North-East and Northern Scotland.

North-East Identities and Scottish Schooling

The Relationship of the Scottish Educational System to the Culture of the North-East of Scotland

edited by David Northcroft

The Elphinstone Institute
University of Aberdeen
2005

ISBN 0-9545682-2-2

Typesetting and cover design by Malcolm Reavell. malcolmreavell@macmail.com

Printed by Webmart Ltd, 13-15 Wedgewood Road, Bicester, OX26 4UL

First published in 2005 by
The Elphinstone Institute
University of Aberdeen
24 High Street
Aberdeen AB24 3EB
United Kingdom

Cover photographs

Front cover: Children outside their School at Echt, Aberdeenshire, at the turn of the nineteenth/twentieth century.
Photograph from David Northcroft Collection

Back cover: Ballogie School, 1920s.
Photograph from Mary Campbell, Dingwall, whose mother is the girl standing on the extreme right.

Contents

Preface

In September 2000, the Elphinstone Institute of the University of Aberdeen sponsored a one-day conference on the topic of 'Local Schools and National Schooling'. It is from this event that the present publication has sprung. A modified version of seven of the papers which were presented then are reproduced here, alongside four others. Each of the eleven pieces was generated by an open invitation which was issued to all of the Scottish institutions recognised as having an interest in the field of Scottish history, education, and social or cultural study. The conference was organised and directed by the Director of the Institute, Dr Ian Russell, and by Dr David Northcroft, who has both edited and contributed to *North-East Identities and Scottish Schooling.*

More generally, the present work has grown out of the defining interests of the Elphinstone Institute, which 'exists to study, record and promote the cultural traditions and language of communities in the North of Scotland and, in particular, of the North-East '. Its appearance is a response to the widely accepted recognition that the distinctive, and within the United Kingdom, distinct Scottish education system has developed its own powerful structures and traditions, and that these have, historically, been regarded as receiving their fullest expression in the North-East . And that, moreover, because, outwith the city of Aberdeen, private institutions have played only a marginal role in the education of its people, the national public school system provides a strong focal point for a consideration of the wider social and cultural context in which the people of the North-East have lived.

It is hoped that 'education' will establish itself as a continuing institutional concern. To this end, the editor of this volume, as Research Associate of the Elphinstone Institute, is currently initiating an extensive oral history programme. The intention is to build up a representative archive of audio-recordings, each to be lodged with its own transcript. Interviewees are being chosen in order to offer a permanent record of a wide range of experiences that will cover a number of backgrounds, settings, and occupational outcomes. A fuller note on the procedures involved is appended to the group of transcripts, which appear as Appendixes 1 and 2. It is important, however, to use this opportunity to record deep gratitude to all of the individuals who have so willingly and trustingly submitted themselves to what has usually turned out to be a two-hour session, most often imposed upon them in their own homes and accompanied by their own generous hospitality – another North-East tradition at work. Any reader who wants to discuss this work, or to offer suggestions, is cordially invited to do so, either through the Elphinstone Institute or to David Northcroft direct (at 01569 730621 or david.northcroft@virgin.net).

For the purposes of this work, the 'North-East' has been interpreted as the area covered by the old counties of Aberdeenshire, Banffshire, Moray, and Kincardine – the former Grampian Region. The city of Aberdeen has not, however, been included within the range of this particular study: its distinctly urban character has yielded a different and very interesting history, one which merits a treatment all of its own. While the education of Aberdeen itself will certainly be a significant part of the Institute's work in this field, *North-East Identities and Scottish Schooling* concentrates upon the rural hinterland and small burghs of the region.

A second important aspect of the total educational experience of the North-East which has, likewise, been under-served in this work is that of the female. Here, we are aware that not one of the formal contributors is a woman. As explained, the invitations to submit were issued to all potentially interested parties throughout the country. It is to be hoped that the failure to attract any female representation is not evidence of another, and notorious, Scottish tradition at work. As with the city, this is a topic that also merits its own study.

Many individuals – and of both sexes – have helped me, not only in the preparation of this specific work, but in my researches into the subject of North-East education, in all its breadth, frustrations, and glory. To all of them, I am most grateful. Finally, the support and encouragement of the School of Education at the University is warmly acknowledged.

David Northcroft

Postscript
Since his unforgettable address to the conference 'Local Schools and National Schooling' in September 2000, Robbie Robertson has, most grievously, died. It is hoped that the inclusion in this publication of the paper that he gave that day will serve to remind us all of what his vivid presence has meant to Scottish education. Wide-ranging, audacious, and stimulatingly expressed, 'The Smokestacks Curriculum and the Coming Lightning' is characteristic of a brilliant and independent spirit who will be much missed.

Chapter One

Introduction: Local Schools and National Schooling

David Northcroft

It is a system of which Scotland has just reason to be proud. Of silver and gold she has ever possessed but a trifling share; nor has nature bestowed upon her the warmth of unclouded sun and the rich produce of a luxuriant soil. But the son of the most humble peasant in our native land has it in his power to approach the fountain of learning and to drink unmolested from its pure and invigorating and ennobling stream

> 'Remarks on Parochial Education' *Aberdeen Magazine* (1832), II, 395-406.

Sir Henry Craik, once head of our Education Department, said Scotland was the best educated country in the world and the North-East counties were the best educated counties in it

> Elsie S. Rae, *A Waff o' Win fae Bennachie,* p. 71.

An old gentleman describing his parish schoolmaster, said, 'aa he taught me was the weight o the tawse'.

> John R Allan, 'The Lad o Pairts', *North-East Lowlands of Scotland,* pp. 228-46.

Scotland Spirals Down to Blissful Ignorance

> (Headline for article on current academic standards), Norman Harper, *Press and Journal,* 28 July 1999.

When the proposal to gather together papers on the historical and cultural significance of school education in the North-East was first made, potential contributors were offered the above four quotations as their stimulus. The first of them sets the tone for the rest, indeed for the topic as a whole. There, in full blown early nineteenth-century rhetoric, is the *Aberdeen Magazine's* own declaration of allegiance to what by then had become a defining national belief.

Its essence lies in the self-consciously proud declaration that, here, in this poor and naturally disfavoured Scotland, the common people are heirs to the riches of a celebrated educational tradition. The article, to which these lines act as the preface, does proceed to give some evidence for the claim that the country's education is heroically democratic in nature. Long before its publication, the Scotch had enjoyed the benefits of a legally binding system of school education. From the little school which, by Act of the old Scottish Parliament, stood at the heart of every one of the country's 940 parishes, any young lad might be able, given the wit and the will, to study his way up to university entrance and on into the professions which lay beyond. At the time of the *Magazine's* writing, this arrangement constituted, as Robert Anderson comments in his piece, an unusually well established and systematic provision. Education in the northern country could be considered truly public – and certainly well in advance of anything that the more haphazard and laissez-faire English were getting up to.

It is, however, the language in which these historical truths are set out that really carries the message. The prose assails us with patterns of national contrast, which are hung with the images of romantic celebration. The rigours of the northern landscape and of its scarifying climate, the opposition of a simple purity of mind to the easier wealth that is to be picked up in a more southerly clime, the linking together of homespun peasants and the ennoblement bestowed by the native education – each of these conceits is orchestrated to beat the patriotic drum. The social facts of a legally founded system of parish and of burgh schools are, in this way, hammered out into the resounding harmonies of binding, epic achievement.

This is, of course, the language of myth. To say that is certainly not to discount it for, as Anderson says, 'myth' is not so much 'reality's' alternative, as an idealized way of representing it. The simplified drama of a nineteenth-century journalist's rhetoric is designed to evoke, once more, the rightful aspirations of a shared and inherited tradition.

This justification does, however, raise a number of issues, especially for a myth which takes 'democracy' to be its defining power. The most immediate of these are to do with ownership – who controls its version of events, whose interests does its continued influence serve, how representative is the image it seeks to portray of actual situations and the people who inhabit them?

As Anderson goes on to explain, a national myth, broadly considered, may serve two types of social function – and he finds evidence for both of them as being at work in the way in which, down the ages, Scotland has sought to project its education. One is to bind the people together into a system of defining belief; the second is to provide the assumptions that will direct their further development. In the nineteenth century, portrayals such as the *Aberdeen Magazine's* image of the humble lad o' parts served, at a time of furious economic expansion and industrialisation, to summon up a still united pride in the democratic strengths of the old parish school ways. If this had an 'integrative' intention, it also laid the basis for a future that would be guided by values such as educational opportunity and academic achievement, and a continued faith in the particular forms these had taken within the Scottish structure of local schools, of lads o' pairts and hard, paternalistic dominies.

The extent to which such a 'crystallisation of reality' may have a positive effect upon the educational future depends upon the nature of the relationship between the situation it claims to represent and the attitudes which are embedded within its form of expression. The crucial test here is, firstly, the extent to which, as the prevailing social and economic circumstances change, it is open to development. And, secondly, its capacity to serve the needs of the ever wider range of interests which such a process will engender.

Here, it should be noted that the *Aberdeen Magazine's* account rests upon the patriotic power of a representation of Scotland in terms of rugged landscapes and humble peasant lads; it derives from a society that was predominately rural and where its people may be assumed to inhabit small agrarian communities which are ordered into the accepted hierarchy of laird-kirk-artisan-farm labourer. In such a stable setting, the cause of democratic advancement could be seen to be satisfied by the prospect of the occasional talented and commendably industrious lad being enabled to study the classics at his village school and thus to ascend a 'ladder of opportunity' (Anderson's 'competitive individualism') that would – and reassuringly, perhaps – for the majority, be always too steep to scale.

Yet, at that very 1832 date, a parliamentary Reform Act was beginning to open up the franchise, and a fellow Aberdeen journal, the *Northern Iris*, was already wondering at the speed of an economic advancement that had seen the city visibly become a modern part of a nation which was now making startling economic progress: 'Poor beggarly Scotland', it trumpeted, 'is become a rich and wealthy nation and "Sawney the Scot" is become a gentleman'.[1] In such a world of flux, how helpful would the *Magazine's* version of the national education prove to be? Would its ritualistic type-casting of Scottish society prove to be both sufficiently durable and flexible to ensure that the further progress would be guided by an impulse that, historically located though it might be, would indeed show itself to be genuinely and expansively democratic? Or would it, rather, serve only to validate practices that sought to perpetuate interests which would increasingly prove to be not so much rooted as bogged down in the pieties of a backward-looking society whose myths, as a consequence, would now lose the right to express anything but nostalgia, evasion and an introspective conservatism?

These are questions which were particularly important to the North-East . An intensively agricultural area of straths and howes, whose lowland plains stretch up towards Scotland's greatest mountain range, its landscape could be described as quintessentially Scottish.[2] And, in education, down the generations which followed the *Aberdeen Magazine's* evocation, a number of developments, such as the Dick and Milne Bequests,[3] combined with an increasingly effective agrarian revolution to substantiate the region's position as the heartland of the Scottish democratic ideal. By the end of the century, the counties of Aberdeenshire, Banffshire, Moray, and Kincardine could portray themselves as a tidy, but testingly hard landscape of hard working farm communities where the parish schools and thriving burgh centres were manned by well equipped dominies who, year on year, would send a talented local hero or two to test his mettle against the academic champions of other like communities in the annual University Bursary competitions at King's and at Marischal Colleges.

So closely did the North-East come to identify itself with the national system that one hundred years after the *Aberdeen Magazine's* pronouncements, Elsie Rae could reiterate the by now familiar boast that the North-East counties constituted the best educated region, in the best educated country, in the whole world. But what exactly could 'well educated' mean when applied to a whole region, which had now come to house several hundred thousand assorted souls, where every adult now had the vote and where the young could expect to enter a range of occupations and life experiences infinitely more diverse and complex than the standard parochial fates of the 1830s? In her *A Waff o' Win' fae Bennachie*, she makes it clear that the North-East's reputation has sprung from the ability of its schools to apply the local values of hard work, self-discipline and getting on in life to the production of star pupils able to hold their own in any company, however Scottish, British or Imperial that might be. But in succeeding in this way, the schools of the North-East were acting as the foremost exponents of a national tradition which, while it favoured the academic prowess of the selected few, sought to surround all pupils with an unrelenting ethos of hard work, of stern discipline, and of well drilled basic subject matter. The sardonic comment of John R. Allan's 'old man' is but a glimpse of the kind of disenchantment which, in the later era of compulsory education, such a regime could elicit among the masses who were never going to win a ten guinea award in the annual Bursary Competition or pass the Highers that would, in later life, earn them the right to go dark-suited to their work. The myth's reverence for past exploits could, moreover, induce a sense of perpetual decline, of which Norman Harper's recently headlined observations are but a latest manifestation.

This is the kind of dissent, or invidious disappointment, which any authoritarian school regime could expect to provoke. For the North-East, however, the commanding presence of the ubiquitous local school could be felt to weigh down upon its young with a specially heavy oppressiveness. John R. Allan's use of his old man witness is, in his *North-East Lowlands*, part of a lengthy chapter on the 'Lad o Pairts'. In it, he describes the almost stock breeding efficiency with which the region's teachers have gone about the task of rearing an educated product that, like the prime beef of the Aberdeen Angus, is marketable all over the world. This is, as he makes clear, an ambivalent tribute. His is a region which has prided itself upon the competitive excellence of all its little schools, but which has also nurtured a culture and, above all, a Doric tongue whose being lay in the very soil of local custom and rural attitude from which the Scottish Education Department run system was attempting, in the name of an exportable academic excellence, to educate its young away.

4

As a wider investigation among the texts which are cited in David Northcroft's *Readings in North-East Education,* would demonstrate, behind the official version of lads o' pairts, of selfless dominies and the parish skweel, there has always existed a more complex and, at times, painful story: for some there is no doubt that 'getting on' was a real and grateful prospect, but there are many others who can point to a schooling that was narrow, over-regimented, cruelly policed by the tawse, neglectful of the less academically inclined and repressively antagonistic towards their home culture. The amount of selective glorification which has been invested in publications such as Elsie Rae's *Waff* and the county branch of the Educational Institute of Scotland's *Schools and Schoolmasters of Banffshire,* has provoked a latter day scepticism of sufficient force to sting the current holder of the position of the Queen's Historian in Scotland, Professor Christopher Smout, into his rasping exposure of the native education tradition as the legalized means of 'trying to smash facts into children'.[4]

But these are words which merely replace one set of stylised beliefs with another – an anti-myth for the commonly cherished one. Between the polarisation of viewpoints, and along the line of 170 years of further development since the *Aberdeen Magazine* of 1832, there must lie a continuing ravellment and unravellment of personal encounter and inherited attitude. Smout's debunking comment, for example, was made in 1977 and in the quarter century since, there has been sufficient time to witness the prohibition of corporal punishment, the virtual collapse of classroom Latin, the spread of a fabulous micro-technology and the swelling of the proportion of pupils who can now look to go on to higher education to some 40 per cent. And in that time, there has, no doubt, been a further decline in the number of Doric expressions that are to be overheard in the average Buchan playground.

Yet, through all the shifts and upheavals, the local school remains the one prolonged institutional experience which almost all the children of the region may be expected to encounter. And, despite it all, its inhabitants continue to regard the term 'North-East' as carrying something more than a merely geographical significance. Against such a complex mix of continuity and upset, of generalised myth and personal experience, the standard histories can only have a limited reach. For those who wish to grasp more of the ways in which the local school and the national system that it represents have come together, both to shape and to complicate the region's distinctive identity and cultural experience, it now becomes important to take the historical and the international perspectives, which Anderson's introductory paper has set before us, out into the individual recollections and the local histories of the people of the North-East.

In a range of different ways the papers which follow attempt to do that.

The first group of titles offers three individual case studies. Their subjects could be considered as standing outside the North-East school tradition, yet, in both a personal and a professional sense, they engage with its essential values. There is the entrant into it at the age of fourteen of the new arrival from the south of England; there is the prodigiously gifted Victorian minister's son who received all of his pre-university education at home and then grew up to become professor at 24 and, ten years later, was tried by his Church for heresy; there is the Buchan railwayman's son who matured into a controversial headteacher and fierce critic of the very system which had educated him up to that position. The responses of this trio – as novice, outsider, and rebel – enable us, by contrast and by opposition, to understand something of the insistent ways in which the orthodoxies of a North-East schooling have attempted to work upon the sensibilities of its human subjects.

The experience in the 1950s of David Northcroft, as an adolescent who was quite abruptly wrenched out of his Sussex grammar school to take up membership of a small village academy, 650 miles to the north, was played out on a markedly more modest scale than those of the other two. But, forty years on, he is able to use his small autobiographical episode as the starting point for a reflection upon the likenesses and the differences in the two systems which, successively, made up his own schooling – and of the extent to which any point of comparison has been over-run by the power of the North-East's self-belief in the distinctive superiority of what it had to offer its pupils. If the assertions to that effect, with which the rector at Aberlour High school confronted him, owed little to any actual knowledge of the curricular experiences that his new recruit had brought with him, they had the authority of a long cultural history behind them. Northcroft's personal anecdote is to be placed in the context of a whole tradition of educational celebration which looked upon Banffshire, and its great lore of lads o' pairts and romantic topographical description, as its very epitome.

In 'Home Education: A Victorian Case Study', Gordon Booth traces the career of William Robertson Smith, who became one of Europe's pre-eminent linguists and anthropologists, and who used those skills to act as a British pioneer of the methods of the 'higher' biblical criticism that had originated in Germany. Yet this was someone who had grown up in a Free Church manse in the relatively isolated location of Keig, on the edge of the Howe of Alford, 150 years ago. His achievements had been made on the back of a schooling which had, until he entered Aberdeen University at the age of 14, been received at the hands of his father and in his own home. The arrangement, as Booth explains, was less idiosyncratically domestic than it might appear. Before he was called to his rural ministry, the reverend William Pirie Smith had been a headmaster in Aberdeen; he had seven children of his own to tutor and they were frequently joined by a succession of guest pupils. His pastoral duties, moreover, were light and within his Free Church manse, he was free to devote himself to building up what became, in effect, a small and coherently organized school. In it, he emphasised intellectual rigour, classical scholarship, the importance of academic achievement and co-operation with his own paternalistic rule: in short, the regular hallmarks of a bracing Scottish education. Yet, in addition, he also offered an immersion in scientific enquiry and encouraged the growth of a spirit of speculative enquiry and of self-expression which was greatly in excess of what the parish school there, or anywhere else in the region, would have cared to permit.

If the intellectual prowess of his eldest son closely chimes in with the hard working academicism of the North-East system, his ultimate fate – an arraignment at the bar of his own Free Church Assembly in 1876 on account of his rationalistic treatment of standard Bible themes such as 'Angels' and the 'Ark of the Covenant', followed by a departure to take up a Chair at Cambridge – exposes the limitations which were expected to be placed upon its personal applications. Smith's fate illustrates Robert Anderson's conclusion that, traditionally, the native claim for a 'democratic' education has rested upon structural, not liberationist, considerations: the way was to be made open to any bright young man to acquire the academic credentials to advance triumphantly into the professions, commerce, or the British Civil Service, but the attitudes he carried with him were designed to substantiate, not to challenge, the prevailing framework of social philosophy and intellectual practice.

If William Robertson Smith had been taught at the parochial establishment at Keig instead of the drawing room of its manse, then he might have been better able to manage the delicate balances that were at play within the local education tradition between individual advancement and any right to a free individualism. One who, a hundred years later, had no such innocence over the extent to which academic democracy could, in practice, mean a highly schooled conformity, was R. F. MacKenzie. In 'The North-East Radical with a Revolutionary Agenda', his biographer, Peter Murphy, traces the development of one who grew up as a railway worker's son in deepest Aberdeenshire and who was, as a pupil at the local school, inducted into that county's daily homage to the virtues of the three Rs, to be drilled into its young by a strict and grimly physical discipline. MacKenzie then followed the well worn route by which the local likely lad goes to university and then re-enters the system as a teacher. But, in his case, with a totally different outcome: he rose to the position of headteacher, first in Fife, then in a large Aberdeen secondary school. There, he determined to use his position to open up the received school curriculum to the freedoms of creative self-expression and a committedly child-centred methodology. This drive was accompanied by what turned into an aggressively polemical campaign against what he had come to see as the repressively Calvinist, life-denying constraints of the 'good' Scottish education which he himself had received at Wartle and whose values he had been expected to reproduce unquestioningly for the benefit of the next generation.

The result was a series of crusading books and, in the 1970s, a notorious headmastership at Summerhill Academy, where his insistence on jettisoning the belt and freeing the syllabus from any authoritarian, facts-serving pedagogy ran him straight into the persistently conservative force of Establishment opinion and, ultimately, the limited tolerance of his employer, the City Council of Aberdeen. The consequence was the rare distinction for a Scottish headmaster of being sacked. His subsequent *Manifesto for an Educational Revolution* was rejected by his publishers as too radical to be worth the handling.

Yet, as Murphy observes, it would be over-simple to type-cast his subject as 'Rebel'. It is not only that a quarter of a century on, his attacks upon the rule of the test and the culture of target-setting and teacher accountability, can seem sufficiently pertinent to arouse a sympathetic reaction – to which the political vigour of Murphy's own re-assessment acts as ready witness – but that R. F. MacKenzie was himself the product of the very system he came to reject. It was its grounding in linguistic precision and in intellectual rigour which enabled him to become such an accomplished polemicist. It had also contributed to an upbringing which gave him the profound and unswerving, if frequently exasperated, love for his native land that he expressed so vividly in his final work, *A Search for Scotland*.

The cross play of forces within the North-East situation can, it would appear, produce a complex adult result, one in which the tensions between personal opportunity and cultural constraints experienced within its schoolings require a more subtle retrospective appraisal than that which is easily available in any general study of the topic. That is why some of the most enlightening reconstructions of what it has meant to be educated within the local schools of the region are to be found in its creative literature.

In the second group of papers, Ian Campbell considers the responses, in their fiction, of two of the country's most striking early twentieth-century writers, the Ayrshire George Douglas and Lewis Grassic Gibbon, whose schooling was received in Kincardineshire. He reflects upon the fact that while an initial, and publicly acknowledged, impetus behind each was an able and a committed parish school dominie, both of them wrote in ways that were sharply critical of Scottish education and its schoolmasters. It is, however, the man from Arbuthnott whose work gives us the more sustained and subtle treatment. Here, Campbell is able to use the apparent contradiction between the life and the literature that was spun out of it, to show how its author's interaction between them enables him to illuminate some of the acute dissonances that growing up in the North-East can generate within its sons and its daughters. If Gibbon owed much to his own nurture within a tightly drawn Mearns community, his adult life, and later wide reading, departed from these origins to such an extent that he became what was very much a self-educated man.

In this respect, he was part of the pattern followed by William Robertson Smith and R. F. MacKenzie. Like them, he, too, becomes caught up in the difficult tug to be felt between the individual's primary experience and the impress of systems of social and cultural formation that are external to it, of which the school is the earliest and, perhaps, most persistent agency. It is a dichotomy which gives his work an essential source of creative energy and which underlines its continued relevance for us today. It is not only in the well known representation of the heroine of *Sunset Song*, and its 'English' and its 'Scottish' Chris, that he deals with the issues of choice and commitment, which switch the individual backwards and forwards, first between the culture of the home and the systematic usurption of it by the country's Edinburgh run Education Department, and then between the old Mearns ways and the beckoning modern world of cities and of industry; there is a wealth of documentary material in which the same theme is explored. There is also *Grey Granite* and, at the end of it, the figure of Chris's son Ewan marching off to a new life in London.

The more general survey of poets, novelists and memorialists contributed by Douglas Young would confirm that 'education' lies at the centre of any cultural analysis of the North-East. But, once more, if the experience of the school is used by them as an integral theme, the attitudes which criss-cross their writing are more critical than celebratory. And this despite the fact that each of them, if to varying degrees, may be considered a product of its lad o' pairts (and, in the case of Jessie Kesson, even lass) system. Again, there appears to be a tension at work – here, between the recognition of a personal indebtedness to, and a wider questioning of, a formative experience, which they have since come to view as exerting a narrowing, dispiriting effect upon the life of their homeland – and upon the capacity of its people to derive satisfaction and joy from it.

A repeated thematic approach in such as Gibbon, George MacDonald, in the poetry of Charles Murray, and in William Alexander's great Aberdeenshire novel, *Johnny Gibb of Gushetneuk*, is the juxtaposition of the two worlds, that of home and that of school and of society: of culture as something you inherit and as a subject-matter that has to be learnt. And in the life story, as well as the work, of Ian MacPherson, there is an example of the lad o' pairts who, after a brilliant early academic progress, threw up his lectureship at Aberdeen University to return to the land, to the hazards of the smallholding and the subsistence of the freelance writer.

But, once more, the outcome is far from one dimensional. If, in the writing of MacPherson and Gibbon, there is recreated the individual experiences that suggest that in the soul-life of the children of the North-East, it is the culture of the land, and of the Doric tongue that it has fed, which provide the well springs of a true 'education', there is also the knowledge that it is the powers of intellectual organization and of literate expression acquired at the parochial school, which have given them the ability to understand and to communicate these truths.

Together, what these accounts of past schoolings suggest is the importance of reconciliation. There is the balance that is to be struck between the impulse towards individual fulfilment and the set expectations of the community, between the fabled ideal and actual circumstances, the culture of the home and the drive by the educational system to train in its subjects a capacity to meet the less immediate demands of a wider and more impersonal society, between the difficult task of reconciling the intimacies of a North-East upbringing with the pressures exerted by the world at large. And, running through all these tensions, is the problem of the deeply felt and preciously mythologised North-East past.

Can a satisfactory future, given the weight of its inheritance, be constructed out of this past? To what extent, and how, may the values and the structures, which were gradually accumulated during 300 proud years of public education, be drawn upon to serve the twenty-first century and do so in ways that will achieve growth rather than be a severance?

For Derrick McClure, the issue of language is crucial to any decisions which should be made concerning the curriculum and the forms of expression which it should nurture. Robert Anderson observes that whatever else has distinguished the nation's educational system, it has not been the attention it has paid to the specifically Scottish. This omission has certainly included its literature and its languages. For the North-East child, brought up within a vibrant local culture, the exclusion has been especially severe. Douglas Young comments that for a writer like Gibbon, the refusal of the school to admit his or her own Doric into the classroom not only throws up a disjuncture between the home and the school but assaults the growing child's own sense of identity.

Sunset Song, however, was written from a situation which, seventy years later, has now slipped away. Pupils, McClure reports, are no longer beaten for using their home language in class. The old, unquestioned insistence that 'Standard' English was the hallmark of the educated young Briton, and that any variation of it is to be condemned as slipshod ignorance, has now been superseded by an easy-going tolerance. But, as he goes on to protest, that is all it is. Recent research into the attitudes of the region's primary pupils towards Doric has exposed little more than confusion with regard to its status, its range of usage and its relationship to English. Doric deserves better than that: it is a pre-eminent example of how a local speech can develop its own distinctive character, the part that it may play in what is a well-defined regional culture and of how it may generate a robust and varied literature.

A working knowledge of Doric is, alongside that of English and its great literature, McClure states, the birthright of every North-East child. The failure to teach it, as opposed to merely allowing it, is to be seen as part of a general loss of nerve among teachers, who have been caught up in their age's excessive reaction against the certainties of the past. In particular, they have been undermined by the socio-linguistic arguments of the 1970s and 1980s, which asserted the equal validity of non-Standard dialect forms and exposed the way in which judgements as to what constitutes 'good' speech have, in the past, been infiltrated by social class attitudes. But the consequence is that teachers have now been rendered wary of appearing to impose any linguistic standards at all.

To McClure, such permissiveness is indicative of the extent to which we no longer inhabit a securely ordered mental world. The withering away of language instruction has taken place at a time which has also seen the final postwar collapse of any general acceptance of a social framework that granted Scots a fixed place within a Great Britain which stood at the culminating point of a great imperial history. What is now required is a new synthesis, one which will balance the former pride in what constitutes that general knowledge, which properly belongs to all educated young persons, with an appreciation – and taught where necessary – of the richness of their own North-East heritage. Such a programme should also be guided by an understanding of how language may best function within any advanced society and of the range of expressive and communicative forms necessary to its sustenance.

'Uncertainty', Derrick McClure concludes, as he faces outwards into the current welter of relativism and ever shifting values, 'is not a principle by which individuals or communities can live'. It is warning to which Robbie Robertson responds by asking us to go out and embrace the turbulence which others would have us regard with a more measured caution. He has the sense of us all as being in the early stages of a fast moving culture which will be irresistibly pluralistic in character and be impelled by the infinitely various, libertarian possibilities opened up by an exponentially developing micro-technology. It is one which will place unlimited powers of access, of selection and reconstruction at the keyboard fingertips of all North-East children. He sets these bewildering, dancing riches against a current curriculum which he considers to be fixed in the era of linear top-down knowledge, of 'coal and steam'.

It is vital that educationists develop forms of learning which will be propelled by the dynamism of what he terms the Information Curriculum. Yet despite the visionary enthusiasm with which he projects this future onto our screens, Robertson also recognizes that the multi-dimensional, non-stop drama of the global village can disorientate and overwhelm. It is this realisation which leads him to argue that the micro-technologically energised, lightning-fast future must be properly earthed and that the new curriculum has to be rooted in the experiences of the past. Here, the North-East child is especially fortunate, for he and she stand on the solid ground of a rich and intimately felt culture. The new technologies can be used – and by the children themselves – to maintain contact with an inheritance which may now be experienced as a participative venture, and not left behind to become a mere historical artefact. It is the ultimate reconciliation.

The papers which make up *North-East Identities and Scottish Schooling* have been collected together around the proposition that the school is a significant and universal experience, one that has a communal as well as an individual dimension. Moreover, this has been especially so in the North-East of Scotland, which is both a self-consciously distinctive region and the home of a celebrated version of the national educational tradition.

The particular system, however, by which the school seeks to work on the development of the individual, intersects with that of the home and the encircling community in ways that create tension, even conflict. Running through all the pieces of this collection is an implied question: what has been the nature of the contribution of this nationally organised local institution to the shaping of the consciousness of those who live and work within the region to their sense of themselves as a people who have their being within the 'North-East'?

In considering this issue, a number of focal points have emerged. The claim has been made that in Scotland the educational system has always belonged to the people, but how 'democratic' has it really, in practice, proved itself to be? Scots have been able to enjoy an inheritance of a centuries old history, which may, however, simply have resulted in a backward-looking and introspective regime. The native virtues which have supposedly informed that progress may each of them be balanced against their countercharge – that the work ethic, the regard for academic excellence, the respect for a merited authority, the piety and the realism of 'getting on' have been used to distract from the Calvinist joylessness and narrowness of it all. How complete, then, has the nationally directed curriculum been, both as an engagement with the full range of North-East experience and as a preparation for a satisfying later life, whether led within its boundaries or further afield?

What this collection of papers has done is to make us aware of the extent to which the school system has sustained its self-belief by embodying its purposes in a series of exemplary stories and has sought to justify itself in national terms by building up its own mythology of patriotic achievement. It has also demonstrated the range of accounts which, down the long years, have both supported and challenged the traditional narrative – the historians, the politicians and public figures, the literary artists, the commentators, and the educationists who have all been able to look back on a lifetime's achievement, which, for better or for worse, was launched in the local school.

Terms such as 'democracy', the 'people', the 'local community', and 'personal experience', however, indicate that their kind of evidence can never, by itself, be enough, that it is important to read and to listen to an ever wider spread of witness that would take us right into the first hand memories of those who are usually called 'ordinary' people. In part, this would be to test the mythology against the common actualities, to set the formative workings of the school against those of the home and the local community. But it would also be to see how closely the national educational story has woven itself into the individual record, there, perhaps, to join in, to complicate and to shape further the North-East adult's sense of what he or she has, or might have, become.

A reading among the texts which David Northcroft has cited in 'A' Yon Skweelin' will help the interested student to penetrate further into these questions, especially as he or she moves from the 'general histories' into the more intimate 'biography' sections. But even the most personal of records is, once prepared for publication, something of an artefact, one which has been shaped and selected into a construction of experience. For this reason, a small set of interview transcripts is included in the Appendix. These were generated as part of an ongoing exercise in oral history, the aim of which is to build up an extensive archive of first-hand recordings of people talking about their own schooldays in the North-East. At present in its early stages, the intention is to accumulate a wide range of direct testimonies that will capture a broad cross section of recollections, not only of school life but of its unfolding role within a number of authentic local lives. Taken together, the interviews should carry a wide social and cultural significance, as well as offering insights into its immediate subject.

The work is, as yet, in its early phase: some thirty-five ninety-minute recordings have been now completed. The sample which appears here can only be regarded as offering a number of preliminary pointers as to how, in the setting of actual North-East experience, the matters raised by the more formal papers on 'North-East Identities and Scottish Schooling' should be explored.

Five interviews (somewhat abridged) are set out in the first section of Appendix 1. They are presented without analytical comment: the intention here is to allow the North-East experience to speak for itself. Yet it is evident that, even at this early stage, they could be said to provide an experiential critique of the themes which have occupied the preceding papers in this collection. As an illustration of how this body of witness promises to deepen our understanding of the way in which the local representative of the national school system has been at work upon the developing consciousness of the North-East child, the major concern of 'language' has, for Section 2, been selected for critical commentary.

The audio-taped witnesses make a series of revealing comments on the way in which their local schools went about instilling into them an acquisition of Standard English as the one acceptable medium of classroom discourse, and, at the same time, of expelling their native Doric from the entire curriculum. Strategies of punishment, admonition and linguistic suppression were widespread. It was a policy, zealously adopted by the local teacher and driven by the centralised forces of the Codes of Scottish Education Department and its ubiquitous inspectors which, in most cases, discriminated against the child's own nurture and communal culture. Frequently, it led to a sense of bemused alienation and resentful disablement. It immediately placed the child of working-class and rural origin at a disadvantage. To this extent, the language regime enforced by the public education authorities could be said to give the lie to all those traditional claims of a classless 'democracy', the 'people's' school and the birthright opportunity to 'get on'.

It would, however, be misleading to treat these highly personal statements, made at the remove of 50/60 years and more from the events they recollect, as a straightforward exposure of historicised tales and official constructions – to make smart conclusion that what these speakers have done is to oppose the favoured fond myths with a cutting actuality. A more considered scrutiny of the testimony, one that is alert to the cross-currents which flow across these accounts, and to the subtle processes of memory building which have defined their final shape, would come to appreciate that the goal of a direct match between the later recollection and the supposed 'real' event is illusory. In the case of the Doric, it is not so much the brute fact of suppression which enlightens as the interplay of the school circumstance and the mature individual's later evaluation of its longer-term impact on a development, which, while representative, will always be a personally interested outcome. So, too, does the spread of reaction across the witness range – from pragmatic acceptance to an appreciated bilingualism, to a life-long sense of inhibition that is both intellectual and social – and with a number of overlapping points in between. And in the process of arriving at these judgements, the hard-edged detail comes to be intermingled with a consciousness of what is 'typical' and what, in juxtaposition, is memorably singular, as does the individualised drama of personal origins and singular temperaments with an adult's retrospective awareness of the wider context of traditional values and social role-play. In this way, the North-East voice, in whatever accents it has learned to express itself, is joining the individual career to the community experience, its present to that past – and in short, is involved in an individual's reworking of the national myth.

On the evidence of this sample, the Elphinstone Institute's archive of oral history promises to enrich our understanding, not so much of what 'really' happened, but of the range and complexity of responses, both immediate and life-long, that a North-East schooling has engendered in its people. More than that, it should have the power to involve us in the very processes of memory and of response by which the local experience of the nation's education system has taken on its own North-East identity.

Notes

1 *Northern Iris*, 'Bye-gane Days', April 1826, pp. 94-97.

2 The North East '…is the most Scottish part of Scotland' according to Elsie Rae in her essay on 'The North East: Its Folk and Language', in *A Waff o' Win' fae Benachie* (Aberdeen: Bisset, 1930), pp. 67-82 (p. 68).

3 The Milne Bequest (from the estate of Dr Milne, late President of the Medical Board of Bombay) was established in 1841 and offered annual grants to parochial schools in the region in return for their agreeing to teach 25 poor children free.

   The Dick Bequest (from the estate of James Dick, a son of Forres who went on to make a fortune as a sugar merchant in Jamaica) operated from 1833 onwards. Annual supplements were to be made to the salaries of those teachers – 'that neglected though useful class of men' – who were able to meet certain academic criteria. It had the effect of ensuring that a much higher proportion of the dominies of the North-East counties were of University degree standard than elsewhere in Scotland.

4 Christopher Smout, 'The Scottish Identity', in *The Future of Scotland*, ed. by Robert Underwood (London: Croom Helm for the Nevis Institute, 1977), pp. 11-21. In a recent communication with the author, Smout added, 'In the years since this was written, much has changed, and I would not say this now'.

Chapter Two

Northern Identities and the Scottish Educational System

Robert D. Anderson

Questions of national and regional identity are currently a fashionable topic, but the distinctiveness of Scottish education has been seen as a mark of Scottish identity for at least two hundred years. It is held to be more developed, or more democratic, or at least different in various ways, especially of course from English education. Some years ago the present author tried to trace the way in which the myth of the 'lad o' pairts' developed in the nineteenth century, both in discussions of educational policy and in literary sources, and he has argued elsewhere that myths are not just fictions, but crystallisations of reality which can have a positive effect on those paths of development which are chosen or avoided.[1] To use the words of Robert Gildea, in *The Past in French History*, a myth is 'a construction of the past elaborated by a political community for its own ends.'[2]

Gildea is cited because a comparative perspective is useful here. Historians and social scientists undoubtedly see educational systems as central to the formation of national identity in the modern world. And this operates at two levels. First at the level of the elite, which participates in a national culture transmitted through secondary schools and universities, and which identifies with the state which embodies that culture.[3] And second, especially since the introduction of democratic politics, elementary education has had the task of teaching the masses to be loyal citizens, the school being one of the few compulsory experiences through which everyone has to pass. It is no coincidence that the Education Act of 1872 (and its English equivalent in 1870) followed closely on the extension of the franchise to urban workers in 1867–68. At both elite and popular levels, language, literature, history, and religion are the elements through which the national identity is defined.

Across this social dualism, however, cuts another distinction, between two types of nationalism. 'Integrative' nationalism, in established nation-states, or those newly united like Germany and Italy in the nineteenth century, gave education the function of welding together masses and elites in the new age of industrialisation and democracy. The other type may be called 'emancipatory' nationalism, where newly-conscious peoples sought to define their cultural identity against an alien oppressor. In this kind of small-nation nationalism, which often involved the assertion of linguistic rights, education at all levels was at the heart of the national struggle and of competition for the allegiance of the new generations: the Habsburg Empire provides classic examples in nineteenth-century Europe, while in the twentieth century one could look at Asian and African nationalisms directed against colonial rule.

For an example of integrative nationalism, we can take Eugen Weber's seminal study *Peasants into Frenchmen* of 1976.[4] Weber argued that French peasants did not fully identify with France until after 1870, and that education (along with other forces like railways, conscription, and the popular press) created a new national identity, and one which was not politically neutral but reflected the values of the dominant Republican elite. It was deliberately designed to override older regional and local identities. The village school, and the village schoolteacher who was the apostle of Republican progress, taught the peasant that he (or she, despite Weber's title) was French, rather than Breton or Provencal, and that standard French was the language which the educated must speak rather than local dialects and patois. But they also taught that France was the France of 1789, that it stood for justice, for progress, for emancipation from reactionary and irrational forces (which m eant, for this anticlerical regime, the Catholic religion), and for France's civilising mission in its expanding colonial empire. As elsewhere in the nineteenth century, the elementary school was a modernising, rationalising influence which sought to teach universal values.

For examples of emancipatory nationalism, we may look to many parts of Europe. Czech nationalism in the Habsburg Empire was a classic case of national identity rediscovered and invented by intellectuals through the medium of history, folklore, music, and poetry; one of its most significant moments was the division of the ancient University of Prague into separate Czech and German universities in 1882. There are parallel movements among other Slav peoples (and non-Slav ones like the Romanians) under Austrian or Turkish rule. But the Flemish language movement in Belgium shows that such demands could just as well arise in advanced industrial states. It is characteristic of these language-based nationalisms that they were often not the work of the older educated elites, but of a new class created as education spread among the peasantry and petty bourgeoisie, led by priests, schoolmasters, doctors and other semi-rural and small-town intellectuals.

Another interesting (and northern) example, though perhaps less known, is Finnish nationalism, which, in the nineteenth century, was directed politically against Russian rule and culturally against Swedish dominance, as Swedish was the language of culture spoken by the educated classes even if they were ethnically Finnish. Here the University of Helsinki had an absolutely central role. Both professors and students were involved in the rediscovery of peasant society, the transformation of Finnish from a peasant dialect into a literary language, and the elevation of folk culture into high art; the best known example is the *Kalevala* epic, known to us usually through Sibelius but originally created out of peasant oral traditions by the Helsinki professor Elias Lönnrot.[5] Every summer students would depart for the countryside, and live with peasant families to absorb their traditions and learn from their supposed folk wisdom.

But how do these models apply to Scotland? Standard nineteenth-century nationalism saw national allegiances as exclusive: the citizen owed loyalty to the nation-state, and any other loyalties – to supra-national bodies like the Catholic church, to international ideologies like socialism, to regional or particularist values – were suspect. Today we are more willing to recognize plural or concentric loyalties, and it is clear that this was very much the case for nineteenth-century Scots, for whom Scotland, the United Kingdom, and the British Empire were all centres of attraction. For the elite, a practical interest in careers outside Scotland was a mainspring of university reform. But for the Scottish middle classes in the nineteenth and twentieth centuries, these wider loyalties, and solid political unionism, were quite compatible with a vigorous cultural nationalism, expressed through pride in Burns, Scott, and other Scottish heroes, a complex of ideas most recently explored by Graeme Morton.[6] It was also compatible with intense local and regional loyalties, and with civic pride focused on the major cities, as any historian who has looked at nineteenth-century newspapers will be aware.

How far these feelings were shared by the less articulate classes is not so easy to say. The record of the two world wars suggests that British if not imperial loyalties were strong by 1914. But had ordinary Scots, like Weber's French peasants, been local in their vision until the school brought wider horizons? Was there a difference here between Highlands and Lowlands? Did ordinary people have their own wider horizons, created by emigration, military service, or seafaring? Family links could make Canada or Australia seem very familiar, a form of imperial interest different from that of the elite Scots aiming at jobs in the Indian empire. These are questions which still need exploration. One of the merits of Tom Devine's book *The Scottish Nation, 1700–2000* is its stress on the importance of emigration in the early twentieth century:[7] Scottish schools were forming future Canadians and New Zealanders as well as future Scots.

In many countries, education taught nationalism through the content of the curriculum. But in Scotland the system was notoriously cool in its attitude to specifically Scottish culture. Scottish history and literature, not to mention the Gaelic language, were neglected in the universities, and long campaigns had to be waged to establish chairs in these subjects. In the schools, the establishment of a national state system after 1872 replacing one run by the churches inevitably led to a dilution of Scottish character. The basic task of elementary education, teaching the 'three Rs', was in any case much the same everywhere. Only when this was accomplished was there scope for more cultural content in the shape of history, literature, or geography. As a matter of fact, there seems to have been more Scottish content in these than is often thought, especially before 1914; but where specific 'civic' instruction was given, it was undoubtedly 'British' in tone.[8]

It is also notorious that Scottish students and intellectuals had little if any interest in Scottish folk traditions. Many of them came from the countryside, but the last thing they wanted was to go back there or to learn from peasant wisdom. Education in Scotland was a way of getting out – out of the villages and small towns into professional life, out of Scotland altogether. This was as true of the North-East as of any other region, as we know from the data about the destinations of Aberdeen university graduates, figures which are more complete than for the other Scottish universities.[9]

Consequently a distinctive nationalist intelligentsia was lacking, at least until the 1930s, and this contrasts both with Ireland – where the Gaelic language movement was an authentic example of a 'second level' intelligentsia of priests and schoolteachers, with significant consequences for the intellectual life of the independent state – and with Wales, where both religion and language provided impetus for the movement of cultural nationalism which created the University of Wales, a distinctive school system, and a myth of a cultured people which has strong analogies with the story of the lad o' pairts.[10] The essays which Hugh MacDiarmid published in the *Scottish Educational Journal* in the 1920s, republished in the 1970s as *Contemporary Scottish Studies*, were a one-man attempt to kick-start the creation of a similar intelligentsia.[11] To some extent this succeeded in the 1930s, but even then the 'Scottish Renaissance' in literature was slow to have much impact on school or university teaching.

If it is not the Scottish content of Scottish education which created identity, where could this be looked for? In the first place, in religion. Until very recently, the main cultural differences between Scotland and England had their roots in the different paths taken by the Reformation. High Scottish culture, including what is now called the Scottish Enlightenment, was profoundly marked by Calvinist religion, and George Davie's famous identification of the 'democratic intellect' can be seen as an attempt to provide a secularised version of this religious tradition, his own attitude to which is significantly ambiguous.[12] When popular education developed in the eighteenth and nineteenth centuries, its function was above all to make children into good Christians, and preferably into good Presbyterians, or Episcopalians, or Catholics. The Irish and Welsh examples show how important religion can be to national and communal identity, even in the absence of linguistic or ethnic divisions. In Scotland, much of the character of the traditional parish school came from its embedding in the social and cultural ethos of the church and its institutions, especially at the parish level – what historians have recently begun to call the local state or 'parish state'.[13] Even the formation of elected school boards in 1872 did not change this much at first, as ministers were elected to them in strength, and the traditional teaching of the Shorter Catechism was normally retained.

This document was often held to have formed the Scottish character. As the leading expert Simon S. Laurie, Professor of Education at Edinburgh University, put it in 1876:

> The intellect, the will, and the arm of Scotsmen, have done, we flatter ourselves,
> their fair share in creating the British Empire, and they have done it all by

virtue mainly of their breed, and by such restricted education as Arithmetic, Latin and the Shorter Catechism afforded.

Or, as he repeated in 1892, 'the Shorter Catechism has done more to make Scotland efficient in the world's work than mathematics and chemistry can ever do.'[14] But where is the Shorter Catechism today, where indeed religion? The rapid secularisation of Scottish life in recent years has left the churches with little institutional power, and many feel religion to be a divisive rather than a uniting force. Scottish national identity can no longer be identified with presbyterianism without offending many Scots who have different allegiances, including non-Christian ones. So multi-culturalism is now the order of the day in education.

Even less politically correct are racial explanations, so popular in the nineteenth century (Laurie's 'breed'). The Aberdeen Professor of Anatomy, John Struthers, in the 1870s explained why Aberdonians had a headstart in life's struggle:

> The people along the east coast are a different race, with Scandinavian blood and larger heads, industrious, careful, and pushing, in marked contrast to the naturally lazy, superstitious, Gaelic-speaking race of the north-west coast.[15]

That was certainly one form of northern identity, and a common one when physical anthropology and social Darwinism seemed to provide scientific justifications for national differences. It was part of a rhetoric – about the Protestant, enterprising, freedom-loving island race – which was as much 'British' as Scottish.

If religious or ethnic explanations of Scotland's educational identity are discarded, we are left with structural ones: that its distinctiveness lay in the relationship between schools and universities, the opportunities given to lads o' pairts, the contribution which education made to social mobility, and the relative absence of class barriers within the national system. These claims frequently appeared in nineteenth-century discussions of educational policy, often coupled with invocations of the spirit of John Knox. According to Andrew Carnegie in 1903, Knox 'made Scotland a democracy while England remains a nation of caste.'[16] Such ideas persisted in the controversy in 1921 over the Scottish Education Department's Circular 44, which rejected any move from a two-tier system of post-primary education to 'secondary education for all',[17] and in the influential report of the Scottish Advisory Council on Education in 1947, to which James Robertson, Rector of Aberdeen Grammar School, made a large input; the Council itself was chaired by Principal Hamilton Fyfe of Aberdeen.

For it was generally agreed that the Scottish ideal reached its purest form in the North-East. The myth was celebrated in works like *The Schools and Schoolmasters of Banffshire* by William Barclay (1925) and *The History of Fordyce Academy* by D. G. McLean (1936). Laurie derived his inspiration from his many years spent as Inspector of the Dick Bequest, and when an Association for Securing Higher Instruction in Scottish Rural Schools was formed in 1912 to protest against the Scottish Education Department's policy of centralising secondary education and to defend the teaching of Latin and Greek in village schools, one of its moving spirits was John Harrower, Professor of Greek at Aberdeen.[18] The Dick Bequest, which subsidised the provision of graduate schoolmasters in rural schools, worked along with the Aberdeen University bursary competition to make the direct link between parish and university more long-lasting here than in most parts of Scotland. It was aided by a social structure in which small farmers and local artisans remained a significant force, and in which the class polarisation brought about by industrialisation was very limited.

Indeed, educational opportunities of this kind had not been uncommon in pre-industrial Europe. The poor scholars who once went to Oxford and Cambridge to study for the Church were squeezed out from the seventeenth century onwards, but in the Protestant parts of Germany this tradition lasted until 1800 or later. In Württemberg, for example, a national scholarship examination sought out meritorious boys and financed them through secondary schools and then through a special residential college for theology students at the University of Tübingen; some of the most famous names in German intellectual life rose through this means.[19]

The parish school and the ideology associated with it always stood for competitive individualism rather than collective democracy, and never offered the same opportunities to girls as to boys aiming at the ministry or schoolteaching. Critics like T. C. Smout have seen Scottish education as characterised by conformist and hierarchical values rather than egalitarian ones,[20] and in the twentieth century radicals like A. S. Neill and R. F. MacKenzie struggled with limited success against powerful conservative and narrow-minded forces.

The lad o' pairts ideal was also based on the kailyard idyll of rural life, and appeared in popular literary forms just as industrialisation and urbanisation created nostalgia for a vanishing way of life. In fact, Scotland had never been a peasant society in the sense that France or Finland were. Nineteenth-century rural life was organized on capitalist lines, and dominated by the landowners. Even after 1872 this remained partly true. Despite valuable work by Andrew Bain, we still know rather little about the workings of rural school boards, but it looks as if the authority of landowners, ministers, and employers only really crumbled in the 1920s, after county education authorities had been created by the 1918 Education Act.[21] Since then, of course, the mechanisation of agriculture and other economic and social changes have largely destroyed the historical continuity of parish structures and rural ways of life.

As a guide to action today, is the structure of Scottish education really so different from England, or any advanced country? At the margins, significant differences remain.

There are higher participation rates in university education, and staying-on rates in schools. The Scottish Parliament has shown its commitment to opportunity through its policy on student fees.[22] Highers remain a broader examination than A-Levels – though not as broad as is often claimed, and England seems to be moving in a convergent direction. If historical differences between Scotland and England are lessening, while Scotland's religious and ethnic homogeneity can no longer be sustained, one can also hardly ignore such factors as the global mobility of labour and the loss of domestic control of Scottish industrial and commercial employment. In the educational sphere, the commercialisation and Americanisation of popular culture makes it difficult for schools to instil any distinctive ideal into children, and the internet means – at least for its more visionary enthusiasts – that colleges and universities need no longer be tied to fixed locations.

The historian cannot help feeling that Scotland had much more national character and was far more genuinely different from England in the years before 1914 when political unionism was at its height. Is it therefore a paradox that as global forces grow, there seems to be a new thirst for regionalism? Perhaps this reflects feelings of powerlessness which seek identity in the local and familiar rather than the abstract machinery of the state. Or perhaps, more positively, it reflects a resurgence of the old phenomenon of concentric identities. As the nineteenth-century nation-state seems to lose its meaning, regionalism has popular appeal, while the elites may find in Europe a transnational ideal to replace the Empire which was once so important in integrating Scots into the British world.

Notes

[1] R. D. Anderson, *Education and Opportunity in Victorian Scotland: Schools and Universities* (Oxford: Clarendon Press, 1983), pp. 23-26. Other treatments are: Robert Anderson, 'In search of the "lad of parts": The Mythical History of Scottish Education', *History Workshop Journal*, 19 (1985), 82-104; Andrew McPherson, 'An Angle on the Geist: Persistence and Change in the Scottish Educational Tradition', in *Scottish Culture and Scottish Education, 1800-1980*, ed. by Walter M. Humes and Hamish M. Paterson (Edinburgh: Donald, 1983), pp. 216-43; Lindsay Paterson, 'Traditions of Scottish Education', in *Scottish Life and Society: A Compendium of Scottish Ethnology*, Vol. 11, Education, ed. by Heather Holmes (East Linton: Tuckwell for the European Ethnological Research Centre, 2000), pp. 21-43.

[2] Robert Gildea, *The Past in French History* (New Haven: Yale University Press, 1994), p. 12.

[3] See R. D. Anderson, 'Nationalism and Internationalism: European Universities before 1914', *Aberdeen University Review*, 54 (1992), 334-45.

[4] Eugen Weber, *Peasants into Frenchmen: The Modernisation of Rural France, 1870-1914* (London: Chatto & Windus, 1976).

[5] Matti Klinge, 'Finland: From Napoleonic Legacy to Nordic Co-operation', in *The National Question in Europe in Historical Context*, ed. by Mikulas Teich and Roy Porter (Cambridge: Cambridge University Press, 1993), pp. 317-31.

[6] Graeme Morton, *Unionist-Nationalism: Governing Urban Scotland, 1830-1860* (East Linton: Tuckwell, 1999).

[7] T. M. Devine, *The Scottish Nation, 1700-2000* (London: Allen Lane / Penguin 1999), pp. 84-102.

[8] R. D. Anderson, *Education and the Scottish People, 1750-1918* (Oxford: Clarendon Press; New York: Oxford University Press, 1995), pp. 193-220.

9 R. D. Anderson, *The Student Community at Aberdeen, 1860-1939* (Aberdeen: Aberdeen University Press, 1988), pp. 138-40.

10 Christopher Harvie, 'The Folk and the Gwerin: The Myth and the Reality of Popular Culture in 19th-century Scotland and Wales', *Proceedings of the British Academy*, 80 (1991), 19-48.

11 Hugh MacDiarmid, *Contemporary Scottish Studies* (Edinburgh: Scottish Educational Journal, [1976]).

12 George Elder Davie, *The Crises of the Democratic Intellect: The Problem of Generalism and Specialisation in Twentieth-Century Scotland* (Edinburgh: Polygon, 1986).

13 Devine, *The Scottish Nation*, pp. 84-102.

14 S. S. Laurie, *The Training of Teachers, and Other Educational Papers* (London: Kegan Paul, Trench, 1882), pp. 32-33; see Anderson, *Education and the Scottish People*, p. 266.

15 See Anderson, 'In Search of the "lad of parts"', p. 90.

16 Anderson, *Education and the Scottish People*, p. 261.

17 Scottish Education Department, *Education (Scotland) Reports, etc.*, issued in 1920-21 (Edinburgh: HMSO, 1921).

18 G. G. Ramsay, *Association for Securing Higher Instruction in Scottish Rural Schools: Statement of the Aims of the Association*, introduced by John Harrower (Aberdeen: Rosemount, 1913).

19 Anthony J. La Vopa, *Grace, Talent, and Merit: Poor Students, Clerical Careers, and Professional Ideology in Eighteenth Century Germany* (Cambridge: Cambridge University Press, 1988).

20 T. C. Smout, *A Century of the Scottish People, 1830-1950* (London: Collins, 1986), pp. 223-30.

21 Andrew Bain, *Opportunity Transformed: The Social Composition of Popularly Elected School Boards in West Lothian (1873-1919)* (Cardenden: Fife County Council Services, [2000]); Andrew Bain, *Towards Democracy in Scottish Education: The Social Composition of Popularly Elected School Boards in Fife (1873-1919)* ([Linlithgow]: the author, 1998).

22 For the new political opportunities, see Lindsay Paterson, *Education and the Scottish Parliament*, Policy and Practice in Education 1 (Edinburgh: Dunedin, 2000).

Chapter Three

From South to North: Education in Memory and in History

David Northcroft

This paper will necessarily begin – and conclude – with an anecdote, and a personal one at that. Both its content and the form are central to what has to be said about the ways in which 'a good Scottish education' is constructed, rehearsed, and then passed on into the national history.

It was early September, 1956; the setting is the Rector's study at Aberlour High School, Banffshire. I was then the 14-year-old son of the recently appointed exciseman at Cragganmore Distillery, ten miles further up the valley and, as his latest enrolment, this was the occasion of my introduction to Mr William Wood MA. The meeting was, like the man himself, short and to the point. The week before, I had been a pupil at Lewes County Grammar School, some 600 miles to the south, in Sussex. My father began to explain what a well thought of establishment that was, what a good start to a secondary education it offered its pupils. As he spoke, he suddenly sounded rather loud and very Home Counties English.

He didn't get very far. After a couple of minutes, Willie Wood promptly cut in: 'I'm afraid, Mr Northcroft, he will find the standards much higher here in Scotland than what he's been used to. And he'll have to work harder too.'

What this paper would like to suggest is that, for all of us, organized education begins with some form of an encounter. And that, although in the writer's case, individual circumstances gave his introduction into it a particularly sharp edge, there have always been a complex of forces at work – some social, some mythopoeic – which have combined to load the child's entry into the systematised world of the local school, here in the North-East of Scotland, with a historical significance. In places like Aberlour or Aberchirder or the Mearns, going to school is at once a personal experience and a cultural process. The infant comes to it from an intimately domestic environment, which the school now confronts as representative of the National System. From the very first day, its teachers, and the codes and values they steer by, will set to work upon the young individual in order to effect a change in outlook, as well as capacities, and not just as a limited episode but through a long drawn out, carefully constructed and deliberately formative procedure.

In a democracy, an intervention into the lives of its members of this insistent magnitude requires explanation. The rhetoric, by which it has been justified, used to talk about 'training' and 'civilising'; of late, 'development' and 'growth' have been more favoured. Polemic of this kind is common to all such systems, of course, but in Scotland, the daily business of the classroom has been further enlarged by a form of discourse, which has habitually sought to place it within the wider context of the country's chronicled history and inherited values. There are evident political, economic, and social reasons for this: at school level, these forces have been translated into a series of traditional practices that enter, and then participate in, the individual's localised upbringing, to make of it, later, an exemplary narrative, a contribution to the collective wisdom, or the basis for a fondly recounted anecdote.

The coming together of North-East child and national institution has, then, always been more than a mere academic transaction that may be accounted for in rational terms. Instead, our memories have placed it into a landscape of assumptions, of individual expectations, of social intentions and of shared recollection. It is, for better or for worse – and usually as a mixture of these qualities – a cultural induction. And as Mr Wood's comment revealed, in his Banffshire corner, the outsider's initiation could be charged with a significance that stretched it back into the tensely self-conscious history of a nation and its continuing identity.

This personal drama of 1956 was, in fact, only part of what was going on for the actors then involved in the immediate occasion. Running through the simple act of school enrolment, a deeper script was being acted out. Both Rector and new boy were locked into a framework that was beyond their own making; actions and reactions on that day had been bequeathed to them by respective histories which belonged to the larger story of Scottish education, and its implicit, inbred comparison to that of its southern neighbour and British partner. This is what enabled Willie Wood, squaring up in a pokey room in a small and sparsely populated parish of upper Banffshire, and quite ignorant of the curricular background of the adolescent incomer who flinched before him, to announce that what now lay ahead was bound to be tougher and more substantial than anything Sussex could possibly have offered. And, interestingly, his new pupil had also come to the meeting with his own satchel of received impressions which this Rector was now confirming. Both his parents and teachers at Lewes, including its couple of expat Scots, had already warned of the hard work, the academic rigour, of the leather belt in place of the bamboo cane. That a Scottish education demanded higher standards was something he just knew about his new country, along with Ben Nevis, the Tay Bridge disaster, the six months of snow and the necessity of choosing between Celtic and Rangers as successors to Brighton and Hove Albion.

He was to discover that none of these anxiously transported beliefs was precisely predictive. During the ensuing four years at Aberlour, he was to deal with a syllabus which was entirely familiar to him, except for the wondrous addition of Robert Burns, one in which the teaching relied on the same routines of didactic exposition, of note-taking, memorisation, exercises, and end-of-term examination.

Whereas at Lewes, being whacked had been a daily fact of life, in his northern academy he never once saw a tawse in anger. There wasn't even that much snow. Teachers called him by his first name, and he discovered the Dons.

Those five minutes of unease in the Rector's office were an actual event; the attitudes which infused them belonged to the myth of Scottish education, and of the self-regarding contribution to it made by the North-East corner.

The blending of myth and actuality, and of the combination of generalised history and specific happening which holds them together in the collective memory, have created North-East Education. Its schools belong, of course, to the nation as a whole and to the larger traditions that the Scottish system projects. The parishes and small burgh communities of Aberdeenshire, of Banffshire, of Moray and Kincardine have, however, come to claim a special proprietorship over them. The local collections, held by the University of Aberdeen and by the City's libraries, are filled with area histories, biographies, pamphlets, and travellers' tales which testify to that ownership. Pick up the essays collected within a generic title such as W. S. Bruce's *The Nor' East*[1] and you will find that the local school is at the heart of an opening chapter by which he lays before us a cherished evocation of the region. In it, may be revisited the stories of peasants who valued education so much that they stinted and starved to enable their boy to study the Latin, of dominies who gave their scholarship to forty years of hard service in some shut off glen, of lads o' pairts who 'cultivated literature on a little oatmeal'. You will also come to the statement, made definitive by its source in the Scotch Education Department's all-seeing, all-managing, first ever Secretary, Sir Henry Craik: 'Scotland is the best educated country in the world, and these counties are the best educated in Scotland'.[2]

The administrator's judgement acknowledges a special relationship between the regional part and the Scottish whole. For a number of specific reasons, such as the operation of the Dick and the Milne Bequests as sources of widespread subsidy, and the close working relationship that evolved between Aberdeen's two universities, King's and Marischal, and their catchment, the academic quality of teacher available to North-East schools raced ahead of that elsewhere in the middle years of the nineteenth century. There is also strong sociological evidence – superbly marshalled by Ian Carter in his *Farm Life in Northeast Scotland 1840-1914* – to indicate that, during these years, the great advancement of the area's agriculture led to a finely graded society, now sufficiently resourceful, and driven by an ethos of independent, self-improving endeavour, to support the opportunities for 'getting on' that could be invested in a thoroughgoing parish school system.[3]

But socio-economic factors such as these are only the faintest of backgrounds to an argument which Bruce prefers to pursue through an appeal to a moralistic pride in the frugality, the God-respecting integrity, and the higher purpose of his folk: 'Luxuries are shunned and only necessities are attended to. Yet the cottar will give his children the best education he can'.[4] He is referring here to 'the cauld kail' of Banff and the 'dry wit' which is carried by the accents of Buchan; but through them he is also talking about Scotland. A pair of comments makes the connection firm: 'Scotland has ever been a country of ideals'; 'Scottish independence has not yet vanished from these counties'.[5] It is not that the schools of the North-East are typical of the whole; they sum up its deepest values. They are its quintessence.

Bruce also tells his reader: 'There is no land in which the past is more of a living fact than it is in Scotland'.[6] Mythologised history of the kind that he is reworking seeks to imbue the current scene with the inherited properties of the past, and thus turn chronicle into tradition. It is by this process that its human elements take on iconic status – village teachers become dominies, their prize pupils are lads o' pairts, they are the sons of pious peasant folk and, as a focal point for the whole community, the parochial school becomes the well-remembered skweel. North-East lore sets this cast against a further transfiguring dimension – geography. In Bruce, the actors are made to tread the surface of a rugged terrain whose climatic rigours and slow yielding soil make the land of Banff and of Buchan the looming, external equivalent to the inner values of the peoples.

The production is repeated in Elsie Rae's *A Waff o' Win' fae Benachie* (1930). In a work which guides us through a range of topographical and historical features, the key statement comes when she announces: 'If I were asked what was the most outstanding thing about the people of the North-East, I would say, without hesitation, their love of learning'.[7] The claim is encased in precisely the same binding that Bruce uses: there is the 'frugal' life, the 'plain' behaviours, the stinting and the starving to ensure a secondary education for the bairns; there is the identical tale of a daily ten-mile trek over steep heather slopes by infant feet, intent on winning through to the University of Aberdeen – 'known as the University of the Working Man's family'.[8] And, arching over all, is the repeated assertion that this is 'Scotland', or rather, what a Scotland laid bare of all degenerate and urbanised pretension should be: 'The folk of the North-East are apt to be judged thus because what are common Scottish characteristics are in them more obvious, more intense.'[9]

These two works, Bruce's and Rae's, emanate from the interwar years when the North-East legend was being written up in the forms that would consolidate it for later generations. It was in this period that the earliest hagiographic accounts of Ramsay MacDonald began to be penned. Here, may be cited Hessell Tiltman's *Labour's Man of Destiny* (1929), a work in which the relatively mild climate of the Moray Firth and Lossiemouth's gently sanded shoreline become the scene where 'Nature sounds a perpetual challenge... It is impossible to picture "the lover of soft paths" coming to such a spot'.[10] The biographer continues to load the raw material with the stock properties: the drama already inherent in the phenomenon of the illegitimate son of a farm labourer, who became Great Britain's first Labour Prime Minister, is heightened into an inspirational pageant. The church is a strong influence but it is the dominie – 'that old Scots teacher, labouring in a remote village', John Macdonald, 45 years in the post – which proved to be the vital one.[11]

These works are but fragments, however, when compared to a volume which appeared in 1925, *The Schools and Schoolmasters of Banffshire* (Barclay). Had this writer but known it, it must also have been present on that initiation day in 1956.

In that era, Morayshire still lay on the other side of the Victoria Bridge, which took the pedestrian across the Spey at Aberlour, and the village was very much part of Banffshire. When it was published, the county authorities purchased sufficient numbers to present one to each of the schools within its boundaries. Its large navy bulk would have been there somewhere among the 'Pillans and Wilsons' and the Blue books ranged along Willie Wood's shelves.

Produced by the Education Institute of Scotland (EIS) branch of the county, the work's intention was to document the achievements of Banffshire schools from the earliest sixeenth century records of the Reformation to the latest era of County Boards, established by the 1918 Act. Although it is full of lists, dates, and diligently assembled events, the factual account is filled out with passages from local histories, log books, verbatim extracts of public speeches, sketches of exemplary careers, individual memories, and press cuttings. These are bound together by a style, which reaches up towards that elevation of manner and allusion that can invest a small county's story with the heroic development of the nation's inner soul.

It is, perhaps, in the frequent passages of geographical evocation that the epic scale most clearly announces itself. In the Preface, the compiler, William Barclay, tells the reader that this is 'a county that may be taken as in many ways representative of conditions throughout Scotland'.[12] It is, on the face of it, a dubious claim to make of a tapering finger of territory, some fifty miles by thirty, almost exclusively agricultural, and without a settlement of more than 5,000 inhabitants. It is, however, fringed by a seaboard, which is enclaved by numerous small fishing ports; it also stretches back through a varied hinterland of 'field, pasture, glen, moor, and forest and abundance of running water', up into the Cairngorms, 'the greatest mountainous area of Scotland'.[13] Barclay's schoolmasters stride out over a land which is marked by the elemental symbolism of a country which, historically, has preferred to seek its soul within its rural and more 'natural' past, and away from the industries and the towns that have lately troubled its countenance in the less favoured, more southerly spots.

The note is reiterated throughout a list which begins with the county town itself, whose academy possesses an antiquity which stretches 'back to ancient times', and which, under its 'brilliant and painstaking' – the classic *Banffshire* combination of attributes – Dr Wilson, saw the nineteenth century out with 'hundreds' of bursary competition winners: 'no school in the North of Scotland stood in higher repute, as tested by this touchstone of efficiency'.[14] Alphabetically, the last, some 72 place-names onwards, is Whitehills, which has, like all of those that have gone before it in this county chronicle, also been blessed with teachers 'of high usefulness and much distinction'.[15]

Aberlour appears exactly half way through this great scholastic procession. Barclay's treatment is, in both structure and tone, entirely typical. First comes the grandeur of the setting. Its valley flooring is girded by the granite chain of the Blue Hill, the Convals, Ben Rinnes; for boundaries, it has the clear waters that speed downwards from the Cairngorms – Fiddich, Dullan, Spey. Once it bore the title of

Skirdustan, after Drostan, its 'tutelary saint'; now it takes its name from the point where the Lour enters the rushing waters of the Spey.[16]

The confluence of place and history, and the flood of masters through the centuries; Barclay faithfully chronicles each one. It is when he comes to Charles Grant, thirty years in charge of the parochial school, from 1844 to 1874, that he finds his consummative hero. A local farmer's boy, who went from village school to university and then straight back to teach within the parish, he could truly be described as 'A Model Schoolmaster'. It is worth pausing to ascertain what is meant by this accolade. Grant was, first of all, a teacher with an outstanding reputation for scholarship and for bringing boys on to succeed in the university bursary competition: 'under Mr Grant many lads of Lower Speyside were enabled to place their foot on the first rung of the ladder of success…' But, above all, Grant was a man whose character and way of life summed up the virtues of his own community. 'As fine a type of Strathspey man as could have been found between the two Craigellachies'; he was an accomplished violinist of reels and Strathspeys; he had an inborn love of flowers and made the school garden 'a perfect paradise'; he was an angler of such mastery that he was 'the neatest at throwing the line on the run o' the Spey'. He was as liable to be consulted by the locals on an obscure point of clan history or of local lore as on the Latin poets of the Augustan Age.[17]

It is, however, the moral qualities which bind the accomplishments together and give the man his true meaning. Grant was content to serve his whole life of 85 years, university apart, within 'that storied and beautiful region', never straying further than ten miles from the place of his birth. There, he taught single-handed, seeking his reward in the success of 'his boys'; 'as became his traditional type, nothing gave the old school master greater pleasure than to hear of their wellbeing in the race of life'. In the community at large, he was elder, session clerk, registrar – 'never more active than when working, without thought of fee or reward, for the attainment of some object likely to benefit that part of Lower Speyside, in which his whole active life was spent'.[18]

It is this mixture of specific detail, of elemental setting, of pious valuation and iconic allusion which enables Barclay to claim that his Banffshire breeds a race of dominies who sum up the national whole. 'He was a typical example of the "old parochial", a class of men for whose efforts of self sacrifice and diligence Scotland can never be too grateful'. In identifying this portion of the North-East with the nation, Barclay is making a claim, not only upon the country's recognition of his locality's virtue, but upon their agreed perception of where such quality lies. His is the language of possession as much as it is of definition.

Another way of expressing this kind of relationship between part and whole is to talk about 'belonging'. Grant is so completely of his parish that he also demonstrates what it means to belong to Scotland. But it is important to realise that in effecting this connection, the writer is implicitly making a claim that involves possession too – that he, the author, has a command over the nation's icons, that he has an understanding of the meaning of Scotland. He is taking upon himself the right to define the properties which establish the 'real' Scotland, and the virtues which identify its true sons and daughters.

It is a process of construction which works by selective recall and partisan emphasis. It is, therefore, open to political exploitation. The myth of belonging, as it seeks out an external correspondence in landscape and communal event, may be appropriated, to assist an immediate cause or to justify an established interest. Both these motives may be seen at work in the present example. It is no accident that Barclay gathered his stories together for publication in the early days of post-war reform, a few years after the 1918 Act had swept away the old parish board system and replaced it with the larger unit of the county. In the strongholds of rural education, this development was interpreted as yet another step in the movement by the centralised Scottish Education Department (SED) towards the concentration of secondary level work in burgh centres, and away from the little places – the Ordiquhills, the Tomnavoulins, the Longmanhills – where generations of dominies had given each local lad the chance, in his very own birthplace, to imbibe the Latin which could propel him upwards to university and into the professions.

The one side could muster up the forces of deep set imagery and native emotion: 'under the old and well tried regime, sons of the county were so trained in the classics as in homely moralities that in after life Banffshire was proud to acclaim them as her children. They passed to the big world outside, played their part in the life in a way that brought abounding credit to the county of their birth…'[19] Against this charging rhetoric, the civil servants in the SED could only range the displaced weaponry of modernisation and of bureaucratic efficiency.

Three quarters of a century further on, it is now clear which side prevailed in that particular battle. But if the line of qualities which Barclay, Bruce, and Rae invoked as defining the North-East – piety, the work ethic, parental sacrifice, academic scholarship, getting on, and a landscape so saturated in education that each tiny parish must have its own academy of learning and its own MA dominie – are now sufficiently dated as to require some rearrangement, respect for the ingredients remains. Moreover, the process of mixing together specific incident and emotive response, in order to achieve the myth of a tribal identity, goes on. To offer some quick examples: the lovingly detailed evocation of a personal schooling at Cairnorrie, complete with poem by Flora Garry at its head, by which, in her autobiography *Good Vibrations*,[20] the internationally renowned musician Evelyn Glennie affirms her Aberdeenshire roots; the weekly columns by Bill Howatson and Norman Harper in the *Press and Journal*;[21] and, most vividly of all, the angst and the soul searching, which greeted the recent melodrama orchestrated by the Scottish Qualifications Agency, and which prompted the London-based *Guardian* to blazon on its leader pages a somewhat less anguished article on 'Scotched Myths'.[22]

How we respond to the part played by education in the formation of our North-East character, within the framework of 'Scotland', is a live issue. Given what we have read, the cultivation of a critical attitude towards the North-East educational tradition, and the larger national virtues which it claims to have in its safe keeping, is essential. This should begin with the recollections of the past and of the texts which have enshrined them. Turn back to Barclay and to his exemplary Aberlour. When the new building was opened there in 1897, the event was dignified by a speech from Mr. John R. Findlay, the Laird of the village. He congratulates the school on now possessing a total role of 270, 35 of whom are learning Latin. He lauds it as a handsome proportion; then comes the climactic summation that, over the preceding decade, ten pupils have earned Bursary awards. It is the basis for what comes next: 'The grand fact for us is that Scotland had, one way or another, a national system of education... for 200 years before England... for two centuries it has been possible for every child in Scotland to obtain elementary education, while to many it was also open to acquire a really thorough education at school or college... It had the further merit that nearly the whole people were thus more or less trained in the exercise of their brains, developing the capacities of the race'.[23]

The movement from Strathspey to all of Scotland is made with the facility of a speaker who can rest easy upon a whole tradition of such valuations, as well as his own inherited pre-eminence within the social hierarchy. Yet a moment's reflection is sufficient to raise the doubts. Mr Findlay is referring to a period in which it was virtually impossible for anyone within the labouring classes to finance a university career without the aid of a bursary. At the boasted rate of one award per year, it is likely that of those 270, fewer than a meagre handful will be able to avail themselves fully of their country's celebrated liberal opportunities.

The Laird's speech invokes the defining values of academic achievement, democracy and sassenach inferiority. Against his particular citation of them, it would be worth inquiring into the fates of all those other unnamed High School hundreds. How did the chance of a mouthful of Ovid and Xenaphon strike the average farm servant's lad, on whose obliging future labour the upkeep of Mr Findlay's estate relied? And, in our pursuit of the relationship between professed equality and socio-economic actualities, it would also be worth asking whether any of the good Laird's own progeny were ever among that parochial 270, sharing the hard benches and the hazards of a minority classical education within a class of fifty or so locals – rather than, as had now become the upper class practice, to be sent to the academic security of the city, or to the English version of a 'public school', as soon as they were old enough to stand the parting?

Against such sharp enquiry, the lustrous imagery of lads o'pairts, of paternalistic dominies, socially mixed schoolrooms and the ladder of opportunity, can seem exposed as the justification by myth of a form of social control which is every bit as politically directed as all the efforts of the SED, on the other side, to rationalise the untidy parish structure into a modern, economically focused regime.

The icons have crumbled a bit since the 1920s. The Kirk, and the piety that sustained it, has dwindled to become just one of a range of social agencies hopefully at work upon our young; it is pointless to speak with precious intensity of lads o'pairts when 40% now go on to Higher Education; poverty is no longer justified as character forming experience; farming, and the communal structures which served it, is increasingly peripheral; it is now twenty years since the College of Education had a Latin graduate on its hands.

Barclay's age is, however, no more than a grandparent's generation away. The assumptions which flourished then have driven deep into our sense of what a proper North-East, or Scottish, education ought to be. Its standards and images still provide a reference point. The themes which were raised then – educational opportunity, the relationship of school to community, the role of academic interests, the standing of the teacher – are very much with us. They are, moreover, still as likely to be debated in a discourse, which turns to the personal memory or the inherited folk model, as often as it does to hard data and empirical evidence. And, if anything, the underlying issues of regional and of national identity are, at the beginning of the twenty-first century, stronger than ever.

What then are the lessons from all this history? What should our response be to a record of the past in which the force of myth has been as potent as carefully garnered fact? Given the seriousness of the matters implicated – power, identity, social control, democratic opportunity – the soundest advice might be to do a debunk, that is to get rid of the myths, rein in the memories and fix on the actual data. Yet look again at how the stories of the past are made to enact their present meanings. *The Schools and Schoolmasters of Banffshire* opens with a set scene.[24] It is of a graveside in a country church yard, where, in November 1921, there were gathered all the sons of Mr Charles Mair, who was for over thirty years a grocer and tenant farmer in the far flung agricultural and moorland parish of Grange. He had been a man of private learning, a student of his county's place names, and a faithful Sunday schoolteacher. But what was really remarkable was his lineage: the magical figure of seven sons who went from the local school to the University of Aberdeen, each of whom gained first class honours in the classics. They had then gone on to become headmasters, to fill Church and legal positions, and to take up a Chair of Greek; two had stayed behind to build up the cattle business of their own region.

It is difficult to resist the spell of a scene which is at once recognisably domestic and grandly heroic. The glimpse of those seven brothers, whose talents had flung them apart, but were now reunited in the black of their common homage, is a reminder that the stories, which people tell of their social experience, compel the imagination and engage our sense of common significance in a way that Scottish Office documentation will never do. The real problem in responding to the narrative invitations of Barclay, Rae, Bruce and Ramsay Macdonald to assent to their version of our identity, is not that they tell too many stories but too few. What works of that kind do is to memorialise their subject in ways that both exclude the possibility of further growth and shut out a whole range of alternative testimony. The preoccupation with competitive academic achievement, and upon the ability to win it against the common odds, is so socially exclusive as to undermine the democratic spirit which is claimed for it.

If we are to recover a properly balanced appreciation of the ways in which its famed educational system has both encapsulated and answered the aspirations of North-East people, then what we need are more, not fewer, personal dramas. In each of the narrative authorities cited in this piece, the focus has been upon a tiny minority of singular achievements. We need to dig deeper into the plethora of materials within our local collections, or to be tapped by oral interview, in order to recover the life histories of those whose parish education ended with the Catechism and the three Rs. In the area of agrarian socio-economics, we already have the patient reconstructive work of writers such as David Kerr Cameron[25] and Ian Carter to thank for a deeper understanding of the extent to which sociology and cultural practice have interacted to shape the world of those ordinary masses, who provide the silent extras to Barclay's classroom scenes. Yet, in piecing together their accounts, these writers pay as much attention to ballads and domestic ritual as they do to data concerning land use and market prices. There is an opportunity to bring a similar combination of human concerns and thoroughgoing documentation to an investigation of the formative experiences which the local school has offered its young citizens, both then in the rural past, and subsequently on into a more complex and various present.

But half the population of the North-East have never been anywhere near a chaumer or bothy, receiving their schooling in its one large urban centre, the city of Aberdeen. The attempts to translate the provisions of the rural parish to the growing city in the nineteenth century, and the waves of, first, evangelical and then middle-class philanthropy that attended it, can tell us much about the interplay of social class interests and educational expectation in the North-East. The privately distributed life story of the soutar, Chartist, and later journalist William Lindsay, with its lively accounts of a flourishing self-help movement in the workshops and the back streets around the Hardgate, would be a useful corrective to the version of an all-providing, classless national system. So, too, would the pamphlets distributed by Sheriff Watson who founded Scotland's first 'industrial school 'for the city's infant street vagrants, along with the unpublished manuscript autobiography stored away in a biscuit tin in the basement of the city Central Library.[26]

Indeed, it is important to remember that, whether country or town dweller, half of the region's population have never been eligible to attain the rank of lad o'pairts. Yet, in Christian Watt, the Fraserburgh fishwife who left Broadsea School at eight to become a skiffie and who later turned down the hand of Lord Saltoun's nephew because of 'society's rules', we have been left one of the most remarkable of North-East autobiographies.[27] The testimony of her and of her gender is also required reading.

There are, of course, many other witnesses who could be summonsed to our investigation of how individual memory and collective history have woven in and out of each other in order to create the subtle patterning that, beneath the stylised surface, makes up the educational experiences and attitudes of Scotland's North-East corner. As a final illustration of the extent to which ingrained models continue to shape the interplay of attitude within our present day relationships, I would like to end as I began, with a personal anecdote.

Some five years ago, I was back in the Aberlour area. From the Elgin tourist office, I discovered that it was now possible to visit Ballindalloch Castle, a site which, in my exciseman's son's days at nearby Cragganmore, had been quite shut off from us locals. At the end of the tour, I got chatting to a pleasant, elegantly tartaned woman of my own age, who was anxious to assure herself that I had found everything in order. It turned out to be Lady Clare Macpherson-Grant, the current mistress of the Castle.

I told her that I had once been a local and that, indeed, we must have been of school age at much the same time (though I certainly didn't recall her presence on the school bus that stopped each morning at the Castle's back gate to pick up the sons and the daughters of parents who worked on the Macpherson-Grant estates – she was, in fact, educated by °her own governess within the castle). After a certain amount of tentative half questioning, it was at last established that the Aberlour school I was referring to was not the secluded preparatory establishment where Gordonstoun's future recruits received their initiation into boarding school life, but the plain four-square parochial building, up at the back of the village. For a moment, Lady Clare was a little discomposed at this sudden revelation of class assumptions and did not quite know how to proceed with the conversation. However, it was only a second or so before the North-East's traditional valuations rescued the situation: 'So', she beamed, 'you went to our local school. Well, I bet you had a simply super education there'.

She was right... wasn't she?

Notes

[1] W.S. Bruce, *The Nor' East* (Aberdeen: Bisset, 1929), pp. 9, 13.

[2] Bruce, p. 13.

[3] Carter, pp. 2–5.

[4] Bruce, p. 8.

[5] Bruce, p. 2.

[6] Bruce, p. 3.

[7] Elsie Rae, 'The North East: its Folk and Language', in *A Waff o' Win' fae Benachie*, pp. 67-82 (p. 70).

[8] Rae, p. 70.

[9] Ibid.

[10] H. Hessell Tiltman, *James Ramsay MacDonald: Labour's Man of Destiny* (London: Jarrolds, 1929), p. 20.

[11] Tiltman, p. 23.

[12] William Barclay, *The Schools and Schoolmasters of Banffshire* (Banff: Banffshire Journals, 1925), p. vii.

[13] Barclay, p. vii.

[14] Barclay, p. 18.

[15] Barclay, p. 78.

[16] Barclay, p. 150

[17] Barclay, p. 153.

[18] Barclay, p. 154.

[19] Barclay, p. 2.

[20] Evelyn Glennie, *Good Vibrations* (London: Hutchinson, 1990), pp. 27–33

[21] See *Aberdeen Press and Journal,* 12 November 1999, p. 8; 22 July 1999, p. 8.

[22] Tim Luckhurst, *The Guardian*, 16 March 2000.

[23] Barclay, p. 155.

[24] Barclay, p. 1.

[25] David Kerr Cameron, *The Ballad and the Plough: A Portrait of the Life of the Old Scottish Farmtouns* (London: Gollancz, 1978); see also *Willie Gavin, Crofter Man: Portrait of a Vanished Lifestyle* (London: Gollancz, 1980); *Cornkister Days: A Portrait of a Land and its Rituals* (London: Gollancz, 1984).

[26] William Watson, 'An Autobiography', unpublished manuscript MS, Aberdeen City Central Library, Local Collections.

[27] David Fraser, ed., *The Christian Watt Papers*, 2nd edn (Collieston, Aberdeenshire: Caledonia, 1988).

Chapter Four

Home Education: A Victorian Case Study

Gordon Booth

The urge to educate one's children at home is seldom wholly disinterested. Either the parent is determined to prove a point or else is concerned to protect the offspring from the moral infections of a contaminating world beyond the home. The well-known miseries of John Stuart Mill at the hand of his father's pedagogic zeal illustrate both motives: in his son's words, old James Mill wanted, 'to give, according to his conception, the highest order of intellectual education'[1] and also to preserve his son untainted 'from the sort of influence he [the father] so much dreaded'.[2] The outcome was a severe mental breakdown on the young Mill's part at the age of twenty.

What I propose to describe, however, is a much happier instance of home education, which took place forty years later. The father, William Pirie Smith, had been assistant to the headmaster of the West End Academy in Aberdeen and, having prudently married the rector's daughter, had taken over as head of his father-in-law's prestigious school, then at 216 Union Street, Aberdeen. Smith took a keen interest in the momentous church events of the day and, following the Disruption of 1843, was persuaded to abandon his secure career for the precarious task of establishing a Free Church congregation at Keig and Tough, in the Howe of Alford, where relatively few folk were followers of the Free Kirk cause and where Smith's flock was always to be a small one. His wife, Jane, was expecting her second child when the couple moved to Keig in 1846 and their first son, William Robertson Smith, born in November of that year, was the first child to be baptised in the new Free Church building there. In due course there was a family of seven children in the manse and, from the start, their father set about educating his children at home, eking out his meagre stipend by teaching a small number of other children, both as boarders and day pupils.[3]

That eldest son, William Robertson Smith, was destined to achieve both fame and notoriety. He stands today as one of the two greatest Scottish intellects of the later Victorian period – being matched only by his more famous contemporary, James Clerk Maxwell.[4] Entering Aberdeen University just before his fifteenth birthday,[5] Smith gained the town council's medal for most outstanding student in his final year.[6] In 1866, he went to New College, Edinburgh, having resolved to devote his life to the Free Church cause, and again rapidly made his mark, becoming an expert Hebraist and obtaining the Professorship of Hebrew and Old Testament Literature in the Free Church College in Aberdeen at the age of 24. While a divinity student at New College, he had also become assistant to Peter Guthrie Tait, Professor of Natural Philosophy at Edinburgh University,[7] and gained wide acclaim in scientific circles for his early papers in mathematics and physics.

It seemed a foregone conclusion that Smith would pursue an uneventful scholarly life in Aberdeen for the remainder of his life, but it was to prove otherwise. Commissioned to contribute articles on Biblical subjects for the new (ninth) edition of the *Encyclopaedia Britannica*,[8] the young professor instantly attracted the wrath of his more conservative Free Kirk colleagues because of his rationalistic approach to the Bible and his espousal of the new 'higher criticism' emanating from Germany and Holland. The first batch of articles from his pen – 'Angels', 'Ark of the Covenant', and 'Bible' – led to his swift arraignment on charges of heresy at the bar of the Free Church General Assembly in May 1876. The case dragged on for four years, with Smith's forensic astuteness repeatedly denying his opponents the satisfaction of a conviction, whereupon they ultimately adopted the alternative expedient of dismissing him from his post in 1881. Smith returned to Edinburgh, becoming joint (later chief) editor of the *Encyclopaedia Britannic*a before moving to Cambridge in 1883, first as Reader in Arabic, then as University Librarian and finally as Professor of Arabic, before his untimely death from tuberculosis at the age of 48, in 1894.[9]

Luckily, we know something of Smith's education at home through the memoirs, contributed for his biography by a number of the boarding pupils who had benefited from Dr Smith's talents.[10] These give a fascinating insight into the way in which an education of the highest quality was provided within a home setting, well before the advent of universal public education. William and his brothers seem to have received an education from their father quite as intense as that supplied to John Stuart Mill, but in a far more harmonious learning atmosphere. The young Mill resented having to teach his own brothers and sisters, but the same technique seemed not to dismay the two eldest Smith boys in the least.[11] One vignette amusingly described the daily routine:

> We began with arithmetic or mathematics. Dr Smith told everybody what he had to do for the next hour, and thereafter he took a pinch of snuff and sat down to read a chapter from Alford's Greek Testament, following up with some algebraic work which he performed, like the rest of us, on a slate, until the post came in.[12]

More significant perhaps is the well-recalled description of Dr Smith's teaching method:

> We went on with our work, rising and going to Dr Smith with the answer to each question as soon as finished, and when we stuck we went to him for help in the

same way. Here Dr Smith's system came in, for he simply said, 'Go on', and on we had to go somehow. If we took the right way he repeated 'Go on' but if we took the wrong method he asked us why we did this or that, and we had to reply to his question before we were allowed to alter our method.[13]

Another account of education at the Manse of Keig is provided by W. S. Bruce (later Free Kirk minister at Banff) who had been struggling to obtain entrance qualifications to university and was invited to stay with the family during the summers of 1862 and 1863:

> At noon, Dr Smith was ready for a walk and we boys would join him... The talk was always of some new thing in Science, or some interesting point in literature or stories concerning College days and College Professors... it was quite understood that this walk was itself part of the education of the manse and was yet more a favour conferred than a task allotted. Often out of the minister's pocket would come a volume for our delectation – probably Tennyson's 'In Memoriam', just a few months arrived and getting its first readings from every member, and purchased at the cost of no little self-denial... At another time it would be classical bits of the Poet Laureate in the grand style, such as 'Oenone', or 'Ulysses' or the 'Palace of Art' or some fine lines of Pope or Dryden, or choice bits of Shakespeare. Every beauty was pointed out, and many an eye-opener we got on these healthy hillsides...[15]

The hour-long daily walk, very much in the Socratic tradition, offered scope also for teaching philosophy, history and science, Dr Smith often playing devil's advocate to provoke argument. Bacon, Pascal, Gibbon, Rousseau, and Carlyle were all the subject of lively discussion. But it was the physical environment of these walks which allowed Smith to impart his own deep interest in science to his pupils:[16]

> Dr Smith would stop at a point on the hill where the huge rocks abutted on the path and would give a very graphic description of rock-formation and of the chemical activity of percolating water within stone. We were shown how the Aberdeen granite was clearly of igneous origin and how big Bennachie across the Don had been cooled and consolidated with the cooling of the earth's crust and then shot upwards into the long camel's back and various 'taps' which had become more sharp by subsequent denudation. The wonders of Geology burst upon our vision like some fairy scene in the Arabian Nights. We could scarcely believe all that was said and barely knew that we were learning modern Science, so pleasantly and jocularly was much of it done. We joked at the tea table about Bennachie's back, and would take liberties with the hard crusts of loaf to show the girls how, with a little squeezing, it was the easiest possible thing to produce miniature Bennachies and camel backs... In other walks the talk would be all of the flora and fauna of the vale of Alford... There we got our living Botany as the Doctor told us the names of every plant we passed and its exact place within the Linnaean classification. Everywhere high intellectual aims were pursued, and in

such a kind and engaging way that what was really a lesson looked like a daily treat and there was more of the picnic than the preacher in it. The love of Science grew daily though unconsciously under such fostering care.[17]

There is no doubt that Dr Smith found his eldest son, William, closest to himself in spirit and that correspondingly he related to the young prodigy more or less on an equal footing. Bruce described that affinity well:

> The father and son had many an argument. Genesis and Geology was a favourite topic. Hugh Miller's *Old Red Sandstone* on the one side and *The Vestiges of Creation* on the other gave occasion for very different views, while Darwin's book *On the Origin of Species* had made a tremendous sensation in the theological world… This produced endless talk, and father and son took different sides to some extent… I confess I was lost in wonder at the grip which the young man had of the questions and at the – as it then appeared to me – daring presumption with which he questioned old-fashioned views about the age of the earth.[18]

Darwin's theory had been published only three years previously, in 1859, and it is plain from Bruce's account that both father and son found it revelatory. Robert Chambers had published his *Vestiges of Creation* anonymously in 1844; while anticipating the Darwinian concept of evolution, it was purely speculative, wholly lacking the systematic observation and inductive reasoning which Darwin brought to *The Origin of Species*. The young Robertson Smith, Bruce tells us, had long been fascinated by the saying of Heraclitus, that 'all things are in flux', and so found the evolutionary model irresistibly appealing. Later, under the patronage in Edinburgh of Peter Guthrie Tait, close friend of both William Thomson (Lord Kelvin) and James Clerk Maxwell, Smith was to become intimately acquainted with the contemporary debate over geological time and with the new thermo-dynamic concept of entropy. All those interests stemmed ultimately from that careful yet systematic nurture provided at the Manse of Keig; all moreover had devastating theological implications:

> On Sundays we got, in the garden of the Manse, what we called his [W.R.S.'s] 'Sermons' on these topics, in which he borrowed from Astronomy, Botany, Geology and Chemistry and enforced upon our boyish minds the impermanency of the cosmos and the wisdom of the old philosophers of Greece, for whom he had a great admiration… The world we had regarded as a permanent entity he proved to us was a changeful process, a Becoming. Nothing endured but the flow of energy and the rational order which pervades it. It was another startling eye-opener to a lad like me; and all the more when I appealed to Dr Smith and found that he supported Willie… When I look back now and think of it, I venture to say there were few literary homes in London or schools [such] as Eton or Rugby where we would have got such eye-openers at that time as we boys enjoyed in that humble Manse at the back of the Don. The genius of the foremost science and of the rising philosophy of the age were being implanted in our minds

without our knowing it… The two holidays I spent at the Free Manse of Keig were the best inspiration to study I ever got in my youth. About that home and its discipline there was not a particle of constraint… For the dullard and the blockhead there was certainly no mercy on the part of the boys: but it was not so with the father and mother. With them there were patience, kindness and endless encouragement; and it seems to me no lad could spend a holiday there without coming away with a deep respect for literature and an ardent love of learning.[19]

Lastly, there remains a 'memorandum' of the son, written by William Pirie Smith in 1883, which is of interest in that the father seems almost unaware of how much he had contributed to his son's erudition:

The amount of information which he had at command on all sorts of subjects was quite amazing. I remember once, when he came out with some out of the way observation at table, saying to him, with a tone of surprise, 'Willie, how did you learn that?' 'I just picked it up,' was his reply. He certainly loved books from his earliest years.[20]

Perhaps diplomatically, Dr Smith plays down the amount of time he dedicated to his children's education:

I had my ministerial work to attend to – and was necessarily a good deal away from home among my people and much engaged in preparation for Sabbath work.[21]

But it is plain from the subsequent description of his teaching methods that the father had from the outset instilled a routine of independent learning which served his children very well indeed:

Their lessons were regularly prescribed and then the boys were left to their own resources and they uniformly did their best, just as well in my absence as when I was present, accomplishing all that could reasonably be expected. I am not sure that this method would answer in every case, but certainly in their case it trained them to habits of self-reliance – drew out their latent powers, accustomed them to think for themselves and gave them the pleasure that springs from the overcoming of difficulties… There was no cramming. No cribs were allowed. There was no such thing in the house and so it came to pass that a passage from a Latin or Greek author which they had never seen had no special terrors for them and presented difficulties such as they had already encountered and often surmounted.[22]

So William Robertson Smith and his brothers were trained in the best traditions of Victorian self-help and the Calvinist work ethic, yet under the watchful eye of a parent who provided them with a breadth of curriculum probably surpassing the best of the new city academics of the day. Formal lessons, from 9 o'clock to 4 o'clock, were complemented by the Doctor's 'walks', which appear to have inculcated the best principles of competitive debate as well as the classical tradition of *solvitur ambulando*. As always, it is idle to speculate on the relative contributions of nature versus nurture. The three eldest Smith boys were all intellectually able, but there is little doubt that the insatiable drive to learn was planted in them from the earliest age by their father. Commenting that Willie had casually picked up the Hebrew alphabet before the age of six but 'ceased to concern himself with this and at a much later period had to begin the study all over again', the father remarks in his 'memorandum':

> At the same time it is quite probable that this early taste of the Oriental may have been as a seed dropped into a kindly soil – a seed which was afterwards to spring into vigorous growth and bear abundant fruit.[24]

That 'kindly soil', the nurturing environment of the Manse of Keig, allied to the father's brilliant tutelage, was to result in an astonishing flowering of the young Smith's natural abilities within his brief life span of 48 years.

Robertson Smith's Calvinist background may seem a world apart from the extreme aestheticism of his English contemporary, Walter Pater, yet both were suffused by the adventurous and questing spirit of High Victorian culture and science which aimed to search out new territories of the mind and to uncover fresh, unconventional ways of understanding the human condition. Smith's seminal contributions to social anthropology and comparative religion – which lie beyond the scope of this short paper – evoked subsequent admiration and fulsome acknowledgement from such better known pioneers of modern thought as Emile Durkheim and Sigmund Freud. Yet Smith's own achievements are barely remembered within his homeland. Still less has our national educational system learned to cultivate aright the giftedness of its most able children. Pater's famous words may serve, therefore, all the more appropriately as the epitaph to the memory of this home-educated Renaissance man from rural Aberdeenshire:

> The service of philosophy, of speculative culture, towards the human spirit, is to rouse, to startle it to a life of constant observation… Not to discriminate every moment some passionate attitude in those about us, and in the very brilliancy of their gifts some tragic dividing forces on their ways, is, on this short day of frost and sun, to sleep before evening. With this sense of the splendour of our existence and of its awful brevity, gathering all we are into one desperate effort to see and to touch, we shall hardly have time to make theories about the things we see and touch. What we have to do is to be for ever curiously testing new opinions and courting new impressions, never acquiesing in a facile orthodoxy, of Comte, of Hegel, or of our own.[25]

Notes

1. John Stuart Mill, *Autobiography* (Oxford: Oxford University Press, 1963), p. 4.
2. Mill, *Autobiography*, p. 123.
3. See Donald J. Withrington, 'The School in the Free Church Manse at Keig', in *William Robertson Smith: Essays in Reassessment*, ed. by William Johnstone (Sheffield: Sheffield Academic Press, 1995), pp. 41-49, for a somewhat more sceptical assessment of William Pirie Smith's achievement.
4. Maxwell came of a landed family in Galloway. He was educated at Edinburgh Academy and was Professor of Natural Philosophy at Marischal College, Aberdeen until the amalgamation with King's College in 1860.
5. He was accompanied by his younger brother, George, who was less than 14 on admission to Aberdeen University. Both were the youngest of the students in their year.
6. Because of illness, Smith was unable to sit his final examinations but was awarded his degree on the basis of a bedside *viva voce*.
7. Smith taught physics to that unwilling and eccentric student, Robert Louis Stevenson. Being wholly different in background and temperament, the two men never became friends.
8. *Encyclopaedia Britannica: A Dictionary of Arts, Sciences, and General Literature*, 9th edn, ed. by T. S. Baynes and W. Robertson Smith, 36 vols (Edinburgh: A. & C. Black, 1874-1889).
9. The fullest account of Smith's life and work is John Sutherland Black and George William Chrystal, *The Life of William Robertson Smith* (London: A. & C. Black, 1912)
10. These are preserved at Cambridge University Library, Add MSS 7476.
11. The second son, George, who seems to have been as intellectually able as William, died suddenly, shortly after graduating.
12. Memoir by W. Y. McDonald, Cambridge University Library, Add MSS 7476, M8, p. 5.
13. Cambridge University Library, Add MSS 7476, M8.
14. *In Memoriam* had in fact been first published (privately and anonymously) in 1850.
15. Cambridge University Library, Add MSS 7476, M12, pp. 4-5.
16. Evidence of Dr Smith's familiarity with the latest trends in science is to be found in several of the son's letters from Edinburgh – cf. that of 26.10.1869 to Mrs Smith: 'There was a splendid arch across the heavens yesterday of exceeding brightness. Tait went up to the University to examine it with the spectroscope and distinguished at least <u>two</u> lines (this is for Papa)'. See Cambridge University Library, Add MSS 7449, C150a.
17. Cambridge University Library, Add MSS 7476, M12, pp. 8-9.
18. Cambridge University Library, Add MSS 7476, M12, p.10.
19. Cambridge University Library, Add MSS 7476, M12, pp.12-13.
20. Cambridge University Library, Add MSS 7476, M3 6.
21. Withrington notes how infrequently the father actually attended presbytery meetings and he remarks, 'There is little doubt that the school took him away from church duties'. See Withrington, 'The School in the Free Church Manse at Keig', pp. 46–49.
22. Cambridge University Library, Add MSS M3, 9.
23. The third son, Charles Michie Smith, eventually became Professor of Astronomy at Madras University.

[24] Cambridge University Library, Add MSS M3, 8.

[25] Walter Pater, *The Renaissance: Studies in Art and Poetry* (London: Macmillan, 1873); pbk edn, ed. and intro. by Adam Phillips (Oxford: Oxford University Press, 1986), p. 152.

Chapter Five

R. F. MacKenzie: North-East Radical with a Revolutionary Agenda

Peter A. Murphy

Almost three decades have now passed since the dismissal, by Aberdeen City Council, of R. F. MacKenzie from his post as Headteacher of Summerhill Academy. It is also fifteen years since his death in 1987. A reappraisal of what this son of the North-East contributed to educational thinking and practice – and to Scottish culture generally – would appear to be overdue.

One starting point might be the treatise he wrote following his sacking; 'A Manifesto for an Educational Revolution', he called it.[1] As that title suggests, the work was intended to be a re-evaluation of the Scottish system generally, one in which shortcomings and injustices would be confronted and an incisively new alternative offered. His normal publishers, Collins, refused to handle it; it was, they judged, too radical.

Their judgement is echoed in the words which Harry Reid, the then editor of *The Herald*, incorporated into the Foreword which he contributed to the present writer's biographical study, *A Prophet without Honour* (1998). 'An allegedly democratic and humanitarian education system', he concluded, 'simply spat MacKenzie out'.[2]

In expressing this view, Reid, twenty-five years after the event, voices the outrage which many liberal minded people continued to feel about the system's treatment of one of its most idealistic and eloquent dissident voices. At the time, however, it is doubtful whether this sentiment would have found general acceptance among the citizens and the ratepayers of Aberdeen itself. When it happened in 1974, this author could reflect upon his own experience of four years service, as Head of Summerhill's English Department, under MacKenzie's own crusading leadership; he had, however, also been born, bred and schooled in the city. He knew his fellow Aberdonian and out of that knowledge, composed the following satirical reaction, couched in the local dialect. It duly appeared in the *Times Educational Supplement (Scotland)*:[3]

An Aberdonian's Farewell to R. F. Mackenzie

Whit's that? They've gi'en him the sack?
Nae afore time! Gi'es mair o' yer crack!

Nae man deserved better tae get the shuv…
Gangin' aboot sayin' skweels are places for luv!
Whit next? A' they young anes need nooadays
Is a gweed skelp… nane o' yer sympathy an' praise,
An' sic like trash. A'body kens whit skweels are for…
Ye're there tae learn an' dae whit ye're telt,
Nane o' this speakin' back… that deserves the belt!
Teachers hae enough tae dae in the classroom,
Withoot fowk haverin' oan aboot the impendin' doom
O' Scottish education near deid frae a glut o' exams…
Whaur wid oor lads o' pairts, oor Jeans an' Tams
Be withoot their O-Grades an' Highers as weel?
Na, na, oor kids dinna want a holiday camp, they want a skweel.
Ach weel, maybe things'll quieten doon noo in the Lang Stracht,
Noo that mannie wi' the daft notion's been sacked!

To understand MacKenzie's fate, as teachers, academics, politicians – and as Scots – we need to understand where he came from and what made him hold the views he did, as well as to trace the shape that his career as teacher and educationist took. He was, first and last, a North-East man; this was the region into which he was born in 1910, and where, 77 years later, he died. More than that, he can be described as that most prized of North-East characters, a 'lad o' pairts'. As such, he followed in the tradition of other writers such as John R. Allan and Lewis Grassic Gibbon in using the rural community of that part of Scotland, with its distinctive culture, as a backcloth against which to work out his own vision of life. Mackenzie, in his final, consummative book, *A Search for Scotland*,[4] as well as in his feature articles for both *The Scotsman* and *The Glasgow Herald*, found constant inspiration in the stories and the observations that were bound up with the language and the lore of his North-East. In a *Herald* piece that he wrote in 1954, for instance, he poses the question, 'Is there in the North-East a stronger inclination to enter into the spirit of the past and to understand it by translating the records of the past into the idiom and familiar background of the present?' And he answers his own question by telling the following story:

> Over 25 years ago one summer afternoon a Sunday school teacher in Aberdeenshire was telling his class about the journey of Joseph's ten brothers from Canaan to Egypt to buy corn. It was hardly surprising, the teacher said, that for all these years his brothers didn't know Joseph. But how was it that Joseph knew his brothers?
>
> It was a difficult question, but one pupil shot his hand up at once, with the eagerness of a child who has suddenly understood. He said, 'Joseph would have seen the name on the cairts!'
>
> For that youngster, the gaps in the background of the story that the Bible does not give, had been filled in by his own imagination. Jacob and Joseph and Pharaoh were real people, as real as the Aberdeenshire farmers he knew. There

was Jacob with a pretty big place down in Shechem – it must have been a big farm because he had all his sons working for him. Joseph had struck out for himself and was doing well as manager of an even bigger farm, one owned by a man called Pharaoh. Jacob had told his sons that they would have to go to Pharaoh's farm; it was the only place in the countryside where you could get corn… when they got to Egypt they had been well done to. They had loused and stabled their horses and gone into supper. All this unbeknown to Joseph. Joseph maybe, had been coming up the close in the gloaming when he saw the strange carts. He went across to see whose carts they might be, and there, on a bright plaque on front of each, he would naturally read: JACOB and SONS, MAINS OF SCHECHEM, DOTHAN…[5]

From his father, the stationmaster at Wartle, in the heart of Aberdeenshire, he learned, in particular, to question the validity of the accepted way of doing things; why it was, for instance, that every rural community seemed to be dominated by the triumvirate of Laird, Dominie, and Minister. Had they some God-given right to hold such sway over them all? Similarly, was the sound but stodgy education he had received at the local schools and later at Robert Gordon's College, where he was Dux, all that it was reputed to be? And what about the intrinsic value of the Honours English course he had graduated from – and at considerable expense to his parents – at the University of Aberdeen? This is how he saw it all in retrospect:

> Even today I have difficulty in describing how I felt as a university student from a working class home. The educational landscape was indistinct as if I was seeing it through a fogged-up railway carriage window. An admission of the naivety of what I felt may help to clean the window. I was aware of my father's qualities; but then, I thought, if he is as I believe why is he content to remain a village stationmaster? The current cultural belief was that such people rose, like cream, to the top… the University never repudiated that view… I wanted to know what the university was for, but it wouldn't say. Is the University about giving glittering prizes to those with sharp swords or giving wisdom to ordinary folk? But it was left vague, so that working class folk in Aberdeenshire should continue to believe that the University offered the bread of life to any of the people in the hinterland who sought it. All the University offered, however, was the cultural galsichs of an acquisitive society.
>
> But little of that was clear the day we graduated. The usual greeting was sometimes followed by the query: 'What does it feel like to be an MA?' It was partly humorous, but there was in it a hankering after magic. We replied: 'It's no different.' What wisdom the University had failed to give us we should have to seek for ourselves.[6]

This is what MacKenzie proceeded to do. He actively set out to seek wisdom for himself. He put off settling down to the teaching career which his parents had desired for him and embarked upon an improvised tour of Europe on bicycle along with his close friend, Hunter Diack, in 1932-33. There, he was able to see for himself the advance of fascism in Italy and of Nazism in Germany, as well as the political unrest in the Balkans. This adventure formed the core of the book *Road Fortune* that MacKenzie and Diack got published by Macmillan in 1935.[7] It is full of an acute observation that plays over both the physical features of the countryside and the character of its people. Mackenzie, in particular, had, by the end of the tour, realised that terrible events were about to unfold in Europe. He remarks in his unpublished memoir of that time that he felt a sense of destiny in his being there to record the way in which such events would impinge on the lives of ordinary people caught up in them. 'I want to set down something of this, something about the men and the women I have known, and the events, known or guessed at, that were going on at the back of their minds'.[8]

It was in France during the cycle tour that Mackenzie and Diack had encountered, unannounced but warmly welcomed, a cult figure of the age, H. G. Wells, at his holiday home at Grasse. Wells had already made a significant intellectual impact upon the young Mackenzie through his *Outline of History*. In it, he had discovered a rare ability to put history into a perspective that made it comprehensible to the general reader. 'I was amazed', confessed Mackenzie in his private memoirs, 'and then delighted at the chapters on Caesar and Napoleon. Wells was saying, "I'm a man – they were not more. Lets have a look at them"… these were the words of emancipation. They were the keys that fitted the locks with which my school and university education had enclosed me in a prison of ideas'.[9]

On his return to Britain, MacKenzie successfully applied for a teaching post at an independent school in the New Forest. His time there (1934-36) had a profound effect on his later thinking in education. This school was known as the Forest School and was run by a society called the Order of Woodcraft Chivalry. The keynote was informality. At the primary stages, before the shadow of secondary level examinations could be cast, pupils had complete freedom to stay away from classes. Mackenzie found himself having to take botany. He had no knowledge of the subject and he told his pupils so. In that situation, learning became for both teacher and pupil a process of discovery. In those botany lessons which largely took place in the New Forest, he and his pupils came nearer, he remembers, to integrating education into a full enjoyment of life 'than he had ever been able to since'. And, in his journal, he sums up this formative period in his life thus:

> I was at the Forest School from the age of 24 to 26. It was as if the school had taken me up to a higher place and let me see the kingdoms of the world, broadening my horizons. These two years stand out in my memory. Since then, former pupils have written that for them too, their years there were among the best of their lives. There was freedom and partly, because of that, there was what Geothe (in a letter to Schiller) called 'tranquil activity'. I'd been into the educational future and it worked.[10]

During the remaining three pre-war years, he continued to delay the moment of entry into any fixed employment, preferring instead to find his own free way by a series of short-term jobs. These included some occasional journalism and topical pieces for both the Aberdeen *Press and Journal* and the *Mearns Leader*. He also contributed to the *North East Review*, a magazine run by a group of Left Wing intellectuals who provided commentary on aspects of the North-East scene from a committedly Socialist viewpoint.

In 1940, he was called up and served in the RAF as a navigator until 1945. The training he had to undergo to become a navigator took him to Florida and then to South Africa, an experience which opened his eyes to apartheid and to the great similarity that existed between the Presbyterianism of his own people and the close-knit religious and political exclusiveness of the Afrikaners. But it was the melting pot of the citizen army that made up the great bulk of the British armed forces in the Second World War which most profoundly affected MacKenzie. In his war diaries and in the memoir he later constructed of this time, he marvels at the way in which ordinary working-class recruits could master the most intricate of navigational concepts and the extent to which class barriers were broken down by the sheer need to muck in together:

> The clerk of the Gas and Coke Company found he was making as many marks in meteorology as the university graduate. Traditional drills were universally described as 'bullshit'. Questions half-formulated themselves in drilled minds... Old values were in suspension, and there was a generosity of outlook which made us more accessible to new ideas. It was ironical that these potential generations of a new society were too busy dropping bombs to apply this generosity to a wider purpose.[11]

MacKenzie's early thinking on education had, at bottom, a practical basis, arising out of his experiences in the RAF. There, he had seen for himself the untapped potential of ordinary working-class servicemen who had been released by exposure to the training for skilled jobs in the services. Clearly, school education had failed these people. The realisation prompted him to wonder if it was the academic curriculum that was at the root of the problem – a curriculum based on learning information that had no relevance to the lives of the pupils involved, and in the hands of teachers who were simply going through the ritual prescribed for them by the state of cramming for the eleven-plus exam in the primary schools and the leaving certificate in the secondary schools.

Once the war was over, he had to get himself a job (he had married in 1945). Although he had been doing freelance work for the BBC, and had contemplated making his career there as a writer and broadcaster, it was into teaching that eventually he went. In 1946, he was appointed to teach English at Galashiels Academy. Although he enjoyed living in the Borders, he was frustrated to find that the sort of education that was being offered in schools such as his was no different from what he himself had experienced, and found wanting, as a pupil twenty years before.

His appointment as Headteacher to Braehead Junior Secondary School in Buckhaven, Fife in 1957, at last gave him his opportunity to put into practice the broad philosophical framework he had come to envisage for education. At the age of 47, he still had the drive to make some of the things he had come to believe in emerge into actuality. Although Braehead was situated in an old dilapidated building formerly used by the High School, MacKenzie had the advantage of starting off the school from scratch and of working with a staff that responded to his desire to review the curriculum towards a more humanitarian approach to the pupils in their care. During his years there, his influence was able to create an atmosphere where experiment in art, music, and technical subjects brought about work of rare quality, an effort that culminated in the art department where, especially, his goal of 'tranquil activity' was realised and pupils were able to become immersed in the joy of their work.

The developments in outdoor education, particularly under the leadership of Hamish Brown, the first-ever appointment in a Scottish state school of such a specialist, opened his eyes to the way in which such activities could be exploited for the benefit of pupils from a deprived urban background. As Brown himself puts it in his *The Last Hundred* some thirty years later, 'As far as I know, my appointment was the first in a Scottish state school to do what would develop into "outdoor education". My remit was "to take the boys and girls of Braehead into the wild and do what I liked with them."'[12]

The pioneering work that Hamish Brown did in exploring the opportunities for introducing town-based pupils to the Scottish mountains as a key part of their education, became part of a much wider vision that Mackenzie developed, with the Inverlair project as its centre-piece. Inverlair was a shooting lodge in Lochaber (formerly owned by British Aluminium) that Mackenzie hoped could be transformed by a grant from Fife County Council into an outdoor centre. This could house, on an all-the-year basis, large groups of pupils whose education, while they were there, would revolve round the opportunities that could be gained from living together as a unit and exploring their native land. It was to be a radical programme of learning by discovery:

> We could ourselves put in a new septic tank… teach our pupils how to adapt a water-heating system to our plans for the house. We could keep ponies and bees and get the reeds out of the tennis courts... we could section one of General Wade's roads to see how he made them, and would establish an observatory and also a wireless station in contact with the school... there would be forestry in cooperation with British Aluminium foresters who were prepared to work with us. We could ask the Crofters' Co-operative at Roy Bridge, four miles away, if we could come in with them in their experiments in soil reclamation. Inverlair would also be the base camp from which expeditions would set out across the West of Scotland, using a chain of bothies on treks as stepping stones, never being more than a day's march from a bothy and enabling the pupils to travel light without tents.[13]

Even though the Inverlair project was aborted – Fife County Council decided against it on the grounds of expense and the poor state of the building – Mackenzie kept the dream alive in his inner thoughts: 'The Welfare State had produced the fittest generation of Scottish children who had ever lived and we wanted to resume where the Welfare State had stopped. It might, after all, be only a dream, but the school had a distinguished staff capable of translating the dream into reality, and the goodwill and tenacity to overcome the obstacles. We decided to encourage the dreamers'.[14]

The consequences of such a vision inevitably led Mackenzie into conflict with the authorities. In resisting the claims on his time to prepare pupils for presentation for O-grades; in trying unsuccessfully to abolish corporal punishment; in publicly voicing opposition to an introduction of comprehensive education that he saw as purely an administrative change, Mackenzie clashed with the educational establishment in Fife. As a result, no place was made available for him in the new scheme of things when it was announced that, under the plans for comprehensive education in the county, Braehead was to be phased out.

He had, all this time, been working out his ideas in print, both by articles in newspapers (the *Glasgow Herald* and *The Scotsman*), and by writing a trilogy of books, *A Question of Living, Escape from the Classroom*, and *The Sins of the Children*,[15] which encapsulated the experience of the Braehead years, and his renunciation of the education system in Scotland. It had, he argued, condemned children to pass their precious years of secondary schooling in circumstances that deliberately stunted their imagination and powers of communication, and placed them under an authoritarian regime that made them resentful and suspicious of adults. His books proclaimed an alternative approach to education based on treating children as individuals, whose lives could be transformed within a school environment that depended, not on corporal punishment, but on a curriculum that was suited to the needs of adolescents and taught by adults who loved and respected them individually as unique human beings.

His appointment as Headteacher of Summerhill Academy in 1968 gave him a fresh opportunity to put these ideals into practice. Six years later, however, came the dismissal. His book about the processes which led up to this ending, *The Unbowed Head*, followed in 1976.[16] In it, he concluded that what had been at stake had been more than just the relationships between himself and the majority of the staff, whose unrest had precipitated the outcome; it had been their very understanding of what they were educating young people for. This, he saw, was especially vital in regard to what he calls 'the Dissident Minority' – those pupils who, in every school, just do not fit into the system – for reasons of their upbringing and for their recalcitrant behaviour under the demands of an oppressive regime, but for whom, Mackenzie argued, an appropriate education is as vital as it is for the more pliant majority.

In this sense, Mackenzie could certainly be described as a social revolutionary who publicly sided with the minority, and, in so doing, wished to expose the fundamental flaw at the heart of a public system which, in his view, cynically uses the schools as an agency of state control.

The conflict at Summerhill between the majority of staff who held to a 'traditional' view of education, based on the Scottish values of stern discipline and emphasis on academic attainment, and the minority who followed Mackenzie in seeking a relaxation in the relationships between staff and pupil, and a more child-centred curriculum, mirrored the central dilemma in education that he sought to expose in *The Unbowed Head*. The book could be described as a work of rebellion. It has a sense of indignant anger on behalf of others and an identification with the oppressed, qualities that are exemplified in this extract:

> Gradually I realised the full significance of what was happening when the pupil (William Brown) shouted back at the teacher... it is part of a world movement. In Chile, in the Dominican Republic, peasants, learning to read, were beginning to think their own thoughts and were refusing to be cowed. There was an awakening in which the human being recognises himself as a person, an active subject rather than a passive object, aware that he can improve human situations, and acting with others, change society and make life truly human... People need to abandon the stooping gait and walk tall. They have the ability to cope with the problem of living. If a civilisation doesn't give them that... it denies them the vital thing... and that society is tyranny. Because it denies this to its young people, Scottish education is tyranny.[17]

MacKenzie's radicalism remained with him for the rest of his life. Even after the traumas of Summerhill, he continued to present his case. He was much sought after as a speaker at educational conventions and he took the opportunity to travel in Europe and America, observing the local scenes much as he had done in the thirties. His energy and enthusiasm were intact; his writing was as prolific as ever. There, he pursued the themes of his earlier work: the questionable validity of an educational system which appeared to rely upon corporal punishment and examinations for its very existence. His scathing attack upon the decision to replace the O-grade regime in 1983 with a new regime of Standard Grade assessment illustrates his unswerving opposition to what he regarded as merely cosmetic changes:

> The possibility that there is something wrong in basing the whole of Scottish education on external exams is not one that recommends itself to the educational administrators. When the exams are seen not to work, they react by developing a still more convoluted system of exams, new certificates, one of them at Foundation, General and Credit levels, and the other made up of modules. And similarly, when corporal punishment is abolished, they concentrate on other punishments ('alternative sanctions'). The possibility does not occur to them that it is the requirement to drill dull information into unwilling heads that forces teachers to use punishment and distorts education. The abolition of exams would reduce the need to make schools punitive institution... I know of no single measure that

would do more to release the flow of initiative in our society than the abolition of the external examination.[18]

The consistency of MacKenzie's opposition to the establishment, and the grip that he perceived it to exert on the education process through the sixties, the seventies and the eighties, marks him out as one of the most significant figures of dissent in recent educational history. But MacKenzie's was always more than just an outsider's voice. The powerful polemic encapsulated in the trilogy and in his later *State School*,[19] as well as the controlled passion of the case that he puts forward for his actions and beliefs at Summerhill in *The Unbowed Head,* characterises him as a man with his own vision, one that ranged over the whole range of political and cultural experience, both in the North-East and in the Scotland whose values it typified.

During all this time, MacKenzie got considerable sustenance from his contacts with other educational radicals such as John Aikenhead and A. S. Neill. It was with the latter, above all, that he kept up a correspondence over many years. Neill was best known for the founding, earlier in the century, of another Summerhill – the small independent school in Suffolk which became one of the foremost pioneers of educational 'freedom'. Like his North-East counterpart, he believed that pupils should be given the liberty to develop their own lives without external constraint and to run the school in accordance with their judgements. The abiding influence that permeated the school was Neill himself who, like MacKenzie, was a sworn enemy of an Establishment that, he considered, had so little of his own faith in the goodness of children.

Even in his late eighties, Neill kept up his correspondence with MacKenzie, encouraging him through the benefit of his astringent wit. As this extract from a letter that he wrote in December 1972, when MacKenzie's problems at his Summerhill were beginning to surface, shows, their observations were often flavoured by their native Scots:

Man, that's a hell of a picture you paint of Scots dominies. But English ones are similar… [which] makes it difficult to be an optimist about education. In essence, the Scots are where they were when I wrote my Log in 1915, so it wasn't a surprise when the students of my own varsity, Edinburgh, recommended me for an Honorary degree and the Senatus turned it down… It disna bather me; it just maks me lach. I'm kinda oot o' things noo. Ower tired to see visitors and to lecture… not being able to go to London I see few fowks… I'm past writing, but my life comes out in May, *Neill, Neill, Orange-Peel* – the chant the kids used to greet me with, the wee ones… I hope I'll live to see it out. At 89 I canna have lang. Don't think I fear death since I think it is extinction… That is what annoys me, never to know what has happened to the kids and freedom, to my grand-daughter of 5 months. So bugger old bastard Father Time, says I.

Rumour said you had been ill. I do hope it is wrong, for the world needs bonny fechters like you, there are so few about now… The so-called progressive schools are half-dead…

51

You must feel very lonely amongst the local teachers who are so anti-life. I
admire your sticking to the State system… I ran awa frae it.

Aweel, as guid a New Year as this lovely world of oors… Whitehouse, Nixon,
Heath etc. – will allow'.[20]

During these closing years, many continued to find him a compelling figure,
one who could influence others by the sheer power of his presence. As Elizabeth
Garrett, his former Depute Head at Summerhill, said in an article she wrote for the
Times Educational Supplement (Scotland) in 1975, 'RF stirs deep feelings in the people
who know him well; they love him, are empowered by him or they loathe him for
the way he upsets their certainties and questions their truths; few are unaffected
by him'.[21]

And, indeed, quite apart from the written legacy, MacKenzie appears to have
given those who knew him a sort of spiritual strength, one that arose out of the
courage of a man who was willing, against the odds, to take on the system and to
subject it to scrutiny and put forward alternative strategies. His books, from both
the Braehead and the Summerhill eras, still stand as a vivid expression of his sense
of outrage at the plight of children caught up in what he considered to be a loveless
education system. And through it all, we can see a courage in the face of adversity,
his doggedness, his resilience, his single-mindedness. These were the qualities
very much in evidence in the final years of his life, when he strove, though gravely
ill, to complete his last testament, *A Search for Scotland*, that was to be published
posthumously in 1989.[22] It was written out of an enduring love for his native land
and offers a penetrating analysis of where, at the back end of the twentieth century,
he sensed Scotland to be heading as a nation.

Some of the very best of this book is to be found in his sensitive evocation of
the Scottish countryside, especially in its more remote areas, where his spirits are
refreshed and invigorated by what he sees, and by the feelings it stirs within him. His
journey starts, with 'Grampian', his own region and a brief glimpse of the city, now
invaded by the entrepreneurs of oil and, if still the site of his old Robert Gordon's
College, in it now houses an institution which no longer has fees sufficiently modest,
and bursaries enough, to attract working-class lads like himself. It has, instead,
become fully 'independent' and thus, he claims, behaves like an English, and not
a Scottish, public school. From here, he moves out into the agricultural hinterland
of his native Aberdeenshire. Observation mingles with family and community
memory, the life of the land and the moulding force of the school and the kirk. But
it is the landscape itself, and the language it fosters, which has proved to have the
binding power. He recalls a journey in a guard's van going to Insch and the way
in which the guard, 'his eyes shining', recited Charles Murray's *The Whistle* as they
clattered along:

> The north-east language, 'the speak of the people' was as perfectly attuned to the
> feel of the poem as a fiddle to a bothy ballad. In a strange way the speak of

the folk influences the folk. When I meet local people who speak the tongue I was brought up with and fall back easily into that speech, I have a sense of relaxation and belonging, of being safe and warm… it's a sense of clinging on to the fruitful earth that bore us, being suckled by its breasts. When we lose our native speech, a birthright, we lose something of our wholeness, our integrity.[23]

But what the land restores, the school and its systems has sought to take away. There follow memories of drilled learning, of impersonal 'half-information', and the imposition of a received speech. Yet MacKenzie never quite loses his faith in the capacity of the good Scottish earth to renew the sense of wholeness. But now it is, perhaps, in its wilder terrains, out in the Cairngorms and among the islands, that restoration must be sought. Later in the book, he retraces a journey across Harris and, there, among the seal-life, the profusion of plover and peewits, all scattered along the rocks of orange-gold seaweed, he regains a 'feeling of community with the animate and the inanimate furniture of our parcel of earth'.[24]

This feeling of oneness with 'our parcel of earth' is close to the kind of insights into our pilgrimage on earth that MacKenzie hoped his pupils would glimpse in their sojourns in the Scottish wilderness – insights inspired by their own discovery of the wild places and by the association in their minds of such places with feelings of freedom and of escape. It is but a short step from this sense of spiritual well-being that he hoped his pupils would be enabled to enjoy, to the kind of visionary statement on the nurture of Scotland's children that MacKenzie makes in the chapter 'The Central Highlands'. Here, he invokes the memory of a past school trip:

 In Rannoch I have seen the vision of Isaiah explode into reality. The mountains and the hills broke before them singing and the trees of the fields clapped their hands… we began to get glimpses of how a Scottish cultural revolution might be set in motion. It would begin in country places.[25]

It was this prophetic aspect of his personality which, to many, made him a unique and magnetic human being. Those who worked with him were aware that he was no saint, that he could rage and rant and easily lose his temper, that he was very sensitive to criticism and that this was a tendency that had been exacerbated by the constant brushes with authority and the consequent sense that the 'powers that be' were out to get him. But, at bottom, many would judge that he was not a politician so much as a fundamentally innocent man forced to inhabit, and to combat as best he could, the politicians' world. Old colleagues recall the strong streak of sentimentality that led him to cry quite openly as he watched youngsters at Summerhill performing the musical *Oliver*. Then he would be weeping with his happiness at the skills and composure of pupils from a working-class background as they performed before a public audience.

His biography carries the sub-title – 'A Prophet without Honour'. Few people nowadays can aspire to having the qualities of a prophet. MacKenzie was far from being one in the Old Testament sense. He may, instead, be thought of as a man before his time, one who was largely looked upon as a maverick and as a trouble-maker by those in authority, a man reviled by politicians of all persuasions, and, most crucially, by the great majority of his fellow teachers. He was, with his erudition and his intellectual capacity, an outstanding product of the education system of the North-East of Scotland; but, for all that he owed to the rigour of the academic training it gave him, he became its implacable enemy. He had, by his personal example, done his utmost to challenge the obsession and hard discipline that he had first encountered as a pupil in Turriff and at Robert Gordon's College, and which, he was convinced, continued to blight the Scottish educational system.

These were experiences which led him to develop his own, alternative strategy. It is the one that he set out in the final chapter of his unpublished *Manifesto*, 'How do we go from here?' Although, characteristically, the conclusions are prophetic in tone, the touchstone for his argument is firmly grounded in his intimate knowledge of the traditions of his native North-East:

> Long ago the fisherman on the Aberdeenshire coast would go out to the headland and look over the sea and the face of the sky, and, out of a gut reaction, announce, 'There is a change working'. I sense such a change working in the thoughts and feeling of people throughout the world, the turning of a tide in the affairs of men... The educational revolution has to do with the whole nature of our life on earth. Its sources of inspiration, the deep springs from which it draws its life, are the inner promptings of the human heart, the vague questions, the doubts, often unspoken, that have troubled humanity throughout its tenure of the planet. Concerning the upsurge of one such question in the mind of one of his characters, Neil Gunn said, 'You saw it – but you have not yet brought it into your head in order to put words on it'. The change that is happening is that more human beings are becoming aware that they should have the freedom to bring these private doubts into their heads and put words on them.[26]

In the end, his answer is to put his faith in a simple plea for hope in an increasingly cynical world. The conclusion is this: 'There is no future for humanity unless we are all involved in creating it. To do that, we need a change of heart in the way we regard out children and the upbringing of them. That simply is what I mean by the educational revolution.'[27]

It is a hope which, now into the second decade since his death, awaits a realisation that, it could be argued, is further off than ever. It is questionable whether the inert and self-serving system which he saw all about him in his younger days, both as North-East pupil and as a Scottish teacher, has become more liberal. Although outwardly, technological innovation is threatening a revolution of sorts, the fears and the dictates of the past would still, it appears, be with us. Certainly the current preoccupation of administrator and of politician with league tables and with performance targets, set within a regime of 'assessment for all' would appear to confirm the values by which the young R. F. MacKenzie had been schooled some eighty years ago in his own Aberdeenshire. In this, his own North-East country, his is a prophecy that is yet to be honoured.

Notes

[1] The author is grateful for the generous and ready co-operation of the MacKenzie family, in particular of R. F. MacKenzie's widow, Diana MacKenzie, who has made available to him the full range of the numerous personal and unpublished papers which were compiled during the whole course of his adult life. These include private journals, diaries, memoirs, and correspondence. The present paper draws heavily upon this material as does the author's earlier *The Life of R. F. MacKenzie: A Prophet Without Honour* (Edinburgh: Donald, 1998).

[2] Murphy, pp. v–vi.

[3] Reproduced in Murphy, pp. 4–5.

[4] R. F. MacKenzie, *A Search for Scotland* (London: Collins, 1989).

[5] Murphy, pp. 67–68.

[6] MacKenzie family papers. Reproduced in Murphy, p. 15.

[7] Hunter Diack and R. F. MacKenzie, *Road Fortune: An Account of a Cycling Journey through Europe* (London: Macmillan, 1935).

[8] Murphy, p. 29.

[9] Murphy, pp. 10–11.

[10] Murphy, p. 51.

[11] Murphy, p. 32.

[12] *The Last Hundred: Munros, Beards and a Dog* (Edinburgh: Mainstream, 1994), quoted in Murphy, p. 64.

[13] Murphy, p. 62.

[14] Murphy, p. 64.

[15] R. F. MacKenzie, *A Question of Living: Common Humanity and Public Education* (London: Collins, 1963); R. F. Mackenzie, *Escape from the Classroom* (London: Collins, 1965); R. F. MacKenzie, *The Sins of the Children* (London: Collins, 1967).

[16] R. F. MacKenzie, *The Unbowed Head: Events at Summerhill Academy 1968-74* (Edinburgh: Edinburgh University Student Publication Board, 1976).

[17] MacKenzie (1976), p. 60.

[18] MacKenzie (1976), p. 52-53.

[19] R. F. MacKenzie, *State School* (Harmondsworth: Penguin, 1970).

[20] Murphy, pp. 134-35.

[21] Murphy, p. 127.

[22] MacKenzie (1989).

[23] MacKenzie (1989), p. 25.

[24] MacKenzie (1989), p. 192.

[25] MacKenzie (1989), p. 169.

[26] MacKenzie family papers

[27] Ibid.

Chapter Six

Looking Back

Ian Campbell

It is one of the ironies of Scottish fiction that so much of it should be about education, and so much has been written on the lads o' pairts who benefited from that education – and that two of the main beneficiaries of the system, 'George Douglas' (George Douglas Brown) and 'Lewis Grassic Gibbon' (James Leslie Mitchell), should have so reviled the system which launched them on their writing careers. In Ochiltree and in Ayr, George Douglas Brown escaped from the bitter poverty of his childhood through the care and encouragement of John Smith of Coylton and William Maybin of Ayr – before going on to Glasgow University, then Oxford, and the inconspicuous encouragement of professors who brought a difficult student through personal and family problems to the outset of a successful career. Small wonder that *The House with the Green Shutters* is dedicated to William Maybin: without Maybin, Brown's publishing career would never have taken off.

Yet the educational system, and educators in general, are mercilessly pilloried in Brown's acerbic picture of Scotland in the second half of the nineteenth century. McCandlish the schoolmaster in Skeighan is an ineffectual puppet, while Bleach-the-boys, the bitter dominie of Barbie, gives hardly a thought to his charges while he devotes himself to the private study of Adam Smith in his study. When he does give a thought to young Gourlay in the novel, he quite clearly sees the horrible mistake Gourlay's father is making in sending an unready and hyper-sensitive boy too young to the city:

> 'They're making a great mistake,' he said gravely, 'they're making a great mistake! Yon boy's the last youngster on earth who should go to College.'
>
> 'Aye, man, dominie, he's an infernal ass, is he noat?' they cried, and pressed for his judgement.
>
> At last, partly in real pedantry, partly with humorous intent to puzzle them, he delivered his astounding mind.
>
> 'The fault of young Gourlay,' quoth he, 'is a sensory perceptiveness in gross excess of his intellectuality.'
>
> They blinked and tried to understand.

'Aye man, dominie!' said Sandy Toddle. 'That means he's an infernal cuddy, dominie! Does it na, dominie?'

But Bleach-the-boys had said enough. 'Aye,' he said dryly, 'there's a wheen gey cuddies in Barbie!' – and he went back to his stuffy little room to study *The Wealth of Nations*.[1]

Now, this is as much parody as is the worthy dominie who self-sacrificingly populates the pages of the kailyard, and brings on 'his' loon to the bursary competition, and the academic life beyond. But it is a key to the plot of Brown's novel that an educational system which offers a relatively open access (only relatively – most of John Gourlay's contemporaries in Barbie follow the route of Swipey Broon into dead-end jobs), simply lets Gourlay down. Spurred on by his father's brutal desire to match Wilson (whose son, utterly without imagination, wins a University place through hard repetitive work), Gourlay is beaten through the rote-learning necessary for University admission, but completely unsustained by individual attention once he gets there. Ironically, his sole success – winning the Raeburn essay prize – draws him to his teachers' attention, and directly leads to his tragedy, spurring him to drink and to an inflated self-importance which he cannot sustain.[2]

Few moments are more vivid than the insight into Gourlay wrestling in his student digs with this limited articulacy, trying to put on paper the ideas which teem in his mind and eventually drive him to drink and to suicide. Imagining an Arctic night:

> He saw a lonely little town far off upon the verge of Lapland night, leagues and leagues across a darkling plain, dark itself and little and lonely in the gloomy splendour of a Northern sky. A ship put to sea, and Gourlay heard in his ears the skirl of the man who went overboard – struck dead by the icy water on his brow, which smote the brain like a tomahawk.
>
> He put his hand to his own brow when he wrote that, and, 'Yes,' he cried eagerly, 'it would be the cold that would kill the brain. Ooh-ooh, how it would go in!'
>
> A world of ice groaned round him in the night; bergs ground on each other and were rent in pain: he heard the splash of great fragments tumbled in the deep, and felt the waves of their distant falling lift the vessel beneath him in the darkness. To the long desolate night came a desolate dawn, and eyes were dazed by the encircling whiteness; yet there flashed green slanting chasms in the ice, and towering pinnacles of sudden rose, lonely and far away. An unknown sea beat upon an unknown shore, and the ship drifted on the pathless waters, a white man dead at the helm.[3]

Not for young Gourlay to spot the outrageous borrowing – Gustave Doré, Stevenson, Arnold, James Thomson – for Brown is not only evoking the opulence of Gourlay's imagination, but enjoying himself as he parodies the teenager's overblown style. A good dominie would have cured him of that; but that is just what Gourlay in the novel did not have.

Like Brown, Grassic Gibbon did have such a friend in real life. Alexander Gray's benevolent presence is all over the early chapters of Gibbon's life, as it is in the displays of the Grassic Gibbon Centre in Arbuthnott which clearly illustrates the gulf between the reality of Gibbon's early life as young James Leslie Mitchell of Bloomfield, and the success of the novelist who, in distant Welwyn Garden City, was to make a brilliant career in a short space of time before his untimely death. Like Brown, he kept in touch with his early dominie; like Brown, he did not spare him in the pages of his fiction. The village schoolmaster who early on encourages Chris Guthrie in Kinraddie is let off relatively lightly, but the teachers in the Academy (a pillorying of the author's hated year in Stonehaven before he voluntarily left secondary education for a life in journalism) are ineffectual or crude, as they are in Gibbon's other autobiographical fiction.

Gibbon had passed through his own John Gourlay phase, and Ian Munro in his early biography quotes from the essay books which Alexander Gray preserved in Arbuthnott school.

> Mr Gray affirms that these are the only exercise-books he has ever kept – and he has kept them for over half a century!

Written at the age of thirteen, these essays reveal many of the thoughts of an unusually fertile mind. Reading them it becomes clear that this boy is deeply aware of his own land and already is searching for words to describe it, the words he was to find so surely twenty years later in *A Scots Quair*. With the gift of eye and mind to portray familiar places, he was able to provide a vivid description of his own district:

> In front stretches a sea of green intersected here and there with small fields, or a winding road disappearing in the waving masses of foliage. There is the silver Bervie, and the old church, while above the huge pines and waving beeches may be seen a solitary column of smoke from Arbuthnott House.[4]

But the inexperienced pen does run away:

> What an irresistable [sic] feeling of power comes when on a calm clear night you gaze up at the millions of glistening worlds and constellations which form the Milky Way. 'Tis then – and then only, that one can realise the full power of the Creator and the truth of the wild dream of the German poet. There is no beginning, yea, even as there is no end.'

With Gray's help, and with the lonely discipline of years spent while an enlisted soldier, tapping at his typewriter in his spare time, Gibbon learned to pare his prose down, even if he never lost the mannerisms of style, particularly in his Middle-East-set tales, of which another few years might have cured him.

It was to Alexander Gray, his Arbuthnott schoolmaster, that Gibbon wrote:

> You were the only schoolmaster from whom I ever learned anything. You used to say you were not so greatly interested in what I said, but in the manner of saying it.

And it says a lot for his reviewing acuity that Compton Mackenzie wrote of *Sunset Song* in the *Daily Mail*, before he had any personal acquaintance with Gibbon:

> I have no hesitation in saying that Sunset Song, by Lewis Grassic Gibbon, is the richest novel about Scottish life written for many years. Mr Gibbon is the first of our contemporary Scottish writers to use the dialect with such effect… There is internal evidence that he had already struggled hard to acquire a mastery of English prose before he ventured to approach his present task. It is experience which has given him the right to experiment.
>
> The language is often coarse and sometimes brutal, and the statement of facts is always unequivocal. Mr Gibbon can summon Robert Burns as witness for the defence. Indeed the comparison with Burns is constant in the reader's mind, for Tam o' Shanter runs through Mr Gibbon's prose all the time.
>
> The theme is the extinction of the crofters by the conditions of the modern world. I am myself optimistic enough to believe that Mr Gibbon's epic elegy is premature, but such optimism only makes me more grateful for this superb lament which shows what is in danger of being for ever lost.[5]

There are themes here which are central to this paper: the fact that Gibbon learned his trade the hard way before venturing to experiment: the fact that he used his perfected style to look back and lament, but also to experiment and to attract the reader's attention to the present, as well as to an 'epic elegy'. For what Gibbon does in *A Scots Quair* is to look back quite superbly – *Sunset Song*, to be sure – but also to look forward, using the full lyric power of his achieved style (*Sunset Song*) to punch home the message, particularly at the end of the first part of the trilogy, that while the dead whose names are on the war memorial may have been the last of the peasants, the last of the old Scots folk, the future belongs to a new generation of Scots who have their own lives, their own language and their own dreams ahead.

Central to Gibbon's ability to look back in this extraordinary, challenging way was his own position as a North-Easterner who had drawn his creative inspiration from life in Arbuthnott and its surroundings, but whose mature writing life was to be spent in London, far from 'home'. Indeed, central to a great deal of his fiction is the outsider's stance, either the outsider to the community (his own position, as an adolescent who could not wait to get out of Arbuthnott) or, more intriguingly, as the outsider who returns to native parts for a holiday. Here is *Stained Radiance*:

> It was three o'clock in the afternoon before they were through the pass in the mountains, and Leekan station came in sight. They got out. A place of corrugated roofs, red-painted, odoriferous, with drooping-headed horses in the railway yard.

Through fir-trees, half a mile up a road, glinted the red granite of Leekan village. Then Thea cried, 'Dad!' and danced up the platform, and put her arms about the neck of a man, and hugged him.

She brought him to Garland. Garland shook a broad, brown hand, calloused, and with serrated edges.

'Hoo are ye? Od, ye maun be tired wi the journey. An Theey's a gey responsibility, I'll warrant.'

He said this in a slow, careful, doubtful voice, speaking carefully and slowly, knowing that all Englishmen were half-wits. Showing tobacco-stained teeth, he smiled cannily. He was of middle height, thick set, with enormous shoulders. A brown beard streaked with grey lay over the craggy whiteness of his collar and false front. He wore a suit of thick tweeds. His eyes were small and friendly and shrewd and oddly timid.

He was Thea's father.[6]

He might have been Gibbon's own father, though in Gibbon's case the bride he brought back to Arbuthnott on visits was as native as himself, her father the fictional Long Rob of the Mill, the author's neighbours at Bloomfield overlooking Arbuthnott. But there was to be no going back in Gibbon's life to the North-East he had longed for in his fiction and in his marvellous essays in *Scottish Scene*. *Scottish Scene* deserves more attention than it has yet had, though Gibbon's essays there are now firmly back in print.[7] Nicely poised between nostalgia and hard-edged realism, they reflect no doubt the author's own feelings as he struggled to overcome his family's distaste for the fictional Kinraddie in *Sunset Song*, and his own sense that he had left the North-East behind once and for all, except for occasional pangs of real need – such as the one which brought him North in his last summer to finish *Grey Granite* in Aberdeenshire, since the novel simply would not allow itself to be written in Hertfordshire.

But the point does need to be made: he ached for a Scotland he simply could not accept as an everyday home:

> Autumn of all seasons is when I realise how very Scotch I am, how interwoven with the fibre of my body and personality is this land and its queer, scarce harvests, its hours of reeking sunshine and stifling rain, how much a stranger I am, south, in those seasons of mist and mellow fruitfulness as alien to my Howe as the olive groves in Persia. It is harder and slower harvest, and lovelier in its austerity, that is gathered here, in September's early coming, in doubtful glances on the sky at dawn, in listening to the sigh of the sea down there by Bervie. Mellow it is certainly is not: but it has wings, by great moons that come nowhere as in Scotland, unending moons when the harvesting carts plod through great thickets of fir-shadow to the cornyards deep in glaur.[8]

So, a full-length quotation from one of these understudied essays, is very much to the point: how does one look back on experience, and then what does one do with the memory?

In the days of my youth (I have that odd pleasure that men in the early thirties derive from thinking of themselves as beyond youth: this pleasure fades in the forties) men and women still lived largely on the food-stuffs grown in the districts – kale and cabbage and good oatmeal, they made brose and porridge and crisp oatcakes and jams from the blackberry bushes in the dour little, sour little gardens. But that is mostly a matter of the past. There are few who bake oatcakes nowadays, fewer still who ever taste kale. Stuff from the grocer's, stuff in bottles and tins, the canned nutriments of Chicago and the ubiquitous Fray Bentos, have supplanted the old-time diets. This dull, feculent stuff is more easy to deal with, not enslaving your whole life as once the cooking and serving did in the little farms and cottars' houses – cooking in the heat of such a day as this on great open fireplaces, without even a range. And though I sit here on this hill and deplore the fusionless foods of the canneries, I have no sympathy at all with those odd souls of the cities who would see the return of that 'rich agricultural life' as the return of something praiseworthy, blessed and rich and generous. Better Fray Bentos and a seat in the pictures with your man of a Saturday night than a grilling baking of piled oatcakes and a headache withal.

They change reluctantly, the men and women of the little crofts and cottar houses; but slowly a quite new orientation of outlook is taking place. There are fewer children now plodding through the black glaur of the wet summer storms to school, fewer in both farm and cottar house. The ancient, strange whirlmagig of the generations that enslaved the Scots peasantry for centuries is broken. In times gone by a ploughman might save and scrape and live meanly and hardly and marry a quean of like mettle. And in time they would have gathered enough to rent a croft, then a little farm; and all the while they saved, and lived austere, sardonic lives; and their savings took them at last to the wide cattle-courts and the great stone-floored kitchen of a large farm. And all the while the women bred, very efficiently and plentifully and without fuss – twelve or thirteen were the common numberings of a farmer's progeny. And those children grew up, and their father died. And in the division of property at his death each son or daughter gathered as inheritance only a few poor pounds. And perforce they started as ploughmen in the bothies, maids in the kitchens, and set about climbing the rungs again – that their children might do the same.

It kept a kind of democracy on the land that is gone or is going; your halflin or your maid was the son or the daughter of your old friends of High Rigs: your own sons and daughters were in bothies or little crofts: it was a perfect Spenglerian cycle. Yet it was waste effort, it was as foolish as the plod of an ass in a treadmill, innumerable generations of asses. If the clumsy fumblements of contraception have done much. Under these hills – so summer-hazed, so immobile and essentially unchanging – of a hundred years hence I do not know what strange master of the cultivated lands will pass in what strange mechanical contrivance: but he will be outwith that ancient yoke, and I send him my love and the hope that he'll sometime climb up Cairn o' Mount and sit where I'm siting now, and stray in summery thought – into the sun-hazed mists of the future, into the lives and wistful desirings of forgotten men who begat him.[9]

This pulses with personal involvement, the memory of life on the farm in its grey boredom as well as its nostalgic beauty at harvest time, the ceaseless routine, the strain of childbearing on the women (a theme of *Sunset Song*, of course), of financial pressure on the whole family. Gibbon's own childhood was spent in a struggle for survival – Bloomfield was a small croft – and his enlistment in the armed forces speaks volumes for the extremity to which a lonely and fastidious man was driven by poverty during the Depression, simply seeking to survive – but at the price of communal living, brutal conditions, and almost total lack of privacy. Gibbon's own letters – many of them in the Arbuthnott Centre, and many now in Edinburgh where the marvellous collection of manuscripts is in the care of the National Library of Scotland – speak of the ambiguous feelings he had, looking back on Arbuthnott. He was amused as well as hurt by Arbuthnott's rejection of his portrait of his childhood village:

> The amount of stupefied indignation *Stained Radiance* seems to have raised! Mrs Gray disapproves, my mother is shocked, my sister-in-law is coldly polite, the *Daily Sketch* has a hysteric fit over my 'brutality' – and Boots bans the book from their shelves as '. . .' Most papers refuse to review it at all, and the booksellers are scared to display it complete with its shocking cover...[10]

Gibbon was aware that his originals, looking back, were all too identifiable: he wrote to Alexander Gray that 'The particular locality has such a close resemblance to Arbuthnott and the Howe o' the Mearns generally that I was forced to insert a few entirely fictitious topographical details in case some enraged Reisker or other fauna sued me for libel', and the maps on each end paper of the early editions of the trilogy are slightly, but definitely, confused in detail to make too easy an identification of the original impossible. [11]

But looking back, Gibbon was also aware he was saying goodbye to a way of life. The quotation from *Scottish Scene* says so, explicitly, often, with real feeling: the countryside Gibbon looked back on had changed both literally and less obviously. Literally, with savage depopulation of the First World War and its associated stripping of woodland and mechanisation of agriculture: more subtly, in the arrival of motor cars, of small domestic conveniences, in the replacement of the bothy system with the more scattered family farmhouses. And the language of his youth had gone, too, caught in the same magnificent elegy the minister prognoses on a way of life, as well as the dead of Kinraddie, in the last pages of *Sunset Song*. In his review, Compton Mackenzie had written of the novel that 'The theme is the extinction of the crofters by the conditions of the modern world', but this hardly does justice to the stealth by which Gibbon introduces change in all three parts of the trilogy, underlining once and for all the need to read all three rather than merely to savour the more immediate pleasures of *Sunset Song*. While Chris leaves behind the lives of the crofters of Kinraddie, to move to the Manse in Segget and the lodgings in Duncairn, those changes Gibbon wrote about were still happening in the farm houses she had left behind – the kirks continued to empty after her second husband died in the pulpit – and the Scots language she had grown up with yielded imperceptibly with each generation to the attractions of a seat in the pictures and a slice of Fray Bentos for tea.

When young Ewan Tavendale says of his life and schooling in Segget that 'Scotch was rubbish, all ee's and wee's, you didn't even speak it in the school playground. And the other kids had mocked you at first, but they didn't long, with a bashing or so'.[12] – he was very likely reflecting his creator's own experience, Gibbon's own impatience with the diet of literature offered him in school, 'Burns, silly Scotch muck about cottars and women, and love and dove and rot of that sort… Poetry was rot, why not say it plain, when a man kissed a woman or a woman had a baby?'[13] But then Gibbon had the tact to embody that impatience in the Scottish Chris and the English Chris, and to make the point that neither could live quite without the other, even if the Scottish Chris does eventually become the controlling influence. Chris has known her own share of good schooling in Kinraddie, and bad schooling in the 'academy' where the teachers despised her farming background, and wished to make of her a cloned schoolteacher. That she had wished to become the 'English Chris' to escape the life of the farm came to worry her – part of the pleasure of reading *Sunset Song* is the alternation between the possibilities which life, and education, throw up to Chris before she takes control of her own life.

The man who could write of Scotland with such nostalgic pain from Welwyn had hardly left behind his early years, and his early language. *Cloud Howe* and *Grey Granite* sadly record the thinning-out of the Scots Blawearie spoke and exulted in, becoming the spinners' more urban speech in *Cloud Howe* and finally the sad jumble of Scots, English and sub-Hollywood which Gibbon satirises as the speech of Duncairn in *Grey Granite.*

When the minister says, unveiling the war memorial, that *'a new spirit shall come to the land with the greater herd and the great machines',*[14] he is not being needlessly obscure. What Gibbon's whole artistic effort in the trilogy and in much of his other output tried to achieve, was a sense that this change is inevitable, is not necessarily evil, is something we must learn to live with because it is life in its raw essence. Inevitably, few around that war memorial understood the message – 'folk stood dumbfounded, this was just sheer politics'[15] – but by the end of *Grey Granite* more people might see Gibbon's intention, in the enigmatic way he closes off the double plot of Chris and Ewan, one marching to a new world and a new challenge in England, the other somehow ending her Scottish plot on the last page without the author very clearly indicating how her end comes. For it has not come: the balance between the Scottish and the English Chris still sways, given a new impetus by Ewan's departure, and more subtly by the social divisions which still very obviously wrack Duncairn, and beyond it the whole of Scotland, the whole world. *A Scots Quair* is not interested in a closure which solves the tug at the heart of Scotland – least of all by looking back to a golden age which Gibbon clearly thought never existed. Curiously few have commented on the shadowy figure Chris glimpses as her family struggles through the blizzard to their new home in Kinraddie:

> Far out of the night ahead of them came running a man, father didn't see him or heed to him, though old Bob... snorted and shied. And as he came he wrung his hands, he was mad and singing, a foreign creature, black-bearded, half-naked he was; and he cried in the Greek *The ships of Pytheas! The ships of Pytheas!* and went by into the smore of the sleet-storm on the Grampian Hills, Chris never saw him again... '[16]

Chris perhaps did not see him again, but in the last pages of *Grey Granite* she would be in a better position to understand why that early Scottish peasant would flee the coming of the Greek ships that brought with them civilisation, enslavement, and all the problems which 'progress' would bring to Gibbon's twentieth century. Gibbon the Diffusionist, in his science fiction, his anthropological writing and in his Scottish fiction, saw any golden age there may have been in the distant past, before Egypt and the dawn of what we call civilisation. Chris, looking over Echt on the last pages of *Grey Granite,* realises there is no going back, to that age, or indeed to the Echt of her childhood. Life moves on.

Which brings us back to Lewis Grassic Gibbon of the Mearns, who outgrew his Kinraddie and embodied that outgrowing in the marvellous sequence of *A Scots Quair.* Like George Douglas Brown, he had reason to be grateful to the schoolmasters who helped him outgrow it. Like Brown, he may have found it expedient or even necessary to parody the limitations of that system, even if the odd gifted individual escaped it, and looked back with affection and gratitude as well as with a sardonic realisation that there is no going back. With that artistic distance, Gibbon wrote with passion as well as with accuracy about the sunset of the way of life he had known in his youth; when he finished the trilogy in 1934, Europe was approaching another moment of change and had Gibbon lived beyond the Spring of 1935 he would have had the challenge of writing about that other New Age. Instead, he left a picture of change in 1911-34 in *A Scots Quair* which remains challenging for its affectionate looking back, and simultaneously for its refusal to take refuge looking back. The old Scotland died in 1918, the minister insists,[17] the novel underlines, the trilogy hammers home. When Chris takes Robert, her second husband, to Blawearie after the War, it has gone, now just for 'sheep they pastured now on Blawearie, in the parks that once came rich with corn...' Chris's story points forward, just as Gibbon's memories of the North-East point forward. Only the land endures.

Notes

1 George Douglas Brown, *The House with the Green Shutters*, ed. by Dorothy Porter (1901), pbk edn (Harmondsworth: Penguin, 1985), p. 142.

2 For a fuller discussion, see Ian Campbell, 'George Douglas Brown: A Study in Objectivity', in *Nineteenth-Century Scottish Fiction: Critical Essays*, ed. by Ian Campbell, (Manchester: Carcanet, 1979), pp. 148-63; and Ian Campbell, 'The House with the Green Shutters: Some Second Thoughts', *The Bibliotheck* 10, no. 4 (1980), 99-106.

3 Brown, p. 160.

4 Ian S. Munro, *Leslie Mitchell: Lewis Grassic Gibbon* (Edinburgh & London: Oliver and Boyd, 1966), pp. 17-18.

5 Munro, pp. 49, 75. For a further discussion of Gibbon's style, in strength and weakness, see Ian Campbell, 'The Grassic Gibbon Style', in *Studies in Scottish Fiction: Twentieth Century*, Scottish Studies No. 10, ed. by Joachim Schwend and Horst W. Drescher (Frankfurt and Bern: Peter Lang, 1990), pp. 271-87.

6 J. Leslie Mitchell, *Stained Radiance: A Fictionist's Prelude* (London: Jarrolds, 1930; Edinburgh: Polygon, 1993), p. 84.

7 See Valentina Bold, ed., *Smeddum: A Lewis Grassic Gibbon Anthology* (Edinburgh: Canongate, 2001); Lewis Grassic Gibbon, *The Speak of the Mearns: With Selected Short Stories and Essays*, ed. by Ian Campbell (Edinburgh: Polygon, 1994, repr 2000).

8 Lewis Grassic Gibbon, *The Speak of the Mearns* (Edinburgh: Ramsay Head, 1982), p. 160.

9 Gibbon (1982), pp. 159-60.

10 William K. Malcolm, *A Blasphemer and Reformer: A Study of James Leslie Mitchell / Lewis Grassic Gibbon* (Aberdeen: Aberdeen University Press, 1984), p. 6 (letter to Helen B. Cruickshank).

11 Malcolm, pp. 91-92. For a fuller discussion see 'The Grassic Gibbon Country', in *A Sense of Place: Studies in Scottish Local History: A Volume of Essays commissioned by the Scottish Local History Forum as a tribute to the late Professor Eric Forbes*, ed. by Graeme Cruickshank (Edinburgh: Scotland's Cultural Heritage Unit, 1988), pp. 15-26.

12 Lewis Grassic Gibbon, *A Scots Quair: A Trilogy of Novels ; Sunset song ; Cloud Howe ; Grey Granite* (London: Jarrolds, 1946), repr edn (London: Hutchinson, 1978), p. 277.

13 Gibbon (1946), p. 280.

14 Gibbon (1946), p. 193.

15 Gibbon (1946), p. 193.

16 Gibbon (1946), pp. 41-42.

17 Gibbon (1946), p. 193.

18 Gibbon (1946), p. 207.

Chapter Seven

Education and Some North-East Writers

Douglas F. Young

It is over four hundred years now – or so the story goes – since the wonderful Scottish educational system sprang fully formed from the loins of John Knox, democratic and accessible, so that the Scots became the best educated nation in Europe. And the North-East has often been identified as the region where this Scottish commitment to education is most evident. Apparently every autumn, just after the hairst was in, the roads from every North-East parish to Aberdeen were awash with 'lads o' pairts', each with his bag of meal and his barrel of salt herring, all on their way to the College to prepare themselves to govern India.

A survey of the creative writers of the region – the poets, novelists, and memoirists – would seem to confirm this commitment, for education and the experience of schooling are again and again the subject matter of their writing.

A closer look, however, reveals an interesting feature: that rather than merely celebrating this regional eminence, they do in fact adopt a somewhat revisionist position, exploring the limitations, even the down-side, of this culture of education. Most of the writers I cite in this paper were themselves products of the 'lad o' pairts' syndrome and it is out of the tension between their recognition of their indebtedness and a questioning of its effects that their creativity comes.

Out of this tension comes again and again a juxtaposition of two worlds, the world of home and the world of school, of culture seen as something you learn or acquire and culture seen as something you inherit. And with the shift from one to the other comes a sense of insecurity, and loss of something more natural and fundamental.

Charles Murray's poem *The Whistle*, which Colin Milton has commented upon very helpfully,[1] provides a condensed and very familiar encapsulation of this juxtaposition. Through his music the boy is transmitting a culture which is very meaningful to the folk he lives amongst, and he shows a knowingness beyond his years, but it is not the kind of knowledge that the master is interested in. *His* piping is of the rule of three. The image of the boy being 'shod again for school' implies a constraint of freedom and nature, and the master's burning of the whistle shows just how far out of touch formal education is with the real life and aspirations of the boy.

A fuller, and, perhaps, the classic, working through of this tension is to be found in the case of Chris Guthrie in Grassic Gibbon's novel *Sunset Song*. Her experience of education has so little to do with her day-to-day living, that she is made to feel that she has two selves. The passage begins:

> For she'd met with books, she went into them to a magic land far from Echt, out and away and south.[2]

One of the books she is given is *Alice in Wonderland*,

> And the second, it was *What Katy Did at School*, and she loved Katy and envied her and wished like Katy she lived at a school, not tramping back in the spleiter of a winter night to help muck the byre...[3]

And it goes on.

> So that was Chris and her reading and schooling, two Chrises there were that fought for her heart and tormented her. You hated the land and the coarse speak of the folk and learning was brave and fine one day; and the next you'd waken with the peewits crying across the hills, deep and deep, crying in the heart of you and the smell of the earth in your face, almost you'd cry for that, the beauty of it and the sweetness of the Scottish land and skies. You saw their faces in firelight, father's and mother's and the neighbours', before the lamps lit up, tired and kind, faces dear and close to you, you wanted the words they'd known and used, forgotten in the far-off youngness of their lives, Scots words to tell to your heart how they wrung it and held it, the toil of their days and unendingly their fight. And the next minute that passed from you, you were English, back to the English words so sharp and clean and true – for a while, for a while, till they slid so smooth from your throat you knew they could never say anything that was worth the saying at all.[4]

Gibbon identifies an English Chris and a Scots Chris, and clearly the issue of language is central to this sense of division. In his non-fiction writing he has some interesting things to say about the attitude of Scottish dominies to language – not just their devaluing of Scots, and therefore of the personal identity of the child – but perhaps more interestingly about the kind of English that was given approval, and how this has affected his (and others') ability to operate in either mode.

Perhaps this may be best illustrated by reference to what Gibbon has to say about Ramsay MacDonald in his essay in *Scottish Scene*. For the most part this is a fairly conventional left-wing 'hatchet job' on the betrayer of socialism, but what is very revealing is the way in which he seeks to identify MacDonald's ineffectiveness as essentially a linguistic one, rooted in the rhetorical verbosity of the Scot struggling with English.

He has never succeeded in penetrating behind words to thought: there is, indeed, no evidence that he ever attempted this awesome feat. Even in elementary manipulation of English one is conscious of a curious phenomenon: he is a clever, if rather unintelligent child, engaged in lifting sentences piecemeal from some super-abacus frame and arranging them in a genteel pattern. . . It is the kind of thing that the dux in a little Scots school pens while the Dominie beams upon him (I know, having been such a dux myself, companioned by such a Dominie).[5]

You will recall that Chris's opportunity for education is curtailed when her mother dies and she has to stay at home and look after the house. This makes another point, that for all its glory this educational system was very much for boys, and only for girls if they had nothing better to do. This is evident in many instances, but perhaps most strikingly in the case of Jessie Kesson who, whilst she was writing for the Third Programme, was earning her living scrubbing floors. In her persona of Janie in *The White Bird Passes* she rebels at the fact that, even though her English papers were the best in Aberdeenshire, the assumption by the trustees of the orphanage is that she will go into service.

> Janie found the small Trustee's face. 'I don't want to dust and polish', she told it. 'And I don't want to work on a farm. I want to write poetry. Great poetry. As great as Shakespeare'.[6]

In *Sunset Song*, by the time that Chris's father dies and she can get back into education, she has decided that it is not for her. Her view has become more aligned to that of her mother when she said to her:

> Oh, Chris, my lass, there are better things than your books or studies or loving or bedding, there's the countryside your own, you its, in the days when you're neither bairn nor woman.[7]

So, from Gibbon sitting in his study in Welwyn Garden City, we have a rejection of the values of education in the face of something more fundamental, an attachment to the land itself, which is perhaps the most dominant single motif in North-East literature. Significantly it is at the very point when Chris is about to leave Kinraddie to begin her training to be a teacher that this profound awareness comes upon her.

> And then a queer thought came to her there in the drooked fields, that nothing endured at all, nothing but the land she passed across, tossed and turned and perpetually changed below the hands of the crofter folk since the oldest of them had set the Standing Stones by the loch of Blawearie and climbed there on their holy days and saw their terraced crops ride brave in the wind and sun. Sea and sky and the folk who wrote and fought and were learned, teaching and saying and praying, they lasted but as a breath, a mist of fog in the hills, but the land was forever, it moved and changed below you, but was forever, you were close

to it and it to you, not at a bleak remove it held you and hurted you. And she had thought to leave it all!

She walked weeping then, stricken and frightened because of that knowledge that had come on her, she could never leave it, this life of toiling days and the needs of beasts and the smoke of wood fires and the air that stung your throat so acrid, Autumn and Spring, she was bound and held as though they had prisoned her here. And her fine bit plannings! – they'd been just the dreamings of a child over toys it lacked, toys that would never content it when it heard the smore of a storm or the cry of sheep on the moors or smelt the pringling smell of a new-ploughed park under the drive of a coulter. She could no more teach a school than fly, night and day, she'd want to be back for all the fine clothes and gear she might get and hold, the books and the light and the learning.[8]

It is this rejection of the values and rewards of a conventional academic education in favour of something more primitive and instinctive which is perhaps the key point to make, but given time one could find other critical perceptions of North-East education, from, for instance, our two major nineteenth century novelists, William Alexander and George MacDonald. Both are uneasy about the influence that the Kirk has in terms of both the curriculum and the ethos of the school.

Alexander's own educational history provides a comment on the limitations of the 'lad o' pairts' myth. Coming from a relatively poor peasant background, and highly intelligent though he was, the parish school system did little for him, so that it was only when he lost a leg, as a young man, and was useful for nothing else, that he got an education, largely through the Mutual Improvement system which was flourishing in rural Aberdeenshire in the mid-nineteenth century.[9]

This left him with a dim view of parish schools. In the obituary which he wrote for William McCombie, his mentor when he became a journalist with *The Aberdeen Free Press,* he gives a scathing account of parish schools and schoolmasters.

From infancy it was not to be doubted that there was in this their son a marked individuality of character, combining in some degree the mental and moral features of both parents; and it probably was some exhibition of this, coupled with a distaste for the sports of his companions, that led to his receiving such cruel and even dangerous maltreatment at the hands of the boys at Alford parish school the very first day of his being sent there at the age of seven, that he did not return to school for some three years thereafter. He was then sent to the parish school of Leochel-Cushnie where he continued for four or five years under the charge of Mr Humphrey, the parish teacher. This, we believe, completed his school training; and when we bear in mind how meagre and defective the style of teaching was then in even the best parish schools, it needs not be said that in his case the labour of the schoolmaster had but a small share in his education.[10]

For Alexander this poverty in what the parish schools had to offer was all the more galling because he subscribed sufficiently to the 'lad o' pairts' idea to believe that the North-East had a particular aptitude and appetite for education. In his essay 'The Peasantry of North-East Scotland'[11] he supports this thesis by quoting the opinion of an experienced teacher.

> I now give that of another, a teacher, who, after several years' experience in conducting a school attended chiefly by the children of hinds and others in similar grades of life in a southern county, conducted a school in Aberdeenshire the pupils of which were drawn from the socially corresponding classes. And the unhesitating testimony was that, in point of native shrewdness, aptness to learn, and the desire to get on, the Aberdeenshire bairns were so far ahead of their southern compeers as to form a complete contrast to them.[12]

This gulf between availability on the one hand, and appetite and aptitude on the other, led Alexander to support the so-called 'venture schools', or independent schools, which were springing up all over the countryside in the mid-nineteenth century as an alternative to the parish system, often supported by the Free Church as part of their separation from the establishment.

Alexander's great novel *Johnny Gibb of Gushetnuek* is (amongst other things) a novel about this Disruption, and the need to break the social and political ascendancy of the Auld Kirk and the landed class which it represents. In chapter nine, entitled 'Pedagogical', this religious and political initiative is translated into the realm of schooling. The old parish school is in the hands of the suitably named Rev. Jonathan Tawse, appointed by the kirk session, and one of the army of 'stickit ministers', who seem to have dominated the teaching professions at the time. His real interest is in getting himself a kirk, and so he has little time for his pupils, except the two or three 'Laitiners' or high-flyers that he has each year, and even with them his chief teaching technique is a good thrashing:

> As to his classes generally, Mr Tawse had not much that deserved the name of method in their management; and still less was there of thoroughness in the little that he had.[13]

And so the disruptionists set up a rival establishment under Sandy Peterkin that will serve their more practical needs.

> ... it had been felt by many judicious parishioners that the parochial school of Pyketillim, under Mr Tawse, was too much of a mere high-class academy.[14]

The aim is to develop an education that will not take young people away from the land, and detach them from their traditional culture, but rather enable them to participate more effectively in that way of life. Thus when Johnny's farm servant, the 'muckle scholar', in his eagerness to 'get on' wishes to go back to school as an adult, to learn the basics of land surveying, it is to Peter that he goes. Soon Peter has the majority of scholars, some thirty or so, but at harvest time he loses half of them, and has to take to part-time farm labour himself to eke out his salary. Sadly, however, though the venture school is successful and serves a real purpose, the Auld Kirk establishment manages to close it down; the notion of education as 'a political football' is not a new one.

Practically all of George MacDonald's Scottish fiction is an extended critique of the Calvinism of the Auld Kirk, and its presentation of schools and schoolmasters, in such novels as *Alec Forbes of Howglen*, is determined by that ideological purpose. The schoolmaster of the parish school of Glamerton (MacDonald's fictional version of Huntly) is Murdoch Malison who, despite his name, is not really an evil man, but, what is to MacDonald even worse, one who acts out of a perverted religiosity.

> … the master was a hard man, with a severe, if not an altogether cruel temper, and a quite savage sense of duty.[15]

He is another of the army of 'stickit ministers', who is convinced that even the youngest child is riddled with original sin which he is obliged to beat out of him. Annie Anderson, the young heroine of the novel, is amazed at the master's brutality.

> A fine-looking boy, three or four years older than herself, whose open countenance was set off by masses of dark brown hair, was called up to receive chastisement, merited or unmerited as the case might be; for such a disposition as that of Murdoch Malison must have been more than ordinarily liable to mistake. Justice, according to his idea, consisted in vengeance. And he was fond of justice. He did not want to punish the innocent, it is true; but I doubt whether the discovery of a boy's innocence was not a disappointment to him…
>
> At five, the school was dismissed for the day, not without another extempore prayer. A succession of jubilant shouts arose as the boys rushed out into the lane. Every day to them was a cycle of strife, suffering, and deliverance. Birth and death, with the life-struggle between, were shadowed out in it – with this difference, that the God of a corrupt Calvinism, in the person of Murdoch Malison, ruled that world, and not the God revealed in the man Christ Jesus.[16]

This same religiosity makes him place the reading of the Bible at the centre of his curriculum, but the teaching is carried out with such a lack of humanity and sensitivity that it is counter-productive, causing resistance rather than enlightenment.

> A moment of chaos followed, during which all the boys and girls, considered capable of reading the Bible, were arranging themselves in one great crescent across the room in front of the master's desk. Each read a verse – neither more nor less – often leaving the half of a sentence to be taken up as a new subject in a new key; thus perverting what was intended as an assistance to find the truth into a means of hiding it…[17]

But what makes Malison more than just a stereotype, and indeed a rather sympathetic figure, is the fact that this brutality is not an essential part of his nature, and, as one suspects was the case with many in the profession, he is merely adopting the demeanour that was expected of a schoolmaster. He is playing a culturally determined orthodox role, and the man outside school is very different from the classroom bully.

> I shall not have to show much more than half of Mr Malison's life – the school half, which, both inwardly and outwardly, was very different from the other. The moment he was out of the school, the moment, that is, that he ceased for the day to be responsible for the moral and intellectual condition of his turbulent subjects, the whole character – certainly the whole deportment – of the man changed. He was now as meek and gentle in speech and behaviour as any mother could have desired.[18]

It is possible to include much more about Alexander and MacDonald, both of whom have a lot to say about education – *Alec Forbes* for instance takes its hero into the university at Aberdeen and we have a good account of what life at King's College was like in the mid-nineteenth century – but it is important to find the space to deal with another, and undeservedly neglected, North-East writer.

Ian Macpherson was born in Forres in 1905, and he can be seen as the archetypal 'lad o' pairts', coming from a humble background but achieving great academic distinction. His father was a shepherd, and Ian spent his early years near Newtonmore. His sister has given the present author a picture of a very free and happy childhood, guddling for fish under the banks of the River Calder, and she ends with what appears to be a very telling comment.

> I didn't notice any quirks in his personality then and no mention of him being brainy. We were just a lot of kids being happy together.[19]

But then he went to school, and left the Highlands to live in Kincardineshire-perhaps the move is significant, for now the brains came into play. Success at school seems to have been his way of pleasing his mother. He won a bursary to Mackie Academy, Stonehaven, and in 1924 he was Dux of the school. Two features of his schooling add to our picture of the downside of the 'lad o' pairts'. One is bullying and victimisation of anyone different. Gibbon notes the contempt that the metropolitan sophisticates of Stonehaven had for country kids, and for Macpherson things were worse because he still showed signs of being 'Hielan'. His widow wrote later:

> A school friend there spoke of him as 'proud, wild, shy and sensitive'. As in the way of the young his fellows would have liked to gang up on the Highland outsider but Macpherson's formidable physical strength and ferocious temper quickly ended any incipient bullying.[20]

The other point that tends to be forgotten is that for many children from the remote areas secondary schooling meant living away from home. More than twenty years later, Macpherson wrote in an article in *The Glasgow Herald* of the trauma of this. He had been watching a film,

> … and all at once I remembered being a child, twelve years old, and leaving the elementary school near my home to go to a secondary school twenty miles away. My mother had found lodgings for me there and left me with a Bible and a shilling. I had spent all my previous life on farms, amongst my people and the familiar fields, and meal-hours and beasts.
>
> When the first day in my new school was over at last I hurried away from the other children to escape from the town.

And he concludes:

> When one is uprooted for the first time one ceases to be the child one was.[21]

Macpherson came to Aberdeen University and in an English class that was rather impressive – including the writers John R. Allan and Catherine Gavin – he was outstanding. He got a First, won the Seafield gold medal, and Professor Jack took the unusual step of adding a handwritten note to his class certificate, which begins:

> Mr Macpherson was the most distinguished student in the English classes during his four years study in Aberdeen. In the Final Honours Examinations he was awarded First Class Honours and all the University prizes as the first student of a very good year.[22]

Jack's respect for Macpherson's academic distinction led to his being given a post as his assistant and he spent two years lecturing there. The plan was that he would then go to Cambridge to do postgraduate work and pursue an academic career. But then he did a most remarkable thing – and one which, perhaps, embodies the main thesis of this paper – he turned his back on the whole academic way of life and the values implicit in it, and became an early drop-out or 'simple-lifer'.

Now married, he and his wife found a derelict cottage in the middle of nowhere, between Laggan and Dalwhinnie, and he spent the rest of his life just trying to survive in the place where he wanted to be. Latterly he rented a hill farm on the edge of the Dava Moor, and it was there that he was killed in a road accident in 1944, another in the tragic catalogue of Scottish writers to die young.

Macpherson published four novels – he wrote six but two are unpublished – the best of which is the last, *Wild Harbour*,[23] which is a seriously good novel. But for our purpose the most relevant one is the first, *Shepherds' Calendar*,[24] published in 1931, because, largely autobiographical, it deals with the tension between home and school, the culture of learning and the culture of inheritance, on which this paper has focused.

The novel centres on the Grant family, from the farm of Dalarn at the foot of the Cairn o' Mount, and particularly the son John. John Grant has brains, and he becomes the battleground over which his parents fight out their differences of value and aspiration. When his father becomes ill, John has to leave school to help on the farm. He does not mind this because it has only been his sense of duty to his mother that has kept him at his books. But she feels that he is being deprived of his opportunity of a better life, and when father dies she makes a huge financial and personal sacrifice to get him to the university. But he does not want to go, for, in a way that echoes, but predates, *Sunset Song*, his attachment is to the land itself.

> The land called him. His promise and his mother's affection held him. The earth called him, to be its master and its slave, to break it and use it, to glory in his strength pitted against its strength, and be broken at last. The peasant blood of his race cried out against his treachery. His mother would die, his need for keeping the promise pass. That was too late. If he failed the land this time there could be no turning back, no return again to beasts and newly-turned soil, and the chances of the year. If he dared to come back, too late, to the lonely country, he'd know it knew he was a failure. He'd feel its hostility, waiting, to get him at last, make dung of his fearful body. There was no compromise. . . He loved her more than he could say. But the land, the land, everything that did not change and did not seem to care.[25]

Nevertheless, mother has her way, even though she does not really want to lose him, and so in a tragic comment on the power of the culture of education we have a poignant ending where neither of the two is happy but both believe they have done right. Out of duty he goes to Aberdeen, and out of self-sacrifice she is left, with just her servant girl, to walk a stony road alone.

> She sent Sally to bed and read the Bible until failing light ended her lonely worship. In the dusk she walked along the road. She passed the crow woodie. She passed Dalarn, where strangers lived. She walked up the road as she walked with Allan when he took her first to Dalarn. She saw places as they were twenty years before. She heard her own young voice call home her first cows to their milking. She walked up the road to the head of the valley. She walked amongst boulders and the crumbling ruin of the world until morning.[26]

The message may stand as a final comment on North-East education.

Notes

1   Colin Milton, 'From Charles Murray to Hugh MacDiarmid: Vernacular Revival and Scottish Renaissance', in *Literature of The North*, ed. by David Hewitt and Michael Spiller (Aberdeen: Aberdeen University Press, 1983), pp. 82-108 (p. 87).
2   Lewis Grassic Gibbon, *A Scots Quair* (1932–34), rpt edn (London: Jarrold, 1959), p. 36.
3   Ibid.
4   Gibbon, *A Scots Quair*, p. 37.
5   Lewis Grassic Gibbon, 'Representative Scots 1: The Wrecker: James Ramsay MacDonald' in *Scottish Scene*, Lewis Grassic Gibbon and Hugh MacDiarmid, (London: Jarrold, 1934), pp. 95–108 (p. 95).
6   Jessie Kesson, *The White Bird Passes* (1958), rpt edn (Edinburgh: Harris, 1980), p. 151.
7   Gibbon, *A Scots Quair*, p. 33.
8   Gibbon, *A Scots Quair*, pp. 97–98.
9   See Ian R. Carter, 'The Mutual Improvement Movement in North-East Scotland in the Nineteenth Century', *Aberdeen University Review*, 46, no. 156 (Autumn 1976), 383-92.
10 William Alexander, *The Aberdeen Free Press*. 13 May 1870, p. 5.
11 William Alexander, 'The Peasantry of North-East Scotland' [1884], in *Rural Life in Victorian Aberdeenshire*, ed. by Ian Carter (Edinburgh: Mercat, 1992), pp. 48–53 (p. 51–52).
12 Ibid.
13 William Alexander, *Johnny Gibb of Gushetneuk*, rpt edn (Edinburgh: Douglas & Foulis, 1927 ed.), p. 55.
14 Alexander, *Johnny Gibb*, p. 56.
15 George MacDonald, *Alec Forbes of Howglen*, 3 vols (London: Hurst & Blackett, 1865), I, 30.
16 MacDonald, *Alec Forbes*, I, 30-31.
17 MacDonald, *Alec Forbes*, I, 28.
18 MacDonald, *Alec Forbes*, I, 105.
19 Letter to the author, 3 March 1997.
20 E. Macpherson, 'Ian Macpherson', *Leopard Magazine*, May 1973, pp. 19–22 (p.19).
21 Ian Macpherson, 'The Heather on Fire', *Glasgow Herald*, 11 April 1936, p. 4.
22 Class Certificate in possession of Macpherson's daughter, Mrs Jane Yeadon.
23 Ian Macpherson, *Wild Harbour* (London: Methuen, 1936).
24 Ian Macpherson, *Shepherds' Calendar* (London: Cape, 1931).
25 Ian Macpherson, *Shepherds' Calendar* (Edinburgh: Harris, 1983 ed.), pp. 271–74.
26 Macpherson, *Shepherds' Calendar* (1983), pp. 278–79.

Chapter Eight

Stands Doric Where It Did?

Derrick McClure

In the spring of 2000, the distinguished and justly popular Doric writer Sheena Blackhall conducted a research project on the attitudes to the local dialect among primary school children in Upper Deeside.[1] Sheena Blackhall has immortalised in several of her writings the reactions of a clever, fluent and sensitive child to the traditional educational policy of enforcing the use of English and prohibiting that of the mither tongue; and her research (used here with her kind permission) provides interesting evidence of the ways in which the climate has changed since her own schooldays.

That it has changed, and changed in some respects for the better, there can be no doubt. When the Doric and its status are discussed in public, someone in the company invariably recalls being punished in school for using Doric words or expressions: those days are gone, and for this we must give unreserved thanks. The old assumption that the function of Scottish education was to produce children fluent in standard literary English, instilled at the cost of a total enforced abandonment of the mither tongue, was unequivocally misguided; but by now its harmful results have been sufficiently exposed and its faulty ideological basis sufficiently demolished. Children from Doric-speaking homes are still taught to read, write and speak English – an educational necessity which it would be totally unrealistic to deny, and which is certainly not going to change in any future that can be seriously envisaged – but the use of the local dialect is no longer seen as a punishable offence. Most teachers pay at least lip-service to the idea that it should be allowed some measure of recognition, and some (if still only *some*) individual schools and schoolteachers actively encourage its use by the children at least in certain educational contexts. This, as far as it goes, must be regarded as a sign of improvement; and most of us would now welcome it as such. And yet, questions remain. In abandoning the old assumption, have we really made progress, or merely crossed a *pons asinorum*? A change for the better has indubitably come, but has it come for good reasons or bad – for the reasons that admirers of Scottish language and literature have been presenting for decades or for other reasons entirely? And can we look forward to further improvement, or is the token amount of attention now paid to Scots in the schools as much as we are ever likely to achieve?

The old belief in the sanctity of Standard English arose in an age of certainties. Not only in the educational field but in all walks of life, people lived and moved in a world where truth and falsehood, right and wrong, good and evil, were as unequivocal as black and white. You needed to speak properly in order to get on (the concepts of 'speaking properly' and 'getting on' being unexamined elementals); therefore no Scots words, expressions or pronunciations were to be tolerated: it was as simple as that. And the intolerance of Doric as of any other speech form except Standard English was the reverse side of a strongly positive and entirely respectable attitude: a belief that English was of enormous value, as the language of some of the greatest literary achievements in the world and the vehicle of a leading force in European and international culture, and that the ability to speak and write it with grace, skill and elegance was not only a social and vocational asset but a genuine achievement, to be striven for and displayed with pride.

For good or ill, things are no longer so simple. The vast social, cultural, philosophical and ideological changes by which this secure underpinning of life's activities has been worn away, leaving us to make our way in a more confusing and uncertain world, are far beyond the scope of this short paper; but there is no doubting that they have affected the educational field, and the place of Doric within it, as they have affected all other aspects of life. And when we look today at the status of the mither tongue in education, whether as a medium of conversation, a vehicle for poetry and prose texts to read in class, or a subject for study and discussion, what we find is a truly appalling degree of confusion and incomprehension.

Sheena Blackhall's dissertation includes a generous sampling of the responses she received from Primary 7 children when questioned on the way they felt about the local speech. Here is a small selection.

Aabody in my faimly spikks Scots. I like Scots best.[2]

I like Scots. It shows I'm Scottish.[3]

My favourite language is Scots, because some folk canna understand it and it annoys them.[4]

Some o the wirds in English are strange.[5]

Some people don't like to speak it out in the playground, but I've heard them speak it in the village.[6]

I just use Scots at home because I'm a bit embarrassed to use it with my friends because they sometimes laugh.[7]

I canna really speak it because I'm frae Aberdeen.[8]

I rage him [the child's dog] in English and I'm nice to him in Scots.[9]

I like to speak to my cat in Scots and English. If I was being silly and playing with it, I'd speak in Scots. If I was being sensible I'd speak to it in English.[10]

Sometimes I get fed up o the Aiberdeenshire accent. Aabody we ging tae visit says the same thing, "Ay, ay. Foo're ye deein!"[11]

It sounds like another language, like German or French.[12]

I don't understand it and I think it's horrible.[13] (This child has always lived in Ballater and has Scots-speaking parents and grandparents.)

The above selection of quotations is taken verbatim from her dissertation. They are clearly a variegated bunch. No attitude appears to be dominant: some children claim to like the Doric and others to dislike it; some are reticent about using it and others use it freely; some have (or could imagine having) it reserved for particular purposes. At the very least, the evidence of these quotations and of Blackhall's entire thesis shows that children are no longer brought up to regard their home speech as 'bad English' to be avoided at all costs. But how *are* they brought up to regard it? Has the new attitude of tolerance towards the Doric (and correspondingly to other varieties of Scots) led to a clear understanding of its origins and its status past and present, of its distinctive pronunciation, grammar and vocabulary, of its significance as an integral part of the life and culture of the local community through many generations, of the interest and merit of the literature produced in it? The answer, quite patently, is that it has not.

The progress which has been made, in fact, turns out on examination to be almost entirely negative: we have abolished a deplorable fact, the active suppression of Scots as a matter of educational policy; but have put very little of value in its place. Schoolchildren now *may* use *some* Scots; teachers *may* make *some* attempt to encourage it, if they so desire and if they are prepared to do so on their own initiative and with virtually no official guidance. And nothing of moment will happen if they do not take up those opportunities. The official assumption now seems to be that the survival and development of Scots is something which really doesn't matter either way. Between this and the older assumption that Scots is something to be stamped out, which reflects less credit on national policy and on the national mindset which gives rise to it? Under the old dispensation, we were disastrously wrong but at least we knew what we were trying to do: now it seems that we – that is, the shapers and operators of our national education policies – neither know nor really care.

It was in the 1970s, with the movement largely associated with the Edinburgh-trained sociolinguist Peter Trudgill, that a seismic change in educational attitudes occurred: local dialects and sociolects, slang and cant, and all non-standard forms of speech, instead of being regarded as vicious aberrations to be eradicated by an enforced imposition of the standard, came to be seen as equally valid *alternatives* to standard English. Trudgill in his seminal book *Accent, Dialect and the School*[14] argued the point (already well recognised by professional linguists) that judgements on speech forms were often social rather than linguistic in origin: that is, they were not objective assessments of the speech form itself, but were conditioned by listeners' perceptions of its speakers or of the conditions in which it was spoken. If professional-class people regarded working-class accents as 'ugly' or 'slovenly', it was because of the associations which the accents aroused, rather than any inherent quality in the sounds. This was impressively demonstrated by experiments. Native speakers of French, when asked to listen to recordings of a professional-class speaker from Paris, a working-class speaker from Paris and a working-class speaker from Montreal, uniformly rated them in that descending order of attractiveness; but listeners who knew no French, hearing the same recordings, showed no consistent preference whatsoever.[15] A randomly selected group of students was divided into two sub-groups, of which one listened to a recorded lecture delivered in RP and the other to one delivered in a Birmingham accent. Overwhelmingly, the first group judged the lecturer they had heard to be confident, well-informed and in commend of his material, the second judged theirs to be somewhat clumsy, unsure and generally unimpressive: but both groups had actually heard the same lecture delivered by the same bi-accentual individual.[16]

These experiments were, perhaps, naïve by standards of contemporary sociolinguistic research; but they had the wholly salutary effect of showing that when someone expressed the opinion that a given speech form was 'bad', his judgement could not be taken as a valid assessment of the actual expressive potential of the speech form in question. A statement like 'He's got a horrible Glasgow accent' conveys the speaker's own idiosyncratic reaction to the accent so described, but does not identify or describe any objectively verifiable quality of it. This is not to deny that such a reaction may be very real and very strong, nor that a response like 'A Glasgow accent's *not* horrible!' will have no effect whatever on the original speaker's feelings; but the statement does not refer to any scientifically detectable inferiority in a Glasgow accent as compared to, say, an Edinburgh one; and could not because there *is* none.

Trudgill and many other linguists of the period produced a large amount of evidence (much of it, admittedly, anecdotal) to support the thesis that all speech forms, whether international standard languages, traditional local dialects or sociolects of urban working classes, were equally capable of expressing all that their speakers wished or had any need to express, and were equally capable of being developed, if necessary, to express things that they had never expressed in the past. (This view is undeniably simplistic, and illustrates the fact that linguists – including the present writer, of course – are as prone as anybody else to allow their statements to be influenced by extra-linguistic ideology. The notion that the total expressive power of any language is invariably the same as that of any other language simply cannot be maintained: if Navajo or Yoruba has tens of thousands of words, English or Russian has *more* tens of thousands; and if the vocabulary and the idiomatic and stylistic range of Navajo were to expand to equal those of English it would no longer be the same language, just as modern English is not the same language as Anglo-Saxon. What *can* be maintained is that the capacity of *individual speakers* to express themselves linguistically varies only with individual variations in knowledge, practice and skill and not with the language they use: an adult speaker of Navajo will know the entirety of his language whereas an adult speaker of English will know only a fraction of his, so that no-one is automatically advantaged or disadvantaged by being born into a community which uses one language rather than another.)

From the assumption that no language can be said to be better or worse than any other, Trudgill proceeded to argue that the same was true of dialects and accents; and from this, to present the case that locally or socially marked features should be recognised as legitimate speech forms, existing as integral parts of the identity not only of the community but of each individual speaker; and consequently that children with such features in their speech should not be prevented from using them or taught to regard them as 'mistakes', but encouraged to maintain them with pride. Attempting to eradicate the local features in a child's speech, it was suggested, would be more likely to result in confusion and loss of confidence than in a willing adoption of the standard; and would, in fact, constitute a breach of human rights in contributing to, and helping to perpetuate, an entrenched social discrimination against users of speech forms other than the standard. This argument, as far as it goes, would be hard to criticise on either educational or humanitarian grounds.

Unfortunately, the educational orthodoxy which arose as a result of the case presented by Trudgill and others took the implications of their argument far beyond reason or even sense. There is no case against recognising the historical, social and cultural importance of non-standard dialects; but to adopt an 'anything goes' attitude – to assume that schoolchildren require no guidance or instruction whatever in the use of language, or that mere ignorance and illiteracy bestows on a speaker the status of a potential (or even an actual) Sheena Blackhall or James Kelman – is patently a dereliction of all educational responsibility. One aspect of the revolution in educational principles and practices which occurred in the third quarter of last century is that young Conn Docherty's encounter with Mr Pirrie[17] is no longer a regular occurrence in classrooms all over Scotland; another is that students in university English departments are routinely placed in remedial classes to stop them from making errors in punctuation and sentence construction, which their parents could avoid in primary school.

One reason for the more tolerant attitude towards Scots in the schools, that is, is the naïve and stultifying assumption that any form of language is as good, or as bad, as any other: hardly a credible, or creditable, motive. A second and equally simplistic one, I suspect, is political rather than educational in origin: the loss of status of English literature and the English language with the decline of Great Britain as a world power.

Here again, a perfectly tenable ideological position has been misapplied to produce results of which the discreditable aspects far outweigh the beneficial: on the one hand, school-leavers now often have some knowledge of Grassic Gibbon or Edwin Morgan, as also of various Indian, African, or Caribbean writers, who would have been totally ignored in the schools twenty years ago; on the other, they have no knowledge whatsover of the general outline history of English (much less Scottish) literature, what used to be regarded as the Great Tradition having no more place in their mental furniture than in that of a Yanomami.

A primary school headmaster of the writer's acquaintance, about five years before the date of writing, was ordered by visiting inspectors to get rid of a set of Arthur Mee's *Children's Encyclopaedia* which stood on the top of his classroom cupboard. The fact that this compendium is a magnificent treasure-house of stories from many times and lands, of poems suitable for children of all ages and stages, of interesting and useful projects in craftwork and simple science, of reproductions of the world's great works of art, of information on animal and plant life – that it is in many respects an educational resource as valuable as it ever has been, comparable to nothing produced in recent times – did not weigh against the fact (equally indisputable, of course) that it presents an almost laughably simplistic and partisan view of English history: and apparently the teacher could not be relied upon to preserve his charges from being misled by this, while making use of the valuable sections of the books for their education.

This pernicious witch-hunting leaves more than a suspicion of its presence in attitudes to language and literature. That the English language and the magnificent corpus of English prose, poetry and drama (English in the national sense) were consciously utilised in the service of the British imperial project is not in doubt. However, the intrinsic merit and value of English literature – on any showing, one of the greatest national literatures in the world – is wholly unaffected by the fact that the British Empire is now history; and the fact that standard literary English no longer needs to be taught as a passport to important and prestigious jobs in colonial administration is not an argument for not teaching it at all. It is entirely right that the status of the English language and the literary canon should be examined and questioned: this movement has led to important and valuable re-assessments, and to the re-discovery of many neglected writers, especially women. But the current fad of denying children access, or anything but token access, to the great English writers of the past – by implication, attempting to excise the English national literary achievement from popular awareness, as was for generations the accepted policy towards the Scottish – is indefensible on any grounds whatever.

And if Scots has been able to creep in, to a small degree, through the crumbling woodwork of the English cultural edifice, there are no grounds for pride in this. Scottish literature, including that part of it which is written in the Scots language, can and should form a major part of the curriculum in its own right: the fact that ever since the Union it has been overshadowed, or eclipsed, by English literature has always been a national disgrace. It should not have been necessary to wait for a general questioning of the status of the entire English literary canon to restore the Scottish to its proper place. And though it may satisfy our atavistic national instincts to observe the displacement of England's literary and cultural achievement from its once-unquestioned status as the model for the rest of the world, we are surely capable of seeing the whole issue in perspective. The English (or British) imperial enterprise is a fact of history: multi-faceted like all great historical processes, with both glorious and shameful aspects. The utterly preposterous notion of writing it in its entirety out of the collective consciousness, or the equally absurd assumption that the British Empire should be spoken of, if at all, in the kind of shamefaced tones proper to a discussion of the Third Reich, are symptoms of a truly incredible degree of intellectual and moral immaturity.

The position which Scots linguistic and cultural activists have been arguing for decades is not that the mither tongue, in whichever of its many forms, is entitled to the same degree of basic tolerance as, say, a Brummy accent or the imperfectly-learned English of immigrants from the Indian sub-continent. It is that Scots is not only a national language with a centuries-old pedigree but the vehicle of one of Europe's great literatures; and as such is the inalienable birthright of every Scottish citizen. And not even the most ardent cultural nationalist, at least in his cooler moments, has seriously denied the greatness of English literature, or argued that it was necessary to displace it entirely in order to allow the literature of Scotland a place in the sun. Scottish literature, surely, is strong enough to assert and prove the justice of its own claim to respect.

As was noted at the beginning of this essay, we are now living in a world in which old certainties have been abolished by findings which have shown that language and the facts regarding its use are vastly more complex than our predecessors realised. The result of this is that the *thesis* of a monolithic Standard English before which all other related forms had to yield has been replaced by the equally simplistic *antithesis* of an absolute parity for all speech forms: the former standard itself, all regional dialects, all sociolects, even the spoken and written forms of children who have not yet become fully competent in the language and foreigners who have learned it imperfectly. We now require a *synthesis*, by which the findings of modern linguistic thought will be applied to produce, not the present situation in which the various forms of Scots are tolerated on the ignominious assumption of 'anything goes', but one in which they can be encouraged and allowed to flourish as part of a proud and vibrant national culture with lively regional variations. As a step towards this, let us examine the facts which modern sociolinguistics has brought to our attention, and consider the valid and the invalid corollaries which they suggest.

1. Standard English, like all standard languages, owes its status to a historical accident: it is not intrinsically superior to other speech forms, and neither has nor has ever had any divine right to be used in preference to others.

False corollary: Standard English therefore deserves no particular respect. No great effort should be expended in teaching it, and children should not (or at any rate need not) be expected to write or speak it according to formerly accepted canons of spelling and grammar.

True corollary: The origins of Standard English are an interesting historical study, but they do not affect the fact that it *is*, and is certainly going to remain, a language of international importance, with established canons of spelling, grammar and style according to which it is studied and used throughout the world. Ability to read, write and speak it acceptably is, if anything, not less but more indispensable now than at the end of the nineteenth century. On the other hand, it was never the case that acquisition of Standard English could only be at the cost of abandoning a native language or dialect; bilingual and diglossic communities are common, and case-studies now abound of societies where each individual has full command of both a national or international language and a local speech-form.

2. Among the nation-states of Europe (and elsewhere; but it is still a local phenomenon and not a universal fact) language is an integral part of national identity. A measure of affection or hostility may come to be attached to any particular language as a result of the interplays of the historical relations between nations.

False corollary: English, as the imperialist language *par excellence* of the nineteenth and first half of the twentieth century, must be forcibly 'demoted'. Little or no attention should be paid to English literature of the past.

True corollary: Recognition of this fact should lead to a liberation from its pernicious influence. To reject the English cultural achievement, and the language in which it is couched (which is accessible to all Scots) in reaction against England's historical record is to betray the same mindset as the embittered old Cavalier in Scott's *Woodstock*, who furiously upbraided his daughter's suitor for leading him to praise some lines of poetry which he did not know were by Milton.[18] And in any case, the events of history, by definition, are gone. The English nation is no longer a threat to the distinctive and independent cultures of other nations, including our own (this statement would not be true if the word *language* were substituted for *nation*; but that is a different issue). Scottish schoolchildren have, through their native languages (for English has been a native language of Scotland for centuries) the birthright of both Scottish and English literature; and should be trained to appreciate both.

3. Geographically marked dialects are the results of long-term historical developments and are specific manifestations of the universal tendency in language to fissiparate and diversify: they are neither imperfect attempts at the standard language nor degenerate or corrupted versions of it.

False corollary: Any form of speech is therefore in every respect equal to any other; and all must receive complete parity in education: from which it follows that no attempt must be made to correct any form, spoken or written, which any pupil should happen to produce.

True corollary: Before applying this fact to an assessment of a given case, it is necessary to be certain of the historical status of the speech form under examination. Buchan Doric is an excellent example of a local speech form which has developed a highly individual character, a close association with a well-defined regional culture and a literature of remarkable size and quality. Glasgow urban demotic, by contrast, is of much more recent development, its cultural status is more problematic, and its literary development slighter and also more idiosyncratic and more ideologically assertive. The concept of 'equality' is meaningless: each case must be assessed on its own merits – and what is certain is that the speech form of any given area is of more immediate relevance to the local inhabitants, including children in schools, than any other.

4. In stratified societies, differences in speech often correspond to differences in social class. Value-judgements of the quality of the speech of one class made by speakers from another may be based on strong conditioned reactions, but they are not assessments of the actual linguistic efficiency of the speech-form under judgement.

False corollary: There is therefore no need to 'correct' a child's speech in the sense of attempting to remove stigmatised features such as glottal stops: the response of 'if you don't like it, it's your problem' is sufficient.

True corollary: The problem is a serious one in the field of social interaction, and a cavalier dismissal of the reactions of people with inbuilt negative feelings towards certain dialects and accents is likely to be as unproductive as a heavy-handed attempt to eradicate the stigmatised accents entirely, particularly for the pragmatic reason that such people will often be in the position of prospective employers. What is called for here is a greater degree of understanding, among all parties, of both linguistic and psychological facts: the imparting of which, a major responsibility of classroom teachers, will not be achieved by replacing one naïve value-judgement with another.

5. Language change is inevitable: even in relatively isolated cultures the local speech is never static; and in the present era of mass media and easy social mobility language is extremely unstable.

False corollary: It is therefore pointless to insist on 'standards'; and especially to imagine that the standards enshrined in grammar-books of fifty years ago will be acceptable to contemporary pupils. Scots, or whatever any Scottish child happens to speak, is acceptable from the mere fact of its momentary existence.

True corollary: Language change is not an ineluctable force but is brought about by human agency; and the fact that standards are unstable does not mean that no standard can exist, or that none does exist for any given place or time. In the case of Scots, though it has never been standardised to the extent that English has, there is no doubt that some measure of standardisation exists, both for the language as a whole and for some at least of its dialects (i.e. those with an extensive local literature, such as North-East Doric). And though it is true that the natural tendency of language is to change, it is equally true that at least in literate and politically developed societies this has always been countered by pressure towards standardisation: the history of languages, in fact, typically shows a tension between *centrifugal* and *centripetal* forces. The historical place of education, almost by its inherent nature, is to contribute to the latter and not the former: certainly it is no part of the duty of educationists to further ongoing changes (even supposing that these could be recognised), still less to elevate instability to the status of a principle. It is patently absurd to imagine that slipshod grammar or spelling must be tolerated because it perhaps represents a language change in process. Scots, like English, exists in well-established and well-defined forms, towards which children can and should be directed.

6. Any speech form which functions as a community language is adequate for the needs of its speakers (this, indeed, is almost a tautology); and any long-established speech form will both reflect, in some mode and measure, and be part of, the distinctive nature of the community as it has developed through its history.

False corollary: There is therefore no need to develop or modify in any way the speech habits which a child brings to the school, as he can get on perfectly well with the habits he has acquired and to alter them would interfere with his personal identity

True corollary: A child's identity is by definition not fully developed; and the most fundamental and most inescapable responsibility of his mentors (parents as well as classroom teachers, and ultimately the entire society of which he is part) is to contribute to its growth and maturing. An individual's identity cannot be separated from his status as a member of the intricate network of communities – family, peer group, region, nation – within which he functions; in defining each of which a distinctive set of language habits plays some part. Classroom teachers, therefore, have a clear duty actively to foster a child's growing awareness of the use and status of his language, or languages, in all their variations and with all their potential for expression: a responsibility which will not be fulfilled by refusing to assume a positive and definite attitude to language behaviour with emphasis on the value, intrinsic and symbolic, of the native speech. And the value of a language like Scots, with its ancient and brilliant literary development and its status as the mother tongue of a nation with a story long and fascinating enough to match any in the world, speaks for itself.

Uncertainty is not a principle by which individuals or communities can live. There is no returning to the straightforward values of former times, nor is it sufficient to replace them with any equally simplistic set: the new complexities must be confronted. But is its precisely by confronting them that the Scots language, and the entire Scottish literary and cultural achievement, can be restored to its rightful place.

Notes

[1] Sheena Middleton [Sheena Blackhall], *A Study into the Knowledge and Use of Scots amongst Primary Pupils on Upper Deeside* (unpublished M. Litt. dissertation, University of Aberdeen, 2000).

[3] Blackhall, p.25.

[4] Blackhall, p.25.

[5] Blackhall, p.25.

[6] Blackhall, p.29.

[7] Blackhall, p.30.

[8] Blackhall, p.25.

[9] Blackhall, p.28.

[10] Blackhall, p.30.

[11] Blackhall, p.27.

[12] Blackhall, p.36.

[13] Blackhall, p.23.

[14] Peter Trudgill, *Accent, Dialect and the School*, Explorations in Language Study (London: Arnold, 1975).

[15] A. D'Anglejan and G. R. Tucker, 'Sociolinguistic Correlates of Speech Style', in *Language Attitudes: Current Trends and Prospects*, ed. by Roger W. Shuy and Ralph W. Fasold (Washington: Georgetown University Press, 1973).

[16] For this and a full account of its experimental context, see Howard Giles and Peter F. Powesland, *Speech Style and Social Evaluation* (London, New York: Academic Press for European Association of Experimental Social Psychology, 1975), pp. 24-27.

[17] William McIlvanney, *Docherty*, Magna Scottish Writers (London: Allen & Unwin, 1975); repr edn (Edinburgh: Mainstream, 1983), pp. 110-12.

[18] McIlvanney, *Docherty*, chapter 25.

Chapter Nine

The Smokestack Curriculum and Coming Lightning

Robbie Robertson

Keeping abreast of moving culture is a major test for education, and ongoing changes are posing a particularly tough set of questions. Technology's never-ending growth, exponentially fuelled by mercantilist needs, is matched by social re-developments at every level, and even these are dwarfed by the profound transformations required of culture by the certainties of onrushing climate change.

Our country seems to be at some kind of crossroads and knowing which way to move is a matter of pressing urgency for the whole culture but particularly for education, which is today preparing tomorrow's citizens for tomorrow's needs. Or should be. But so far as the future is concerned the truth is that little seems to be being done in any planned way. In the world of education we change our habits as a response to immediate needs, usually driven by political will; our awareness of the future is a kind of Brigadoon where we all snooze together. We wake up on the traditional day maybe for new proposals on curriculum and/or assessment change, or for a technological innovation so far-reaching in its socio-cultural implications it cannot be evaded: the computer, say. Otherwise, so far as future needs are concerned, it is business as usual.

Leadership is of clear importance, but this is only one of innumerable difficulties. The bureaucratic leaderships which direct Scottish education are themselves snuggled up in Brigadoon. They are products of their past experience and tend to live there, cautious people, preferring certainty to experiment and ever driven by a hyper-awareness of costs. Furthermore, changes in thinking and personnel are sluggish since bureaucracy tends to self-replicate through its control of appointments. It is usually the lash of government that makes them move. But politicians, another potential source of leadership, have notoriously short-term ambitions, which certainly do not include the addressing of the questions to be asked here.

At every level in the curriculum we now operate, from the epistemological thinking which shapes it, through its content and methodology, to the roles accorded to the teachers, parents and children who tenant it, we see on the whole the past and its dead hand. This curriculum, here called the Smokestack Curriculum because of its inappropriateness to modern needs, embeds dangerous flaws on account of its retro nature, and if we are fully to confront our future obligations we need to interrogate it thoroughly and make essential modifications to it in some planned way. The coming lightning is already brightening our skies, and the storms it brings will be tumultuous.

In attacking the dominant place of the past in education we must be careful, however, to distinguish this from the past's social and personal value. Knowing it as shared experience is an essential awareness for each community. After all, it is declared across the material and immaterial culture of the area. It provides continuity with traditions and ways of life. It offers social bonding through the knowledge of familiar/familial pathways. Besides, this sharing of the past gives security from the dangers posed by change, and also provides one means of reading and evaluating it, thus reducing anomie, and promoting social cohesion. The language of the locality is, therefore, a central organiser of experience. Yet for all its attachments to the past, it is ironic that the Smokestack Curriculum does not handle this side of the educational business all that very well either.

For a region such as the North-East of Scotland, one that has had such a distinctive part to play in shaping and responding to Scotland's past, this observation is a particularly significant one. The negligent, not to say frequently repressive, treatment which its language and its lore have received at the hands of generations of 'dominies' means that those anxious to conserve its culture have little to fear – and much to welcome – from an extinction of the sullen fires that have fed its smokestacks.

As for the lightning, it is already bringing incessant change. What else will it bring? The future lacks definition but what we do now will without doubt affect its nature. Devising Doomsday scenarios is possible as are the envisioning of futures carrying the kinds of social and environmental changes to which human cultures have been responding for many thousands of years, but at no time more demanding than at present.

We can notice general matters, almost truisms, about the future whatever its nature: that there will be a tendency to destabilise the past, as new ways of life, of thinking, of behaviour replace others; that there will equally certainly be requirements, perhaps necessities, for new forms of cultural mastery; that new forms of language will be needed to address the new culture; that there will be a need for innovation and a more than adequate response to change; that there will be a tendency for increased insecurities arising from the very fear of the new. Futures and their direction need not be inevitable. They are to some extent in our charge, but knowing and weighing up the options, devising pathways, require forms of knowledge and understandings which the Smokestack Curriculum neither permits nor develops.

Multiplying such truisms is not demanding, but if we do indeed believe that education is in some way in the complex business of developing future dispositions, then it is truly astonishing that so little seems to be done to develop them – even as truisms – in the current mainstream curriculum. Not that all teachers are failing to work in these directions. Some do, being forced to rise above lack of support from the present policy-makers who give them little in the way of resources and offer little formal acknowledgement of their efforts. That there is a lack of any systematic view of the necessary curriculum is a severe limitation. On that account, work in these important areas is not only random, it also lacks direction, and what is being done is being done in isolated pockets which are poorly related to the rest of the curriculum.

Ultimately, it is not only leadership that matters. The quality at the chalk face is of equal, perhaps greater, importance. Teachers' skills and receptivity are the bedrock on which curriculum change rests. Their temperaments also control what can be done, and its effectiveness. Their attitudes and commitment determine the success of the overall programme. But social change should also require social will, and to do this most effectively requires national debate, and an understanding of the issues which have been so dimly presented by the Smokestack Curriculum, and in culture generally, as to be meaningless for the majority. What follows should be read as the opening shots in such a debate.

Three Curricular Organisations

The present reliance on the subject base for curriculum at both primary and secondary levels is the first weakness of the Smokestack Curriculum. It is obvious that while there are clear bureaucratic advantages in this structure by, for example, readily permitting a manageable structure based on age, ability, assessment, the identification of responsibilities, and so on, there is little correspondence between the content of subjects and their use in the business of life. Knowledge is not reducible into such strands. Knowledge is, of course, a field, integrated and potentially unified, which we all deploy in an integrated, unified kind of way. But the field nature of knowledge is not addressed by the Smokestack Curriculum. Especially in the secondary school, cross curricular working, for example, exists, if at all, as a kind of imponderable, the barriers between subjects too massive to be moved or reduced, the need for movement scarcely perceived as relevant. In the primary schools, matters are more relaxed, but it is the subject base that still dominates assessment and on which structures such as guidance and advice are reliant. The young hang on in a fog of separately arrayed information, lost within which they are taught neither how to learn nor how to think, and receive no overall map of the domains of knowledge they must master and how they interrelate. It is one of the marks of the Smokestack Curriculum that it is disempowering for its students, and that power and control reside almost exclusively, first with the bureaucracy, and then with teaching staff.

The roots of this subject structure are far from modern and can possibly be traced back to Babylon and Ancient Egypt. Such an organisation of knowledge was certainly welcomed into Europe by Pythagoras and Plato, and was one of the proudest features of mediæval culture.

The mediæval curriculum constituted the seven liberal arts, the threefold *trivium* of Grammar, Logic, and Rhetoric, and the fourfold *quadrivium* of Arithmetic, Music, Geometry, and Astronomy. These words describe a three- and four-way crossroads because the paths of knowledge they describe were seen as interconnected at a fundamental level. To ensure an awareness of their interrelatedness at a humanistic level each was also accompanied by its associated metaphysical discipline. Thus Geometry was attached to Geomancy: the relationships between form and spirit, the emotions generally, being considered particularly important for the design of buildings such as places of worship or for the graphic arts.

These precious seeds were preserved throughout the so-called Dark Ages to become the epistemological base for mediæval universities, not only in the Christian West but the Islamic East. The total collapse of the *quadrivium* in Europe came in the late sixteenth century with the arrival of materialist conceptions of Nature and, with it, a parallel emphasis on commercial and economic interests. Such ideological predispositions left no room for linkages between brute reality and its metaphysical subtleties, and turned the learner into a trainee helot destined, in our time, either for academic ermine, dungarees, or for unemployment.

This is the situation at which we have arrived in modern education. Although the skeletons of the *trivium* and *quadrivium* can still be recognised, their spirit has vanished. The systems of analogy, pattern, and correspondence that they promoted out of a belief in cosmic harmony and interconnectedness have also fallen and so has grown the modern structure of mostly detached specialisms, each with its usually impenetrable ideolect, each with its cadre of experts. In the Smokestack Curriculum, which embodies this world view, there is no sense of any overall pattern, nor of the integration of knowledge. The emphasis instead is on mastery, competition, using detached areas of knowledge whose value is usually determined by their value for the world of work or for the inculcation of social behaviours.

Of infinitely more value will be a genuine Information Curriculum, based on what is now known to be the pattern of human learning and the acquisition of knowledge. An Information Curriculum will stress, for example, the direct teaching of thinking and reasoning skills, of research, of cultural knowledge, of aesthetic response and spiritual awareness, of decoding and encoding skills in all the languages – visual, auditory and print – that we have developed as key aspects of an overall view of human communication (see below). These will not be isolated programmes but programmes integrated in a transcurricular way. Learning will be a partnership between the school and the community, with parents involved in the curriculum and holding commensurate responsibilities, with children given a generous measure of independence and control, and with universal access to the contacts and knowledge possible through the Internet.

Such a curriculum will be focused on the individual, more intensively than the Smokestack Curriculum permits, but its primary organisational nodes will be small groups rather than classes; secondary nodes will be provided by the subject bases, now too deeply instilled to be eradicated, and still of value for the purposes of direct teaching. Age will no longer determine the groups' structures. Interests, ability and the ability to learn will be the determinants. None of this is easy to put into effect, of course, but far from impossible. It will, however, require major shifts in the ideological positions of the parties involved. As has already been said, none of this is new, and some simplified elements of an Information Curriculum are already present in Scottish education, albeit in a disorganised kind of way.

The Information Curriculum will also have a different orientation to the learner. The Smokestack emphasises needs: information will proceed from an optimistic base and will emphasise opportunities and success, no matter how minor. Assessment will always be through self and peer processes, monitored as necessary. The teacher and librarian will become guides rather than directors. The dominance of instruction will be replaced by search and research. Eating a prepared diet of information will be replaced by the cooking of individual meals. The current prevalence of the printed page will be substantially reduced to accommodate moving picture and screens, which are children's now preferred means of negotiating information and entertainment.

The Smokestack Curriculum also gives precedence to linear manoeuvres. For example: traditionally and at present, nearly all children proceed in lock-step transitions from class to class, with progress similarly seen in a linear way, whereas children, on the whole, make progress in jumps and starts, almost in random kinds of ways. Similarly, the year is still characterised by the repetition of previous patterns not only organisationally but in terms of curriculum content.

These features represent straight-line thinking. An Information Curriculum will emphasise each child's interests and potentials. It will organise a personal curriculum in terms of step-by-step procedures, perhaps involving repetitions from different perspectives, and always ready to be modified to meet changing situations. Rather than linear, this will be a curriculum based on algorithmic thinking and a closer correspondence to the realities of learning and the learner.

Assuming that our culture will continue on its present path, our future will be concerned with mutabilities of many kinds: fewer jobs for life, more needs for periodic training in new skills, more movement across regions and between continents, greater contacts between individuals from many different cultures, and so on. This future to which we are tending will not be interested in fixed patterns of knowledge. Only the Information Curriculum can address that future and deliver what is necessary: adaptable people, capable of addressing all contingencies, able to acquire new skills readily, autonomous learners, unanxious and unthreatened by change, confident in their abilities to meet all challenges, demonstrating an automatic flexibility, not rigidity.

Only in this way can we claim to be producing that current shibboleth, the lifelong learner. The Smokestack Curriculum is scarcely up to the task, its teaching being dominated by an ancient technique: the exploration of an exemplum followed by problems to be solved based on the exemplum. This technique does not develop cognitive mobility, only immediate learning and a reliance on mostly unidirectional strategies. True life-long learning demands a knowledge of process, an understanding of systems, and an awareness of structures and their relationships.

The Information Curriculum will recognise that both the future and the past must be engaged within the school's activities. To achieve its ends most effectively any socially relevant curriculum must also give its future citizens deep roots from which to address their coming needs, somewhere for their minds to call home. The Information Curriculum will, therefore, be a marriage between past and present, focused on the future but aware that the past provides the palimpsest on which the present and future are both written.

Libraries will naturally thrive in the Information Curriculum and the librarian team will be seen, not as a peripheral resource, but as co-equals with teachers, and be involved in curriculum planning, development, and delivery. Both sets of professionals will share common beliefs. They will see education as a preparation for the world and life; work will be a secondary consideration and its essential skills will be taught on the job. They will take as a right that they have freedom to teach what they and their pupils want. They will be in the paid business of devising their own teaching materials to some agreed pattern, and these will be available free of charge to other contemporaries on the Net.

The Information Curriculum will have three, interrelated dimensions or ranges of activities to be presented across the curriculum. These dimensions will not constitute the whole curriculum but will be significant parts of it. They are: a Scottish (and for the North-East a particular emphasis upon the human experience of that region) dimension (see below); one concerning the UK; and the third dealing with the world. Thus the experience of the past will include not only, say, the Vikings and their incursions into the British Isles, with the Scottish experience given some emphasis, but also Europe, their role in the foundation of Russia and Normandy, their establishment of colonies on Iceland and Greenland, their discovery of America, and the societal and cultural conditions which drove them.

If we are to address the coming lightning in any constructive way the development of such local and internationalist qualities should be at the heart of the curriculum. We live in an increasingly interconnected world, and national perspectives are no longer sufficient. But the world culture which is growing round about us, often stemming from the commercial subcultures of the USA, is intentionally decentred for commercial and technological reasons and presents no ostensible allegiance to any one nation. This lack of any fixed cultural identity suggests dangers for individuals and their well-being, as we rush pell-mell towards our future. The truth is that the Smokestack Curriculum's concerns are at best peripheral to such interests because, denatured shadow from the past, it is scarcely up to the job of providing the essential skills necessary to prepare children to meet their complex future positions in society and culture.

In the unrelated conceptual spaces of the Smokestack Curriculum there can be no attempt to grow organic skills such as thinking and inventiveness, to develop powers of analogical reasoning, to have a perception of patterns inherent in human culture, to get any sense of an organic unity, not only in nature but in our lives. This is not a concern for the able child, who will learn no matter the curriculum. But little wonder that this curricular starkness is offensive to many, and that many children reject their education as essentially unconnected either to their needs or to their being.

The Scottish Dimension[1]
In the world forming about us no nation is an island. We are now, increasingly, integral parts of a complex world culture with international travel a commonplace, and with national political frontiers eroding all around us. Centrifugal globalising movements struggle with more national, centripetal forces. On that account, the Information Curriculum must encompass the diversity of Scottish indigenous and multi-ethnic culture; it must support processes of integration, and it must also include UK, European and wider world perspectives. Globalising influences must, however, be so managed in the curriculum and in society to ensure the survival of Scotland as a cultural entity, and this can only be achieved if people appreciate their cultures and have been given experiences which help to endorse them. In all these respects the Smokestack Curriculum has failed.

In common with others, Scottish culture is richly varied. The modern nation has a variety of indigenous cultures, often associated with a region or group of regions. These cultures have living histories which are revealed both in artefacts, the earliest reaching back to the Neolithic, and in lifestyles with characteristic features of behaviour, language, and industry. In addition to Gaelic – Scotland's most ancient and increasingly vibrant culture – these include the Norn of Shetland, Orkney, and Caithness, the mix that is the Scottish Borders, and the varied cultures of the cities. The Doric of the North-East has made a particularly distinctive contribution to the overall native mix. While these remarkably resilient regional forces might be thought to fragment and to diminish any sense of a common, national culture, taken together they constitute a shared experience which in the past and now can well be described as 'Scottish'.

All regional cultures should be quintessential features of an Information Curriculum, each making its own special contribution. Giving all learners some sense of this variety should be a curricular aim, but each region's culture should also form a distinctive part of its curriculum. This will create an enriched awareness of place. Culture is now, and has always been, in a process of constant change, and education acting alone can intervene only in partial ways to divert that movement. It is this very process of change, now accelerating within our culture, which requires a well-grounded sense of place, time, and a distinctive culture to guard against the dangers of dissociation and alienation.

When people share a common place they will mostly have in common important ways of life determined by that place's distinctive environment and by their own history, languages, arts, faiths, and beliefs. This place will be regarded, in the first instance, as Scotland, its regions, and local communities, since these are the places from which most Scots derive their identity.

A major task of education is the creation of a sense and awareness of personal, social, and cultural identity, a process necessarily interwoven with the past, present and their conditions. This task requires wider versions of identity than the merely national, and a Scottish dimension should accommodate them. On that account, although each Scot may possess multiple identities, this should have a core located in Scotland since it provides the society, culture, topography and peoples with which the vast majority of Scottish learners most identity.

In creating a sense of cultural identity, nothing is more important than the matter of language, and, in particular, of Scots. Although 'Scots' shares a common historical origin with English it cannot accurately be relegated to the status of a dialect. Stigmatised and eroded in the past, it presently lacks generally accepted formal registers of speaking and writing. Despite centuries of attrition, however, it continues to express itself in variants of different density across the country and is used and understood by possibly two million people. These variants are sufficiently close to one another in vocabulary and grammar to be treated pragmatically as one language, and are codified in an impressive range of dictionaries. Scots has one of the most extensive and distinguished literatures of any of the so-called lesser used European languages and is of abiding interest to scholars around the world. Writings in varieties of Scots continue to thrive today, often in forms of particular interest to the young.

For generations the use of Scots – or, in the North-East, Doric – was discouraged in schools on the false grounds that it interfered with the learning of the national dialect, English. Over the last 25 years there has been increased, but still spasmodic, attention to the potential contribution of Scots language and literature to the curriculum. It remains true, however, that Scots in its varieties has never won the practical support from the Smokestack Curriculum which it merits. Nevertheless, the importance of English within the United Kingdom, and its growing role as the main medium of global communication, suggests that programmes of English language and its literatures should continue to be at the heart of pupils' learning at all stages.

Scottish and regional culture have distinctive features and powerful ideas and, as such, are worthy of study and transmission. This Scottish experience creates a sense of a social and cultural unity, of a Scotland made from a varied past, progressing towards a shared future, and with all the capacities necessary to meet the challenges this progress will entail. In doing so, Scottish culture provides a robust platform from which to explore and to accommodate the larger world, its messages, and distractions. Scottish culture, any national culture, rooted in some real past, but open to new experiences, provides an essential basis for future happiness and a successful passage in a world of incessant alteration.

This position does not, however, imply a passive acceptance, nor a mindless indoctrination through a curriculum which denies conscious engagement. Clearly, critical engagement and debate will be used in the Information Curriculum to promote knowledge, appreciation and discrimination. The young need always to be educated to the possibilities of different interpretations of events, to the debating and challenging of established views. In doing so they should *always* be taught to look outwards, and to draw on cultural influences from other places and other times.

It is the Information Curriculum which will handle such needs best, for the Smokestack Curriculum is derelict, and has always failed, in this regard. It does not recognise that it is indigenous, historically-rooted culture which makes a strong bond between individuals, helping to form their view of themselves, their shared worlds and the world generally. The most important aspects of that culture have been shared by those in Scotland and its regions across centuries, and this should continue to be represented in, and to form one basic approach for, an Information Curriculum.

Communication: A Cross-Curricular Concern

At the heart of all education is the idea of communication. Unsurprisingly, really, since it is also at the heart of culture and society generally. Such a view is not present in the Smokestack Curriculum which, in a characteristic display of incompetence, fails to provide any opportunity to explore systematically the nature of human communication, although it is central to the ways in which our lives are organised. This responsibility has, to some extent, been accorded to English, although it is now known that the essential skills the subject presently handles – reading, writing, talking, listening – represent only a small fraction of the gamut of human communication systems, and are, of course, themselves transcurricular needs. Perhaps it is time for English to become another kind of department with a different role, one that specialises in literature teaching and language theory, offering support teaching to other curricular interests, and responsible for the development of communication skills across the curriculum.

Thinking of communication as a field activity involving, say, cultural knowledge, proxemics, body language generally, as well as spoken, visual and written language, also helps us to see other immediate areas of priority, many of which are unrepresented in the Smokestack Curriculum: the symbolic content of systems such as mathematics and imagery; computer work; local indigenous languages; modern world languages; non-indigenous local languages; watching; drama; music; dance; visual arts; environmental concerns; history; media studies; social and moral education; crafts; sociology; social psychology; philosophy; the cognitive aspects of perception and communication; architecture; business/ enterprise; archaeology and palaeontology.

From even this tentative list, it becomes clear that the Smokestack is not in the business of promoting any cohesion of knowledge. Rather it promotes the maintenance of boundaries with crudely defined, antique, epistemological territories, to be for ever kept distant one from another. Some key disciplines, such as the social sciences, it does not provide for at all at school level.

How might communication be handled by the Information Curriculum? There will, first of all, be a broad framework of progression to include the needs of all learners. This will be established at a national level and be modified by schools to match their specific needs.

Within that framework, each learner will have an individual programme, chosen by the learner in co-operation with a teacher and/or librarian. Different programmes might well have different emphases dependent on interests, abilities and learning rates. The numbers of such programmes a school could provide will necessarily be finite, and be available on computer as summary and as complete course. This finite list should be ever-growing.

We can easily imagine some immediate organising categories: symbolic systems; computing; language; moving and still images; mass media; music, drama and dance; the visual arts; social sciences; world religions; local, national and international history; geography.

All should be signficant permeators and all courses, for every group, will require to have some elements of each, though not, of course, all. These courses will be designed to overlap and will have clear objectives. Thus a course focused on language – local, national, and world – might require elements of symbolic systems, computing, mass media, social sciences, and history. The degree of emphasis will be determined by age, ability, and learning rates, and be related to the direct teaching of thinking and learning skills which will be an ongoing priority for the school experience of every child. There will, naturally, be different emphases for different age groups and abilities. The study of symbolic systems at Primary Year 1 will, for example, necessarily be very different from the more complex approaches adopted by the senior school. One can also imagine a greater degree of inter-relatedness being fostered with increasing age.

The individual programme of each group of learners will be joined to other groups so as to form manageably sized cognate groups. Clearly, each programme might be potentially different from others, but they will share sufficient in common to permit cognate groups to be formed, and to have some degree of collective guidance by the teacher and librarian. Such variations will be seen, not as a disadvantage, but as an opportunity for further learning from other learners, and provide invaluable lessons about the richness of the topic.

Summary Conclusion

Even this crude sketch demonstrates that an Information Curriculum will not be arrived at tomorrow. But some of its proposals can be put into effect now. The

Scottish dimension, for example, could be developed and implemented almost immediately, since a range of documentation and practice already exists to support it. Others, such as thinking and reasoning, and symbolic systems, will require longer to develop and implement. Overall, a time scale of about 25 years should be envisaged, given the massive needs for training and development involved.

An Information Curriculum will require each child from Primary Year 1 onwards to be given a laptop computer with access to the Net and networked to all other computers in the school. Each classroom should also have a computer suite and a range of AV aids. These costs should be set against the current costs of course books and other teaching materials, which will be replaced by teacher-modifiable ranges of texts available on the Net. Similarly, every school will have the complex timetables envisaged here managed by means of computer, with records of some sophistication maintained for the use of teachers and librarians.

Schools in Scotland will be linked nationally and to others across the world. Teachers and librarians will have classes of hundreds, as they teach to more than one location. Pupils will interact across national frontiers. Lessons will be stored on the Net and be accessible to meet the curricular demands of many schools. The essential lesson must be to encourage a sense of sharing, of common quest, and the satisfaction of individual needs. At its simplest level, this must be what an Information Curriculum should be about and which, of course, the Smokestack Curriculum persistently denies.

It is time to start waving goodbye to this retrograde curriculum, and to devise a system more appropriate to our pressing needs. I have suggested one variety here; there are certainly many others.

Notes

[1] Review of Scottish Culture Group, 'Scottish Culture and the Curriculum', a report submitted to the Scottish Consultative Council on the Curriculum, 1998.

Chapter Ten

A' Yon Skweelin: Readings in North-East Education

David Northcroft

'An old gentleman describing his parish school master, said "aa he taught me was
the weight o the tawse."'

John R. Allan, 'The Lad o Pairts', *The North-East Lowlands of Scotland*,
pp. 228–46.*

Despite the evident satisfaction with which John R. Allan inserted this blunt
witness into his account of the educational traditions of his native region,
scepticism and refutation were far from being his own last words on the matter.

The illegitimate offspring of a fifteen year old farm servant girl who then ran
off to America, abandoning his care to the grandparents, John R. Allan had the
kind of background which qualified him for membership of that celebrated species
which furnished the title of his study. He was certainly an individual who 'got on'.
Born in 1906 at Udny, by the 1930s he had become one of Scotland's most noted
young writers; after the war, he returned to his own Buchan to give himself to that
area's other great enterprise, that of farming. But he continued to write: by then, the
exploration of his own Aberdeenshire heritage, in words as well as personal action,
had become a life-long beguilement.

In 1935, he brought out *Farmer's Boy*, not a straight autobiography, he warns
the reader, but 'an imaginative reconstruction of the past'. It is, quite explicitly, an
attempt to memorialize a whole way of life, whereby his neighbours, within the
agrarian community of his North-East boyhood, strove, celebrated and came to their
final rest as one. The chapter 'Unwillingly to School ' is part of that larger intention.
If its title, and the vivid opposition it sets up between the stultifying constraints
of the austere parochial school room and the abundant vitality of the fields and
the woods through which the children daily trudge to get there, speaks of a more
ambivalent response, the ingredients of myth are still present. There is its densely
cultivated syllabus of repetitive skills and rote steered facts, which, by the time he

---

* This chapter should be read with reference to the Select Bibliogrphy, see pp. 162–76

was ten, had granted this farmtoun loon the listed knowledge of all the rivers of the Russias and an apprehension of the storms that swept across the Straits of Magellan. And, in the stark contrast between gentle Miss Thom of the Infant Room and the ferocity of Miss Grey in the Senior, he encountered the boldness of character which finds fertile root in the Aberdeenshire clay. They, like the national system they represent, are blended into the grand human comedy which, on the open ground of this North-East, is, it would appear, freed to take on its own pungent definitions.

How justly to evaluate the quality of a local education, which was so heavily invested with the riches of the national faith in its supremacy, was a matter which Allan never quite managed to settle. In his *Summer in Scotland*, each of the chapters is given over to a geographical theme, all except number eleven. This is 'The Lad o Pairts or, what is Scottish Education?' The native pride, the success in convincing the English 'that Scottish education is the best in the world', the Ladder of Opportunity erected by John Knox and the Presbyterian reformers of 400 years previously, are each moved into position – but so, too, is the personal recollection of a schooling which at times appears to take on the grinding force of a machine: like some potato grader, it shakes out the dirt, the dross, the small and the misshapen, in its driven attempt to wrest scholarship from the hard Buchan soil. A few pages on, comes the complicating ambiguity as he breaks off to tell us, 'I was a lad o' pairts myself, and I offer my own private experience as a tribute to the system'.

Thirty-six years later, in the updated version of his *North-East Lowlands of Scotland*, he is still devoting chapters to 'The Lad o Pairts', still deploring him as a force fed, 'unnatural' species – but also telling us about 'an old man' of his own parish who, quite heroically, spent years saving up pennies from his £4 a year as a hind to learn sufficient Latin to win a bursary and so go to university at the age of twenty-five. 'The old Scots way was hard for those who were short of money. But it had some advantages – few got much of the academic sort unless they really wished it; the desire and the interest had to be there first'. The fact that there were so many who did win through shows that in his North-East, education had become part of the region's ecology: 'the village and the farm people with their little schooling made some effort to overtake knowledge and made some part of it theirs and handed it on as a general heritage a country child breathes in with the air…'

In between times, in 1955, Allan was entrusted with the 'Education' section of the Aberdeenshire volume of the *Third Statistical Account of Scotland*. Dutifully, he covers the statistical ground, with data relating to attendance, school centralization, the incidence of bursary awards and so on. But he also interjects with jokes about teachers who should be certified, not certificated, makes comparisons between Aberdeenshire stock-breeding and Aberdeenshire pupil-rearing and worries about why it is that in this county of democratic academic opportunity so many putative lads o' pairts leave school early and settle for careers in an office or at a trade.

If the full history of North-East education has yet to be compiled, the writings of John R. Allan provide a vivid overview of the topics, the settings and the attitudes which should inform such a study. The variety of forms, the interplay which he achieves between personal experience, general data and the surrounding framework of myth and tradition, along with the ambiguities, subtleties and the oversimplifications which such a mixing generates, also remind us of the critical hazards, and the interest, which such an enterprise offers.

To read into a topic, which has clearly stood for so much in the lives and the memories of those who have experienced its formative powers, and which has bred its own mixed strain of circumstance and of mythology, is to engage in a search for meaning. The Select Bibliography can only give an indication of where that may be located, or rather, how it may be pieced together. But, given the richness of its history and the strength of its characters, any investigation into North-East education is as much an invitation as it is a challenge.

Basic Documentation

The remarkable *Statistical Account of Scotland*, which was overseen by Sir John Sinclair during the 1790s, gives a parish by parish account, arranged under a number of categorical headings, of which 'Education' is one. The specifics are drawn up by the respective parish ministers and are, accordingly, patchy and occasionally idiosyncratic, but, overall, the relevant county volumes give a mass of indispensable detail and incidental insight into the prevailing attitudes of a hierarchical society, where schooling was administered through a union of kirk, master and lairdocracy (the 'heritors'). Note, too, the great array of private 'venture' establishments, as well as an irregularity of attendance that was heavily influenced by seasonal factors and child farm employment. The *'Statistical'* exercise was repeated in both the 1840s and the 1950s, once more using the parish ministers as contributors, but now with the addition of a number of thematic overviews.

The nineteenth century also witnessed a sequence of public inquiries, as the State edged ever closer towards a universal, compulsory system under the dual management of centralized Government department and local Boards. The 1834-37 *Education Enquiry* furnishes full parish by parish returns of attendance, provision and comment; the *Argyll Commission* of the 1860s not only contains full data but offers reports of sample field visits, some written in vividly descriptive prose.

The sequence of reports made by Allan Menzies and Simon S. Laurie under the terms of the *Dick Bequest* from the 1830s onwards likewise contain much interesting evaluative comment. Until they dwindled into the slim policy booklets of the post war era, the 'Blue Book' yearly reports of the Scottish Education Department (SED) ran a substantial 'Northern districts' section.

The Elphinstone Institute, University of Aberdeen, launched its Elphinstone Kist in 2002, a web-based educational resource in North-East Scots edited by Les Wheeler and Sheena Blackhall. Its collection includes a specific 'Education ' section, where will be found some newly commissioned and gathered material, in addition to several of the items listed below. It is a fully searchable and downloadable resource.

General Educational Histories

As to be expected for a region which has been perceived to play such a prominent and representative role in the nation's educational development, the North-East figures extensively in the general histories and surveys of the topic. Two are particularly worthwhile: Scotland (1969) – the author was Principal of Aberdeen College of Education between 1961 and 1983 – is now over thirty years old and, in its lack of critical bite and sociological awareness, has become somewhat dated. But for lucid narration it still has its place.

Anderson's 1995 study is not only much more recent; as a cogent, critically alert treatment it is unrivalled. The basic ground is thoroughly covered, the major themes are identified, and the analytical comment demonstrates a keen awareness of the importance of myth and construct, as well as the socio-economic context.

Anderson has also been responsible for two stimulating articles which carry seminal weight in their respective areas: 'Education and Society' (1985) examines the impact of economic and political forces upon the traditional parochial provision, as Scottish society moved from a primarily agrarian to a more industrialised, urban community; 'In search of the Lad of Parts' (1985) offers lively illustration of the function of the inherited democratic myth, as both a necessary encapsulation of ideals and a form of social justification which distracted attention away from the inequalities that lay behind the lad o' pairts folklore.

The author has recently produced an 'experiential' history of Scottish education under the title of *Scots at School*. Drawing upon the first-hand accounts to be mined in various biographies, local histories and contemporary media accounts, this work is presented as an anthology of extracts, accompanied by a detailed commentary which tracks the development of the nation's schooling from 1750 to the present day. Some 120 pieces are included, of which the North-East contributes approximately one third.

Periodical and Pamphlet Literature

The upsurge in prosperity and reading leisure (see *Northern Iris*, 1826), evident in the 1820s and 1830s, encouraged the launch of a series of short-lived Aberdeen-based journals. In their brief careers, they were responsible for a number of weighty surveys of the national system which, if self congratulatory, are, for that very reason, revealing of what contemporaries valued in the Scottish system and the degree to which the local parochial provision was projected as the outstanding example. A somewhat more subversive version of the impact of a rural education upon a true child of North-East nature such as *Rory McFigh* (1831) also features in some of the serial fiction which enlivens their pages. For these items, see *Aberdeen Magazine* (1831, 1831/32) and *Aberdeen Censor* (1825).

Later, both the *Aberdeen University Review* and the literary pieces contributed to the student-orientated *Alma Mater* contain a number of relevant items, some of them lovingly expressive of the myth-making, memorialising character of North-East self-description that was, perhaps, at its height in the half century leading up to the First World War. The obituary articles on the local dominie hero Billy Dey (1916) are a choice example.

Nationally, the journal of the Education Institute of Scotland, *The Educational News* (after 1918, *The Scottish Educational Journal*) contains much of interest, especially in the more newsy early years. *The News* is particularly strong on North-East affairs during the decades leading up to the First World War, when the region was seen as the stronghold of the traditional parish virtues for the profession's resistance to the centralising, modernising tendencies of the SED.

During the Victorian and Edwardian eras, the locally printed and sold pamphlet provided a ready means of opinion and debate. The Department of Manuscripts and Archives of the University of Aberdeen Library contains thousands of such publications; they include not only discussion of immediate matters like the proposals for a 'National system', or the role of the 'Industrial School' in controlling child crime, but access to a range of related social issues, such as the living standards and cultural expectations of the farm labourer, and the function of the local Presbytery in alleviating poverty.

Since the seminal work of William Donaldson began to appear (1986, 1989), it has become impossible to ignore the vast amount of polemical comment and serial literature that was appearing weekly or so in the numerous local newspapers and magazines that flourished from the middle of the 19th century onwards. Much of this fugitive material was written in an informal, demotic style, which was enhanced by the use of Doric and other non-standard forms. Donaldson makes great claims for the range and penetrating vitality of his recovered material, and, in his commentaries on it, demonstrates the extent to which the columns of, for instance, *The Peterhead Sentinel* and *The Aberdeen Weekly Press* acted as a source of representatively sceptical and irreverent observation on such pillars of Victorian Scottish life as burgh council officials, the Kirk and the education system. He shows how popular columnists like William Latto and 'Jeems Kaye' were anxious to puncture the pretensions of the much vaunted 'democratic' schooling of the time.

School and Teacher Histories

The indispensable Barclay (1925) has already been considered elsewhere in this volume (see Northcroft). Ian Simpson's *Education in Aberdeenshire before 1872* (1947) is obviously required reading. Thorough, if pedestrian, it supplies necessary detail as to curriculum and logistics. Its conclusion is that, after a slow start, in the middle of the century, a number of socio-economic and specific factors (Dick and Milne Bequests) combined to establish the best provision in Scotland – but that achievement was always patchy and dependant on local circumstance and energies.

As many of our rural schools were established or rebuilt during the later years of the nineteenth century, there has recently been a rush of 'Centenary' histories. Not many of them, however, have reached out, either in scope or depth, beyond an immediate local audience. The usual format has been a few oral-bite memories, some bare factual background and extracts from the school's logbook over the years

– and these, in their turn, have tended to confine themselves to the highlights of pupil absences, diphtheria, blocked roads, blocked lavatories and Royal occasion holidays – interesting the first time round but in need of contextual analysis to achieve a wider enlightenment. Here, it should be noted that, while the maintenance of school logbooks has been mandatory since 1872, and that they therefore offer a ready source of evidence, in them headteachers were required to confine themselves to impersonal, procedural entries.

Because of this restriction, the article by Sydney Wood (1991) is particularly welcome. Here he uses the formal records of one nineteenth century upland Aberdeenshire school, Ythan Wells, as a case study example of the physical and cultural difficulties, which confronted the lone teacher in his attempts to fulfil Scottish Education Department requirements among the snow and the sheep. The two 'Education' chapters in the successive *Books of Bennachie* (Young, 1976; Simpson, 1983) also provide some useful comment to accompany their extensive reliance upon the log-books of schools of that district.

Of the school history booklets, *Dunnottar* (Nicol, 1989) (Stonehaven) and *Esslemont* (O'Dochartaigh, 1981) (Ellon area) Primary Schools are among the best. The histories of *Fordyce* (MacLean, 1936), *Kemnay* (Downie, 1995) and *Elgin* (Bennet, 2001) Academies are, however, more substantial and contain portraits of notable teachers as well as eye-witness accounts. The former, in particular, is interesting as an example of the kind of repute which a small Banffshire school could achieve through the magnetism of its academic teaching: in its history, the picturesque and the larger-than-life characterisation is freely intermingled with the documentary. With regard to Kemnay, the 1841 article which appeared in *Chambers's Journal* provides a striking example of the kind of national pride that was ready to be invested in any remote rural school which appeared to be bringing academic enlightenment to the peasantry. For the next century, the sharp pre-war school memories of Hunter Diack (see Biography), a native of Kemnay, neatly cross-refer with the ready praise handed out by the Academy's chroniclers.

An Aberdeenshire Village Propaganda (Smith, 1889) is significant in its ability to give insights into the alternative self-help tradition in education which continued its way throughout the nineteenth century, despite the claimed democratic comprehensiveness of the parochial system. Its communitarian values of mutual assistance, of self-run evening classes and subscription libraries, also stand as a contrast to the more competitive individualistic outlook encouraged by the academicism of the village school. Smith's story is of the celebrated 'Aberdeen and Banffshire Mutual Instruction Union', which rapidly spread from its Rhynie origins in the 1840s and 1850s. His account also includes detail of the formidable autodictat William McCombie, the self taught farmer who built up the largest private library in Scotland and went on to play prominent roles in Aberdeen press and political affairs. Robertson Nicoll's (1900) biography of the Rhynie exile and metropolitan journalist James MacDonnell also gives further details, as well as furnishing a striking example of the hagiographic conventions which governed much Victorian biography, and which thus further assisted in the perpetuation of North-East mythologies.

The same could be said of the sentimental Kailyardism of *Robert Lindsay* (MacGillivray, 1905), the fond remembrance of the simple teacher who gently cared for the bairns of an idyllic upland Kincardine community in the 1830s.

For reasons which are, perhaps, depressingly obvious, biographies of real teachers are a rarity. Flora Youngson's (1995) *Dominie's Daughter*, however, offers gritty insights into the status and living standards of a village teacher of the 1920s (in the Fraserburgh area). The record of her own teaching career is similarly full of telling period detail, as she moves through the social deprivation of the 1930s and 1940s (poor housing and lice) to the expansiveness of the affluent 1960s – her 'Golden Age' – before the cutbacks of a later and less optimistic era. Cormack (1964) is another worthwhile study. Its subject, William Cramond – a noted local historian and distinguished scholar who, nevertheless, had to endure forty years of servitude in a small and largely unappreciative fishing port school during the last decades of the nineteenth century – reveals something of the frustrations and mutual antipathies which often lurked beneath the dominie myth. This Life shows how the use of eye-witness accounts in conjunction with the logbook records can bring the latter to life. Charles Thomson (1936) also delivers more than its subject would appear to suggest: beneath its ominous title of *Scottish School Humour*, is recounted the story of a lengthy career which, while it had its early stages in the Glasgow region, was concluded by twenty-one years as Rector of Buckie Academy – and mixed in with the tiresome reiteration of pupil howlers and parental malapropisms is some interesting material regarding such issues as discipline, employment conditions, inspection and medical welfare. In contrast, Peter Nicol's *Ramblins o' a Dominie* (1995) offers some diverting detail of school life at Peterhead in the 1920s but lives up to the first part of its title rather too enthusiastically to achieve real insight.

The 1999 biography by Peter Murphy of R. F. MacKenzie is an important recent addition. Although his subject achieved his greatest notoriety in the 1970s as the idealistic, child-centred Rousseauesque, and therefore doomed, Headteacher of the Aberdeen housing scheme Summerhill Academy, his own upbringing had been in the heart of Buchan. His educational enthusiasms were largely driven by a desire to live by what he felt to be all that was most humanly vital in that environment. His own writing (e.g. *A Search for Scotland*, 1989) covers a wide spread of interest in North-East and Scottish culture and makes indispensable reading for anyone who wishes to engage with an alternative view of what a North-East education ought to be.

Local journals, *Heirskip, Leopard* and *Education in the North,* have included the occasional piece. One or two of their more useful examples are referenced.

Local History
Although the nineteenth century parish school was intent upon bringing a standardised form of academic curriculum and social control to all Scottish

regions, the character of North-East education was dependent on how that national intention interacted with local community life. Two historians, Cameron and Carter, have constructed rich and striking portrayals of the agrarian society which predominated before the First World War. Cameron attempts to do this as an act of imaginative recreation; Carter brings a generous sensibility to the task which, combined with a well organised sociological method, achieves a penetrating and wide ranging exploration of farmtoun life and culture. Unfortunately, their treatment of the parish school is comparatively slight and over-reliant upon one or two insufficiently examined examples. Carter is especially dependent upon his hero William Alexander (see Fiction), though, in general, his is a most impressive piece of work.

The more specific local histories, which stretch along the shelves of the Aberdeen City Libraries collection at Rosemount Viaduct, are very uneven, both in the quality and in the extent of their education coverage, though almost all of them recognize the central position of the parish school in the development of their communities and give the topic its own section or even full length chapter. In addition, many also include details of the wide variety of venture establishments which, despite the reputation of the parochial system, multiplied their way across the land in pre-1872 Act days. Smith (1875) is a useful compendium of parish-by-parish data, which shows the state of public provision and social development at the time of the Act.

Treatments can range from a fairly cursory list of dates and incumbencies to a devoted gathering together of anecdotes and lore in proud celebration of their own place's ability to represent the traditional virtues of the Scottish way. *Aberlour* (Thomson), *Banff* (Imlach), *Cairnie* (Pirie), *Glass* (Godsman), *Glenbervie* (Kinnear), *Laurencekirk* (Fraser), and *Tarves* (Porter), are particularly choice examples of this tendency. More factually plain, but usefully full, records are supplied by *Birse* (Callander), *Peterculter* (Buchan), *Daviot* (Sinclair), and *Monquhitter* (Duffus). The following combine steadiness of perspective with the warmth of individual memories: *Buckie* (W. Smith), *Fraserburgh* (Jamieson), and *Rosehearty* (McLeman). Much more recently two volumes have appeared – *Stuartfield* (Penny) and *Newmachar* (Bridges) – which in their different ways have acted as models for how a contemporary local history may be put together using the best of modern audio technology and sound documentary scholarship. In each of them, the village school is dealt with in the context of both personal recollection and socio-economic development.

Reminiscence and Comment

John R. Allan's *Summer in Scotland* (1938) is one of a sequence of collections of personalised essays in which an author uses a mix of travelogue, historical data, reminiscence and social comment in an attempt to build up a portrait of North-East life, usually in the context of the essential Scottish values. Reference is made to Rae (1930) and Bruce (1929) elsewhere in this volume (see Northcroft). One of the strongest examples is provided by Brown (1952) who, under the same title as Allan, brings a sympathetically sensitive intelligence to his own exploration of 'Granite and Getting On'.

Of the rest, Beaton (1923) offers a vivid but nicely constrained treatment of mid-nineteenth-century village life in the shadow of the topographical feature which is often made to bulk large as the very epicentre of North-East heritage, Bennachie. The pieces by Allardyce (1913) and Paul (1881), though generally celebratory in spirit, attempt some measure of evaluative comment: Paul is scathing in his appraisal of the region's education in the pre-Dick Bequest days of the early nineteenth century. Gregor (1874) strives for a grand manner evocation of the model lad o' pairts career and succeeds in giving the local myth an extra burnish.

Watson (1905) also shows how personal recollection can work for literary status through a series of carefully crafted portraits, which include the local 'Skweel'. The fine restraint of his writing makes his a not unworthy attempt. Low (1904) tries to do the same in the studied nostalgia of his Bennachie 'Vignettes', which includes the set piece 'The Misses School ', but more easily slips down into that mixture of pietism and pastoral conceit associated with the Kailyard school. More recently, a number of others, such as Buchan (1993) and Ogston (1986), have combined nostalgia with solid incident in ways that recall the memorable role played by the local school in their childhood initiation into the adult world. Carnegie (1980) offers a more florid version: her work is a vivid example of what is a common theme – the contrast between the highly coloured natural world of the fields and the ways outside the school, to the austere regimentation that lies within.

The genre continues to flourish. Within the last few years two publications have used the local school as central to their fond recreation of former days. Stewart (1998) employs her incomer's experiences in the Strathdon area to generate an admiring response to the traditional Scottish strengths, which she discovers to be still there in the 1960s. Gibson (1997) offers a more straightforward recollection of the incidents, the teachers, and the daily treks to school which give her strong memories of Finzean in the 1920s.

The 1996 collection of eight North-East childhoods edited by Lawrence contains some striking material of (mostly) interwar experiences in a range of settings. Schooldays are woven into the general patterns: from the perspective of the 1990s they appear to be part of a stable, ordered world that has now slipped away.

Biography
These are the most prolific and hazardous group of texts. The impulse to give significance to the individual life can lead the author into areas, where the individual experience during the early formative years, is made to take on a particular drama, the iconic properties of which are safeguarded by the distancing of time, locality, and the awareness of later adult success. And in this drive to construct the personal myth, the individual life is often made to achieve identification of self with the greater context of region and, even, of nation. Within this general tendency, a

range of patterns may be observed: those who wish to pass over their schooling as unexceptional, or even to reject its pretensions to offer all its subjects a valued start in life, and those whose claim to have achieved a representatively ethnic success, which leads them to identify closely with this celebrated aspect of North-East life.

In between these extremes, there are a number of examples where incident and response are blended together in a more balanced way so as to offer nothing more or less than a picture of the 'typical' mixed-experience upbringing. But, generally, it is important to ask questions about perspectives and motives, especially those of time and timing. The nineteenth century biography, for example, is ruled by a set of formalised conventions which lead to patterning the life into an exemplary shape; more recently, the author can be inclined to work in those pieces of criticism which create what has become, in many cases, an equally predictable sense of realistic re-appraisal. Yet the last decades have also seen a number of examples which have wished to measure the successes of the past – discipline, work ethic, respect – against a perception of modern day degeneracy and break up.

Within the biographies of those whose schooling was in the nineteenth century, a division may be made between the stories so patterned as to exemplify the traditional democratic virtues, and thus conform to the lad o' pairts pattern, and those whose later success is seen as largely due to their own unaided efforts (though still, thereby, demonstrating the underlying North-East values of piety, work and integrity). The lives of a pair of clerics, Robertson (Black, 1912) and Davidson (Strahan, 1917), are ripe examples of the former, as is Craib (Grant, 1905) at Mortlach in the 1860s and Ramsay MacDonald's (1919) own lustrous account of his Lossiemouth schooldays. The late nineteenth century Schools Inspector, John Kerr, uses his *Memories Grave and Gay* to roam freely over the settings of a long career; the North-East is highlighted as the stronghold of the national traditions – several pages are devoted to Udny as the prime exemplar in his chapter 'Old Parish Schools'.

The first hand recollections of two octogenarian authors apparently blessed with total recall, Murison (1935) and Fraser (1973), give us a less trammelled perspective: the latter is valuable for the precise detail of curriculum and environment experienced in a remote upper Deeside setting of the 1890s, while the former, having attended three different institutions in the Strichen/Old Deer area, before a completion year at Aberdeen Grammar school and then a career as an outstanding linguist, is unrivalled for scope and comparative evaluation. Wilson (1902) is also useful as a balanced, clear-eyed account of Forglen days of the early century. Mention has already been made of the hagiographic treatment of James Macdonnell by Nicoll (1900).

Of the self-made men, the two John Duncans – the minister from Turriff (Allan, 1909) and the Drumlithie weaver and botanist (Jolly, 1883) – give revealing details of the restrictions that could be placed on academic advancement within the vaunted system. The Newburgh experiences of James McBey (1977), whose rise to become a leading artist owed more to articles in the *Boys Own Paper* than to anything he got at the parish school, demonstrate the repressive nature of much Board education, even at the end of the century. A pair of local lads who got on sufficiently to achieve ennoblement – Sir Hugh Gilzean-Reid (Mackay, 1922) and Lord Mount Stephen (Gilbert, 1965) – offer further evidence of early privation and enforced premature school-leaving. The reminiscences of Barclay (1925) have been salvaged to give us a glimpse of the vagaries and vicissitudes which confronted an evidently intelligent and thoughtful 'Unlettered Man' in mid century Buchan. In the twentieth century, *Kincardineshire* (Smith, 1990) has given a sharp account of the way in which social divisions still practised by school staff could impede the progress of a bright lad from the cottar classes. Elsewhere in this volume, Gordon Booth has described the alternative tradition of home education and its remarkable product Robertson Smith: see Black and Chrystal (1912).

The assumptions invested in the lad o' pairts tradition reflected the broader social subjugation of women. Yet Christian Watt (Fraser, 1988) has left us what is probably the outstanding North-East biography. Only two years at school, this was the Broadsea fisherwife of fierce intelligence and belligerent independence who turned down Lord Saltoun's nephew in marriage, fought to educate herself, was argumentative in theology and gifted in phraseology. Her reminiscences, composed during her long later years as an inmate of an Aberdeen mental hospital, are an invaluable social document, which help us to locate the position of education, in both its institutional and its broader sense, in the sociology of mid-century North-East life.

The pattern is repeated into the twentieth century, though with less ritualistic heightening. Bruce (1922) at Elgin around the First World War continues the self-congratulatory lad o' pairts format, while Webster (1981) at Maud, Fraser (1973) in the Garioch, Mackie (1992) at Methlick, Peter (1994) at Salthousehead and Fordyce (1981) at 'Foggieloan' (Aberchirder), provide a wider spread of perspectives, which combine warm appreciation with some solid curricular and social detail. Glennie (1990), with her intimate recollections of Cairnorrie Primary School in the 1970s, extends this tradition into the more recent period. Diack (1962) is notable for the incisiveness of his comments on the continuation of lairdocratic attitudes, at Kemnay, into the twentieth century.

It appears to be too soon for written biographical accounts which would take us into the centralised comprehensive, mass higher education of today. The need to build up an archive of oral evidence is very clear.

Fiction

The earlier articles by Ian Campbell and Douglas Young cover most of the ground (Alexander, Gibbon, Kesson, Macpherson, MacDonald). It is, however, worth pointing to a pair of Lewis Grassic Gibbon works, in addition to the *Scots Quair* trilogy, which recreate lively versions of Mearns schooling, as informed by the author's ability for sharp irony and critical dramatisation: *The Thirteenth Disciple* (1931) and the unfinished *The Speak of the Mearns* (1931). A pair of important women deserve further comment. Nan Shepherd, as a farm daughter whose academic brilliance enabled her to become a lecturer at Aberdeen College of Education, was well placed to explore the relevant issues and, although her fiction contains little direct treatment of schooling, novels like *The Quarry Wood* and *A Pass in the Grampians* offer sensitive treatments of the social and cultural background. Jessie Kesson dedicated *The White Bird Passes* (1958) 'to My Dominie'; the book provides a compelling depiction of a fierce determination to become a writer, despite consignment to an orphanage, and draws upon the difficult personal background which has recently been investigated by Isobel Murray's biography (Edinburgh, 2000), *Writing her Life*. *Glitter of Mica* (1963) catches the social divisions present in a twentieth century rural community, where pupils have been divided into 'senior' and 'junior' levels. It also deals with the tensions between Standard English and regional speech usage – a central topic which has been relatively neglected in the works of this bibliography.

Cameron's *A Kist of Sorrows* is a fictional counterpart to his documentary exploration of traditional rural society. The parish school is seen as the centre of village culture, one which shares in the destruction wrought on it by the invasion of capitalist farming in the late nineteenth century. Neil Maclean (1874) draws on his own Peterhead experiences to offer a more contemporary, but equally romantic, version: his mythopoeic saga *Life at a Northern University* is prefaced by a suitably coloured account of local rugged dominie heroism.

Poetry

The local collections are packed with slim anthologies of work through which the amateur observer has wished to express a personal appreciation, whether in homely Doric or exalted English, of a local life properly led amidst familiar scenes. Many of them include at least one or two efforts at schooldays evocation, usually in conventionally appreciative terms – devoted dominie, homely surroundings, a good grounding in a spirit of secure domesticity, the tawse notwithstanding. This strain reaches far back into the nineteenth century – Ritchie (1881) and MacKenzie (1894). Among the more distinguished examples are Caie (1939), Gibson (1916), Garry (1947) and Abel (1916). Symon (1916) creates a poignant twist to the usual prize-list roll of honour by reviewing the muster of the war dead from one small glen school.

The exploitation of schooldays, as a way of sharpening the focus on what has been lost to communal life in modern times, has continued to the present day. The mood can range from simplistic lament – Rich (1989), Milne (1984), MacDonald (1995) – to a more complex sense of tensions by which the child's need to grow into an enjoyment of his or her own ethnic culture is ranged against the disciplined academicism of the school system. Blackhall, Morrice and Mackie have each written strongly in this vein.

Of the region's other notable poets, Charles Murray (1979) has been discussed by Douglas Young – his *It Wasna his Wyte* (1929) remains the finest evocation of the way in which a North-East education can confront the country child's own 'natural' environment with a mystifying routine of adult externalities, and yet become so familiar a part of the surroundings as to merge, accepted, into it. Although William Thom (1844), the nineteenth century 'weaver poet' from Inverurie, who was (briefly) feted nationally as a second Burns, largely wrote from inside the industrialised urban environment of the Aberdeen textile works, some of his work has the penetration of a universal poet. His reminiscences provide a similarly incisive revelation of the educational realities that awaited most members of the labouring classes of the day, 'even' in the North-East.

The most sustained and informed treatment, in both a poetic and a thematic sense, is provided by *The Collected Poems* of John C. Milne (1963). Milne was himself a brilliant lad o' pairts before the war and, after it, served for many years as Master of Method at Aberdeen College of Education. In poem after poem, he builds up a series of sardonically knowing observations of the North-East scene and of the formative role entrusted to its parish schools. His work is both about Buchan realities and pretensions, and the teacher's immemorial lot.

A phrase from John C. Milne's *Skweelin* has been incorporated into the title of this paper – but the full line from which it comes should also be noted: 'Fut's a' yon skweelin for?'

Appendix One

Five Schoolings: North-East Folk Talk about their School Days

Violet Cassie born 1920: Fraserburgh area, mostly Strichen

James Michie born 1926: Auchenblae and Mackie Academy, Stonehaven

Alan Morrison born 1930: Daviot

David Eric Brown born 1935: Muchalls and Mackie Academy, Stonehaven

Norman Harper born 1957: Alford and Inverurie Academy

Explanatory Notes

The transcripts which now appear represent an early sample, taken from a series of interviews which are currently being gathered together into what is intended to be an archive of first-hand testimonies on the school experiences of a range of North-East people. At the time of writing thirty sessions had been completed: the interviewees are people whose memories stretch back sufficiently far to record a significant sweep of change and continuity. The oldest, to date, is a 100 year old ex-teacher, the youngest a well known North-East journalist (Norman Harper, above). Their adult occupations have included the position of Director of Education, farmer, car salesman, librarian, fisherman, policeman and housewife. If only five of them can be accommodated in this present work, all of them have had lengthy and absorbing individual stories to share; each one of them is worth the listening for anyone who wants to understand more of what, in straightforward human terms, the experience of going to school and growing up has meant to some, at least, of the people of the North-East of Scotland.

The initial witnesses were approached because they were known to the interviewer (David Northcroft), as having been schooled in the region and, subsequently, as having made their careers and led their lives there. The first step, after agreement in principle was gained, was to send them a simple pro-forma of points to be considered, such as 'first day', 'discipline', 'teaching styles', 'syllabus', 'home language/school language'. This documentation did not play a prominent role in the actual interview: in the event, people slipped comfortably into a narrative retelling, prompted from time to time by a question from the interviewer and the occasional invitation to draw things together into an evaluation. The tone of the interviews was informal; they took place within relaxed, domestic circumstances – most usually the interviewee's own home.

No attempt, at this stage, has been made to track the individual or ethnic character of speech. All discourse has been rendered in the conventional 'standard' form, with regard to sound patterns, excepting where the speaker was clearly employing a regional variation for purposes of emphasis. The vocabulary and grammatical construction are, however, as uttered. In the event, a wide range of speech forms was used; while almost all subjects wanted to say something about the Doric, and they were encouraged to speak as 'naturally' as possible, fewer than ten of the thirty interviewed thus far could be said to have been employing even a modified version of it. Of the scripts included here, David Brown and, to a more marked degree, Violet Cassie are among that number.

Recordings were made by an unobtrusive audio machine. Verbatim transcripts were then drawn up, sent to the interviewer with an invitation to make amendments of fact or mishearing and to offer any comment or gloss that was felt to be needed. What may now be read is the outcome of this process, although in a necessarily abridged version. This has been for reasons of space – the shortest interview has been 75 minutes, the longest 120.

The intention now is to adopt a gradually more structured method to the collecting of material. Following this initial scatter-gun approach, the attempt will be made to follow up the themes, which the first sample has indicated, by setting them against a wider and more complete range of individual experience. Areas such as the fishing communities, the suburbs, the council estates, travelling folk, adult returners to education, immigrants, for example, should be added to the farming and the professional education circles which have so far been in focus. It will also be necessary to move more widely across the generations – to set the experiences of parent against offspring, the latter age group against their elders.

This is work for the future. In the meantime, the following early sample is offered in order to provide a personal complement to the more formal and academic pieces which make up the first ten chapters of *North-East Identities and Scottish Schooling*.

Violet Cassie: Interviewed October 2001

I was born at Crimond in 1920. See, I'm at the age when I can now speak about it. It's when they're 30 or so that you can't ask a woman about her age! A working class family; my father was practically a jack-of-all-trades. He was very good with his hands. He was an engineer, a ship's engineer. In the First World War he was in whatever you call them that drive the boat – he was there all through the war, in the minesweepers. Then after the war, like, his main job was in the quarries, them country quarries where they're making the granite stones and that for the roads; he was the one in charge of the explosives.

In between times, when the jobs were scarce, he went on the fishing boats, to Lowestoft and Yarmouth – all down the East Coast. He took whatever jobs were going. My grandfather had a farm and he worked on that for a while and when the time came that there were too many of them at home, and the farm work was scarce – this was during the 1920s – he had a lot of brothers, see, a big family, eleven of them – and then he would go from farm to farm and ask, 'Do you want draining done in the fields?' So, whatever jobs were going, he did. He went and asked for it! He was never on the dole or anything like that. And then at night – if we was needing my shoes repaired – he would mend them, right up to the time when I was working. Whenever we went back to school, we always had new boots, but a new blazer might be more difficult – unless the rabbits were plentiful! There were always rabbits to be found about the Mormond Hill and so they poached. Self-help – what you call foraging!

We moved quite a lot. My grandfather's house was just an ordinary farmhouse, ken: upstairs, downstairs, three bedrooms, maid's room. The house in which I was born had just the three rooms, just an old fashioned kind of cottage. It was named the 'Brick House'. It was all brick – but that's down a long time ago.

But the longest time we stayed in a house, a fair-sized house, was at the bottom of the Mormond Hill – ken where that is? Just below the White Horse, where we spent all our summer days. That was a farmhouse rebuilt for us. But there was no bathroom or anything. But it was a big house; four rooms there was. I had three brothers, one sister. I'm in the middle: Joe, Jean, Douglas, then me, and then William. Douglas died out in Canada, three years ago. Joe, the oldest brother, he stays at Inchmarlo, by Banchory. He's retired, but his son, he's 'Taylors of Banchory' – the shop. My youngest brother's still in Canada and he has a business there, an important kind of business.

I was speaking to my sister last night – I'd forgotten all the schools I was at. It's a whole list! Ken, there's a lot of travelling folk in Buchan – I dinna ken but I might be related to them. We moved wherever the work was, you see. Either that, or the dole, and none of us would have done that! Wherever the job was, there you went! And aye trying to get a better job – that was it.

The first school I was at was Stuartfield. I think I was a year there. I had quite a lot of experiences there. I fell into the dam and lost my new shoes. I didn't get smacked, but, oh, ho! Then I had to wear old ones, with darnings and things. Then I was coming home, up the brae – no cars or anything at that time – but a chap run me over with his push bike and broke my arm. My fault! But Jean was telling me last night, and I'd forgotten, she said, 'See the mark on your arm, that was the chap that ran you over'. I was going to my bed last night – it's still there! Of course, I wasn't very big.

Now, where did I ging frae Stuartfield? Bulwark School! There was only us and another two at that school. Five, that's all. I was there six months – a wee school just beside the road. But they closed it. I went to Maud School. No bikes, no buses – we just walked. About two miles along the road – there were roads. On your boots and walked!

Now, from there… let me think… I went to Blackhills School. That's on the road to Fraserburgh from Peterhead. Of course, half the schools I went to are all closed! Bulwark's closed. In fact, one of my brothers came home from Canada and he was going to video all the places that we'd been – and there's just a tree and a few stones lying. Oh, they'll be very impressed in Canada when they see that!

So I went to Blackhills School. I was there one year. No, I've got it wrong! I went to Strichen before I went to Blackhills. Strichen! I would have been… four schools by then! Oh yes, I'm very well travelled! And we went to this little house; it would have been a farm cottage, a cottar's hoose. But we were nothing to do with the farm, we just rented the house. There was a house getting built for us, rebuilt over on the other side of the Hill. But in the meantime, that house was never very waterproof or anything. So I went to Blackhills till the other house was built.

Now how many's that? Five? I was at Blackhills, it must have been a year – it must have taken that time to build that house. And then we went back to Pluckshill. That was the name of the farm right at the bottom of the Mormond Hill. I went to Strichen School again then. That's where I finished. I was 14 – 1935.

The only thing I remember about Stuartfield School is the singing. The teacher gave me a note home to my mam: 'Would I sing in this concert?' I must have been 5. That's all I can mind about Stuartfield. Whether I'd been scared there or what, I don't know.

Bulwark School I can mind. We were asked to take a peat to the school, to heat the little school. I canna mind if it was every day or not but I can mind on one thing and that's going down the road and taking the peats. And we just stayed at the back of that school. But they closed it.

But a lot of the country schools, the little schools, did that. And you took a can of cocoa and heated it on the fire. That was your lunch. But that all stopped. It wasn't like that at Strichen. At Strichen you got a lunch in wintertime. Soup and bread. The farmers brought loads of tatties and neeps and things and the janitor's wife did a big bowl of soup. That was just in the winter-time. In the summer-time you took your own sandwiches and things.

Because we were almost, but not quite, three miles from the school at Pluckhill… not at the start, but then they started that if you was more than three miles you got a bike from the Education Authorities – as a loan. But if it was under three miles you just walked. Strichen was a secondary school as well. It was a big school. It took them in from Boyndlie, New Leeds, Techmuiry, Memsie, all the little schools from all about. So if it wasn't buses you had to go by bike. You couldn't have walked all that distance.

Strichen was the main school. I was seven or eight when I went back to it. I can mind more about the secondary learning. The day consisted of whatever you went in – quite big classes ye ken, quite big classes – about 30 or so at least to one teacher. The first thing you got was the Bible lesson to start the day, then arithmetic, mental arithmetic – God, I mind that! No, no, without any crowing about it or anything, I was excellent at that. I wasn't scared at all. Not at the spelling either, I could manage that. I was quick on my feet.

I was the one but my brother – because he just couldn't be bothered – his teacher one day, my mum met her in the street – this was my youngest brother, just full of devilment and fun, he was. Miss Grey was the teacher, so my mum went up to her and says, 'How's William getting on?' – just as any mother would do. 'Well,' she said, 'he's not brilliant but he's always so cheerful!' But he would come home and mum would say, 'Well, dear, how did you get on today?', and he would say, 'I got the strap once today, once'. For not doing his home lessons! And he regretted it once he left school and was going into business. But he worked his way up and had a big business in Canada, employing lots of folk and everything. But he regretted not sticking in at the time, did William.

It varied each day. But we had science – I loved science. You were doing all your experiments in a big room, the science room. It was quite well equipped. I can mind getting first prize for doing a description of the vacuum flask; what it was all for and all the different layers. I had to fill my dad's one every morning. We had this awful ill-natured, passionate kind of teacher. We used to get tests and you was just shaking, when he was handing it out and you was just waiting for it. And one of the days, I just hadn't bothered and wondered what he would say. And what did he say? 'You've got splendid brains, girl – when you care to use them!' That was how much praise you ever got. He turned your gas right down.

Oh, he got into fits of temper. He would get you down on the floor and everything. But he was there for all his teaching days. And yet, if you met him out of school: I can mind meeting him once – I was married, with Barbara's dad at the front during the war, walking ben the street in Fraserburgh. And he tapped me on the shoulder and said, 'Hello!' He said, 'Come away!' And we had tea in Lawrence's tea-room and he was just charming!

I was his favourite: he had a favourite boy and a favourite girl. Mind you, it wasn't a good thing, because many the time you'd get tripped up going out the door because you was the teacher's pet. It wasn't a good thing! I got to go to the Post Office to do his post and got a penny when I got back. He stayed at Bricklea; he had a little croft and a housekeeper and a cow. He was just a crofter really, ken. But he was an excellent teacher. But you was scared of him. I wasn't so scared of him but the boys were.

Mind you, it was a good school when I was there, an excellent school. It took you right up to university; it took you up to 18. They came in from New Pitsligo and all around. But this Mr W—, he got his come-uppence once. It was just at the end of term, I can remember this, and I think one of my brothers was in it but it was never proved he was one of them. But two or three of them took him and strapped him to one of the science tables and gave him a good smacking. The boy White from Pistligo, he was expelled but he didn't care, he was leaving anyway.

He really was… he would keep you in at night if it was a bad day and you had a long road home. Douglas, my brother, he's got these blue eyes and didn't really stare but he used to say, 'Stop staring at me, Burnett! Or you'll get the strap!' Douglas wasn't scared at him even when he was in a rage; he wasn't scared at him. Well my father went down – he'd kept Douglas in a few nights and my father had a motor bike and he came home from work. Douglas had this long lonely road – nobody beside us, the roads were bad, it was dark. It happened three or four nights running, so my father came in and asked, 'Is this Douglas being kept in the night again?' First of all, he asked Douglas if he'd been misbehaving to be kept in. But him and another one, it was just something the teacher did. He hadn't done anything wicked or that. There was no vandalism at that time – we was all scared! So, my father went down on his motor bike and spoke to him. I dinna ken all he said to him but he did say he would be down next time it was dark and make *him* do the walk right up to our house. So he apologised.

It was just the science teacher. It was a big school, see. There were teachers for different subjects. Mind you, he was a good teacher as well. You did learn from him. He was good at explaining things. He was just too passionate. He got into such a temper, he would get them on the floor and jump on them! Whatever it was… he was a good teacher. He could bring you through your lessons.

We had English. We would have an essay to write, once a week, probably. We had that many subjects that we had them just once a week practically. Science we had once a week. Arithmetic every day. English would be an essay, maybe next day, poetry or grammar, of course – we had lots of grammar! French we had, and Latin. Now if you didn't take Latin, you would have domestic science – for the girls – and for the boys, woodwork. There was poultry science for the ones who wanted to go into farming. Now what else… sewing! That was your domestic science, and cooking as well. We had a big cookery room. It was well equipped.

Singing and art! For art you did drawing and you would get a country ramble, when he spoke about wild flowers and things… nature study! Geography and history too. I was not awful fond of geography – though I aye passed the tests – but I couldn't say I liked it very much… History I quite liked. It was mostly Scottish history. But I've forgotten an awful lot. What else did we get? Sport, oh aye – in navy knickers and white blouse, oh yes! If it was a fine day, it would be outside in the school playground and you was going at it – we had a proper Drill teacher. If it was bad, it would be inside – we had a gym room. If you forgot to bring the white blouse you were in the bad books. You didn't exactly get the strap but, oh! What a telling off you'd get!

The girls got the strap, as well as the boys. Oh yes, but I can't mind getting the strap much… but, of course, I was exceptional, kind! And I was the favourite of the science teacher – got a penny for going out and posting his letters. I was okay with him. I did it during lessons.

Of course, when I was coming out of the school for playtime some of the boys got on to me, 'Teacher's pet! Teacher's pet!' It wasn't a good thing. I was scared of the teacher and I was scared of my classmates!

But there was only one teacher I was so scared of that I wouldn't put up my hand to answer a question in case I was wrong. It was Miss S—, I still remember her, and it was in primary 5 and I can remember her. I'll tell you why. The time had changed – I can't mind if it was forwards or backwards – a few of us girls – we'd got no watches or anything – and we'd forgotten and there we were out playing. Then all at once, we remembered and we were about four minutes late in coming back into the classroom – and we all got the strap. I mind that yet. It was the indignity of it!

My mum said, 'Do you want me to go down?', and I said, 'No'. Barbara's dad now, and they were a big family, he would have telt ye that if they'd gone home and told that they'd got the strap, they would have been asked, 'And what was ye doing? It must have been something afore they did that to ye!' And then you'd get another dose of it!

Any one of the teachers would use the strap if you was needing it. No question about it! But there wasn't a lot of strapping went on, ye ken. Well, in Strichen there was Miss Taylor, I aye remember her and she was the teacher you got when you were new to the school. She took in the first three classes, five years of age, going on six. She had the big room and that was her job from the time she started till she retired. The bairns adored her; they never heard a raised voice or anything.

There were just differences in the teachers. Not a lot of strapping went on. But I'll tell you, you would never have answered a teacher back or anything. You showed respect for them. There was discipline – outside, as well as inside the school. There was never any vandalism. You would never even have thought about it! There was aye something to do – and the boys would be away poaching at night… There was no time for vandalism. And we all had to help at home. There was nothing in the village, you would have said, never a broken window or anything. There was aye something to be doing. We all had our little jobs to do when we went home at night. It was part of your family.

We respected adults in general. There was never even – not that we were goody-goody or anything – but there was never a question that if any grown up had spoken to you and said 'I don't think you should do that!', we'd never have dreamed of speaking back or of touching anything or anybody's stuff.

The teachers were only friendly to you to a certain extent. We were aye in awe. They might come in about and speak to you – but you'd never go to them. You'd never go up to the teacher and start chatting. Some teachers did show an interest in you. I mind at the school at Boyndlie, the little school there. There was a few crofts round there and they had children, boarded out bairns, foster children from Glasgow – there was a lot of that around the Hill. I can remember Miss Grey and this little girl from Boyndlie and she was sitting greetin' in the class beside me. We'd have been the same age, seven or eight, and so she took her to the front and spoke to her, and the next I knew we had put on our coats and she'd written out a note. There were two shoe shops in the village then, and we was put up with this note, and she paid for this girl to get new boots, new laced up boots. She had chilblains on her feet – oh!, her feet were just… And she'd been greetin' because of them. I can't remember – but Miss Grey never mentioned it, and I was told, 'You don't mention this at home or anything!' She'd bought her the new boots.

Strichen was a busy village. There was the mart, all the farmers came with the cattle on Mondays and we had a busy day. It was a little market town! A bustling little village. There

116

was a good community life – a lot of things: concerts, dances, and we had a festival with competing in singing – we had judges up from London. It was a proper singing festival. Oh a lot of things went on in the village; it was a busy little village. But then, after the mart closed and things like that… they've killed all the little villages.

And you see, all the places round about, like us on a Saturday night, winters and all: mum and dad and us with our coats on, all out shopping, getting all our messages for the week. So, we all went down to the village and everyone was doing the same. The place was bustling on a Saturday night; you were meeting all your chums; everyone was helpful and looked out for everyone. That's what I was saying to Barbara; I'll go back and take a walk around the village and I just don't see it now. But I can mind easily, walking down each different street in the village and kenning a'body and speaking to them all. And those I'd been at school with would be shouting and I'd be saying. 'Wait a minute, I'll be with you!' Right up North Street and High Street and round past the Ugie – everywhere! You don't see those folks now. It was a busy little place…

It was a good place to grow up in. I liked the school. I can only say I had very happy days at Strichen School. I knew I wouldn't be going any further on but I passed all my exams. We got every subject you'd have been getting in any larger school, in the town or anywhere. A lot went from there to the university. But they were mostly farmer's sons and daughters and those who had the money to pay for them. Money was important for how far you went on. There wasn't the grants you have nowadays.

You just finished your school, whenever – at fourteen. That was it! All I ever wanted to do was what my mum had done. Housework you see… no, that's not true, because I wasn't awful interested in housework. But working with the animals and working outside… and the cooking. I learned that at school – just a basic. Then I went to work just two months after I'd left school. It was friends of my grandfather who had a farm beside him. I went there, engaged for six months – that was what you did. One little girl, I looked after her. I lived in and I got five shillings a week. I saved it up and bought a bike. But you got your food – there was nothing to pay. Because they were friends of my grandad, when they got new clothes for their child, I got as well. When they got a new coat, I got one as well. But mostly, when a girl went to work as a kitchen lass or at anything in the house, she was on the five shillings a week and her food.

I was quite happy. Everyone else was doing the same. There was nothing to be unhappy about. Nothing! It was a carefree life, there was nothing really going wrong to us. Then, of course, the war came along. I was eighteen. I was married when the war broke out. I was married at eighteen and a half. Sandy was called up to the army and was away all during the war. And when he came home we had the croft.

Jean [the oldest sister] was just a few days at the school. Half a day a week for six months. That was all. She was so delicate you'd think the wind would blow her away! Yet, she could cope well. She worked at the farm as well. She went to work at a big farm near Strichen. You see, there were no other jobs for us girls. There wasn't shops for everyone to go into. There were no businesses at Strichen or anything. So you just took the jobs there was. And, at that time, that was at the farms – all of them had two or three maids. The farms were the centre of employment.

It was the same with the boys. They left school and went onto a farm, became horsemen of whatever. And that was just what you knew you were going to be. And I don't think anyone resented it. It was just your way of living! The thing is, mostly everyone was in the same position, there was nobody above you. And the people you was working for was working

117

just as hard as you – they were none of them bosses just sitting by. The lady I worked for – we got very friendly because we worked alongside each other and did everything together. You didn't think anything about it!

Only those who could afford to go on did so. The farmer's children, the minister's children – there was Mary, she was in my class; she was the minister's daughter – he had two daughters and both went on – though one wasn't as clever so she went on to the Do' School [Domestic Science], but she was still getting further learning. But Mary went to university and became a teacher. The banker's daughter, she went to university but she left half way through the term and ran away with a boyfriend. What a disgrace to Strichen! Then, there was the shop, Bob Greig's shop: Pat Greig, she was one of my chums, and she went on to further learning. But the war broke out and she got engaged to a Flight Lieutenant lad and went away with him. So, you see, the war made a mess of all our plans; we all got scattered during the war; we all went to different places.

Strichen took you up to university, you see. We all mixed together, we were all treated the same. There was no snobbery or anything – I didn't feel it anyway. Of course, I was aye telt that I was just as good as all the rest! Mum and Dad told us that; my granny and grandad and all. They said, 'Whatever you do, you're as good as anybody else. There's nothing to stop you!'

No, we didn't speak Doric in the classroom. If you did, you got a scolding and if you insisted on doing it deliberately, you got a smack. No, no – it was very confusing when you went new to the school. It was very hard for all the kids, with the Buchan dialect and all that. The first week or two when you got to school, you'd be learning to read out loud – it was like a foreign language – it had to be in Standard English, and ye couldna spik it! In the family or on the farm it was all Doric. You had to learn two languages – and you hadn't much time, you had to learn it pretty fast. I was speaking about Miss Taylor, who had all the little ones: she used to go to the WRI meetings and tell jokes and things about some of the things the little kids said. And this boy, Lumsden – his father was a shepherd – and he went to school, you see and he had on this suit and a little waistcoat and those men at the farm gave him this watch, and he said, 'Gad a'michty, Miss Taylor, is it nae near lowsin time yet?!' She got great fun – but she explained the right way to say it to him, you see. That was the fun – you went to school and it was completely different. You couldn't understand what way you had to change your tongue, you see. You just learned it, just learned it!

School was completely separate from your home life. Whenever you got home and out of the school door, in the playground, it was all Doric, ye ken. It was all Doric! Your teacher spoke English, you see. Whatever accent she had. The two were separate – it was a different language. You couldn't go up to the teacher and speak Doric, not even outside. The teacher kept it up all the time. That was the attitude! Still the attitude, ye ken! It doesn't bother me, it's just my language. I can understand it in a way, not being allowed to use it because you're going to go away because not everyone's going to bide in the little bit they were brought up in, in Strichen or around the Mormond Hill. You're going to be travelling and you've got to have a universal language everyone can speak. You've got to have a language they can speak, and that would have to be English, I think. The only time you got to use Doric, or a Scots word, was in the singing lessons when you had a Burns song of something like that. Then you were allowed to use it. But for just speaking, no!

Ye just had to adapt, ye see! I've a friend next door, we were just speaking about this the other day. She was a dancer, a member of a troupe of dancers and entertainers. She was in ENSA during the war and was on the stage for many years after. It was her career. She's seventy-seven now and has stopped. But the other night, she and some chums, they were doing the can-can – she takes exercises for the over fifty-fives up the road. So she had them all doing the can-can the other night. Some of them are ninety! She said to some of them – ken when the fast bit comes – she said, 'Up your frocks!' and one of them says, 'My skirt's too tight'. They were having great fun. Well, she was just speaking about it – she's Aberdeen, a toonser, ye see, her and me have great discussions about all this – I'm teuchter and she's a toonser – we're aye casting up to each other! So, she's telling me, when she was going to the dancing, when she was just learning it in the town, just starting out on the country dancing – she was a ballet dancer as well – and this day, they were dressing up for some sort of show, and she had on some kind of tutu frock thing. She was minding that her dancing teacher, she says to her, 'Your pants are a bit too low at the back!' And she replies, 'Ma ma hid te shoo them up last necht!' 'Now what if I'd been trying to speak English!?', she says. 'Shoo them last necht!… ' Sew them up last night, you see…'

You didn't use it in the classroom. Ye was scolded – and if you persisted… well! But some schools, they do have Doric classes now. But we've all got into the habit of using English because folk don't understand us if you don't. We've all got into the habit of using English! I've lost all the words of my father's and Uncle Tam's. All the words they used, the real auld Scots words, because nobody would understand what you was saying and so you gradually stopped using them.

We had a good Scots education. All the education you needed, you see. We had a rounded education to fit us for what we needed to be doing. A good solid education, that's what I mean. Plenty of Buchan loons went on to big jobs, you see. It was just a good rounded education. A lot of common sense. I wasn't told I was going to be great or anything – but I wis aye telt I could work for a living. Education does mean a lot to the people of the North-East. Not maybe the higher education, but a good basic education. You've got to have that. The three Rs, you have to have that. Nobody left school in my day not able to do that!

James Michie: September 2001

I was born in Kintore [in 1926] but my family moved from there within the first year of my birth; I then spent all childhood and youth in Kincardineshire on the land.

Father was a cattleman and, because he was a cattleman, he was therefore a farm servant. The economics of the time were such that you were on a contract or fee and you were housed in a tied living and whether you were employed or not, or would have to leave after six months, depended entirely on the whim of the farmer as your employer. Consequently, it was a hard life because you could find yourself after six months putting all the scanty furniture you had on board a box and cart pulled by a Clydesdale horse to go to live in yet another small cottar house in the hope that things might improve and, that this time, you might have a longer time to stay to get some continuity and stability. The wages were extremely low, the conditions were extremely harsh, the working conditions were extremely harsh; you never left the land even under atrocious weather – it could be drenching wet – and consequently a lot of farm workers died long before their time from conditions such a pneumonia or arthritis and all sorts of things, occasioned by the nature of the work, in conjunction with the weather.

This is what happened to my father. I was nine; there were three below me – one sister and two brothers. That leads on to where I went to school. I first went to Fettercairn Primary School. That was for a very short time, a year or so, and then, by virtue of moving from one part to another, I found myself at Fordoun Public School which is now known as Auchenblae Primary School. It was the convention in earlier days to name the school after its parish rather than the major habitation – hence Auchenblae was served by Fordoun Public School.

My mother… she was Mother Courage; she had four of us and she did all the work. She worked in domestic work and also farm work, milking cows or working in the fields, at planting time, hay time and the like. In other words, she was the anchor of the family and was its breadwinner. In those days you didn't have the Welfare State, nor did you have counsellors.

I went, then, to Fordoun Public School. I was there from 1931 to 1939. Till I was thirteen. I went from primary 2 to primary 7, all in the one school. It was a six-teacher school: primary 1, 2, 3 then 4, 5, 6, 7, and the Advanced Divisions, in charge of the headmaster, single-handed. He was the only male teacher in the school; all the others were ladies, neatly dressed in twin sets, skirt and double row of pearls. Every one of them was a miss, unmarried because in those days if a woman married she had to leave employment. There was a full range of teachers: the young Infant teacher and the rather able, experienced ladies in primary 4, 5, 6, and 7. They were good folk and were, of course, a product of the time in the sense that the three Rs were paramount; we spoke when we were spoken to, we sat in serried rows, and were severely punished the moment we misbehaved – and that would be that.

I remember – and this is a little bit of sadness – you were punished if you didn't do the work accurately and timeously. That was quite frequent. I should explain that we were working to the convoy system, that is to say we moved forward at the speed of the slowest. It was not individual learning; it was whole class teaching. I think the teacher was to be commended… in modern times this seems extraordinary, but they were all persuaded that each child was capable of doing what any other child could do. In other words, the doctrine of individual differences had not reached the primary school at that time. If the child could not do the work, it was attributed to some character deficiency. It was almost moral laziness, sloth, lack of conscientiousness.

I remember – I won't mention any names – that there was a boy in my class; he was what we would now call a 'special needs' pupil. He had a terrible time with one teacher in particular, who saw him as lazy, disobedient, and disruptive. But this lad had a blank in reading, so practically every day, [he got] the tawse. This lad, I remember, had his hair cut by his father. Of course, he wasn't a professional barber; what he did was to put a bowl on top of his head, what we called an armchair bowl cut, and left a fringe, which in this boy's case turned into a tuft. This teacher used the tuft to pull him along and quite often used the tawse while he was being pulled along. This teacher – and let's be quite clear, this was one teacher, she was at the extreme – but she was convinced she was right and to that extent she could not be faulted.

The parents in my time saw the school as a place of complete authority and if the children came home having had the strap they sometimes got another one.

Now let us strike a balance – and what I want to stress yet again is she was an exception. The other teachers had more of an understanding of the pupils and were gentle… but in retrospect one is sad that they failed to perceive that by virtue of working to the common denominator, the children's ability was unchallenged, unstretched and as a result they could become fractious. There were no libraries, no books other than the set text books like 'Holmes Arithmetic', like the 'Radiant Readers, One to Five' – and they had to last all term. We read round the class and we sat there waiting while it went round; and, of course, the bright children worked out when their turn would come and switched off. What I am trying to get at is the lack of stimulus, the lack of insight, which stemmed from the inability to accept the doctrine of individual differences.

On the other hand, at the end of the day, all of us came out pretty well from it. At the age of twelve, the whole of us, for the most part, could read, we could write, we could count, and we knew right from wrong. It was a Biblical right, in other words an unqualified right.

The kirk was very important but kirk and school, believe it or not, although cheek by jowl, there was never any social, philosophical, educational communion between the two – we never saw the minister in the school. On the other hand, all of us in the village went to the kirk – morning service, Sunday school, and evening service.

We learnt the Bible from Genesis onwards and also a lot of disembodied facts, like the Plagues of Egypt. In geography it was the capitals of Great Britain, and then the world, and even to this day I can remember 90% of them. It gave you a great sense of achievement. The second thing that is interesting – and this extended to every school – was that there was no attempt to link cause and effect and remedy. In history you just learned 1066 Battle of Hastings, 1297 Stirling Bridge, 55 BC and all that – but we did not know what 'Hastings' or 'Stirling Bridge' meant. That was history; we did dates for the most part. It was a huge achievement, that I could remember all the kings and queens and all the parliamentarians.

We didn't have insight into the ways of mankind. One would like to have understood how Aberdeen came to be Aberdeen but all we got was Aberdeen-granite, Redditch-needles, Glasgow-shipbuilding – we could never remember what Edinburgh was for! One industry for each place – Newcastle for coal… I learned to associate one thing with each city… since five years old. Having said all that, and this is in retrospect, a fat lot of good it did me knowing all the capitals of the world because later I latched on to atlases and other reference books where you could look these things up.

But I'll tell you what though: history did give me a sort of dateline, a temporal structure, an internal map for later times. For example, I have just finished Schama's *Citizens*, which is magnificent, as if you are there – 'I understand, I understand!' Knowing about the French Revolution did help – but all I was really taught was that the French Revolution was a bad thing because the king and queen were executed and Robbespierre, Marat, Danton were all villians.

We were not allowed, when we read out in the classroom, to read out in our own dialect. I must say – and I must be careful here – a lot of people give a superficial impression of what was going on; you see, some people write with venom that Scots were not allowed to use the Doric, Lallans or whatever, that it was all suppressed. The fact of the matter was the medium of teaching was English. That was accepted by parents, by everybody. Perhaps it was a great pity that not enough attention was paid to poetry in the Doric, although we did get some. I think the fact of the matter is that English was universal for teaching and it has become the universal language for human life. English has become the *lingua franca* because dialect, the Doric, is no longer fully understood even locally, far less nationally, and far less internationally. When we have a world language like English it opens the world up to you – then regrettably the local working language is dying out. That is happening quite notably during my lifetime.

Auchenblae Primary School is a beautiful granite building which has added a wing during my own time. The classrooms were all well lit, all airy, there were bare floors, of course, and some had – not all – galleries.

We had placings according to performance. Every Friday there were tests, every Friday we were moved into our places for the following week. As far as the children were concerned, differences in ability or performance were just accepted. On the other hand, in a small village it was all quite important; quite often there were petty jealousies among the parents – 'How is it that your boy... ?'

I recall how I arrived in secondary education. There were fees for the secondary school. They were not high but high enough to be a deterrent for the working class, because it was not only the fees that had to be paid for, but books. The teachers from the school came to persuade my mother to allow me to go on. None of my siblings did; they went into the Army, the Navy; my sister went to Aberdeen. They went into the Advanced Divisions.

The teachers lived in Auchenblae, bar the dominie. They were a very important part, psychologically, of the community. They were leaders of the community. I can elaborate on that. Very briefly, there were seventeen shops, and more important than that, there was a doctor, an advocate, minister and four teachers, the policeman. What is left now? Three shops; the headteacher doesn't live in the place; the teachers do not live in the place. They all commute in by car. There's no policeman. All those people living in the village had a stabilising effect. Now the minister serves three parishes. What now happens is that you don't have the same range of quality, the same leadership in the community. The minister and the dominie were respected by virtue of their office. The teachers were very much respected.

There were wooden floors; the rooms were governed by tiers; we sat in pews. I remember one teacher loved her class and, in the harsh days of the 30s, these are the things you remember with gratitude: every Friday afternoon when the bell rang, this lady would go to the cupboard and take out a bottle of sweeties, of boilings, and each and every one of us got one. I remember that to this day. For us it was quite something.

I think also that when we come to talk about education at that time, some of us did find the school an exciting environment, as distinct from home, irrespective of the teacher's philosophy. If a lot of opportunity was lost, it was by virtue of the system, not the teachers. They didn't have the resources to bring all the abilities to fruition.

Looking back, I've been a little harsh. I enjoyed the school. School was a place of excitement. I think things are always difficult in early and in secondary education – and still are to some extent – because the pupils are going through a long process and can't see the end of it. For example, I taught French and German for five years – I got grammatical, syntactical French – but I also told them about the Folies Bergères, about the Weimar Republic. I remember one boy saying, 'Sir, the stuff you teach – it's about the folk in France!' Because our own teaching was fragmented, because we were taught the how rather than the why, we couldn't see the relationships between things. Because of that, a lot of teaching didn't use our ability; we were going through a mechanical process.

They didn't use the local environment; there was no local history. There was some nature study. We all came from the country – we used to gather flowers on the way to school, but by the time we got them to the teacher they were hanging – but the teacher accepted them like a bouquet. There was some nature study but not in any 'environmental' way. We didn't go out of the classroom; specimens were brought in. It was book learning.

I have a great picture of the art lessons. Right the way through school, we had a packet of Reeve's crayons and we were given a Reeve's four-by-four sheet of drawing paper, sometimes coloured, usually brown, and this was our palette. Things had to be photographic. I remember when we came to tulips and houses and things like that, we used the rubber a lot and, of course, that was punished, with a rap. Art was something fragmented. As we graduated, we got a paint-box, but, again, we were limited to four inches. Whereas, if you contrast that to a school like Rothienorman in the '70s, '80s, there it was all individual; individual pots and a large sheet of paper, and all wore smocks like artists. It was a question of 'What would you like to paint today?' I remember a visit to Rothienorman. All of them were rapt in their work, in their creations. I went up to one boy who was working away, the tongue protruding from the side of his mouth with all the effort. I stood by him, watching him. Finally, wishing to offer some encouragement, I said 'That's a fine horse you're doing!' 'Na, ya feel – that's not a horse, it's a coo!'

But that's nowadays. I remember those old art lessons. They had a great impact on my educational thinking. It isn't a question of materials, of form. Professor McMurray always said education is just learning to be human. I've always stood by that principle. I've been a controlled Liberal. I developed my philosophy from what I got as a pupil, not as a rebellion against it. On the contrary, my schooling gave me the basis for thinking about human relationships and, above all, to ask myself how best acceptable relationships could be built and, therefore, it seemed to me that the first thing we should look at is humanity and its interests. I don't think this sprang from Auchenblae itself, but it could have done, partly.

The other people in the class, most of them, well, quite a few went to Mackie Academy but by no means all. For the most part, they went into domestic service or on to the land – became an orra loon, a horseman, cattleman and so forth. Some of the girls maybe got jobs in the bank or as a shop assistant. There was an infrastructure in Auchenblae that needed servicing.

But very few went on to an academic course. There were some who could have gone on but lack of money stopped them; they had to help support the family. But even sadder than that, there was the feeling of 'learnin's nae for the likes o us'. The fact was that their family had always been in that situation and they just accepted it; there was a kind of fatalism. I had difficulty myself – there was a feeling that I might get too big for my boots, that I wasn't fitting into the world that was meant for me. Some didn't want to get on or to get out of it. No. My mother was surprised that I got on as well as I did. There were other things on her mind. She came from a working class family, Aberdeenshire, Kemnay, on the land and in those days – well all the sisters were in service, her brothers on the land.

I can tell you this much: my aunt Nancy, called Nella, had the opportunity to try to study to be a doctor… this was the other great driving force, to see that people got the opportunity. I'm not saying that all of them should be crammed to enable this, but they should be put in the way of things so that they could get the chance to get on. There was the opportunity to get on for some. I should explain this to you, irrespective of what I have said about the nature of the teachers, when I came to the age of twelve, it was assumed that I should go on to the land. What else could one do? The times were such that it was quite out of the question to think otherwise. But three teachers, plus the lady with the sweeties, persuaded my mother to let me go on. That is why I am sitting here now!

You can have no idea what that meant. I was aware of what was going on. I was aware of a moral imperative, that I should not, dare not, fail. There was a huge imperative weighing on me. Even more so when I went to university. I had to justify the sacrifice made. People talk blithely of the lad o' pairts and think what a wonderful thing it all was, but, behind it all, there were a large number who weren't able to go on. Quite a number who could have gone

123

were denied – for various reasons, the main one being economics, the inability of the family to sustain education. But the other reason was that they had never had anybody in the family who had gone. In fact, this still exists today – in Mastrick, in Torry. They had never had the tradition. Social determinism is still there, in the town.

People ask me, and I ask myself, if I had gone on the land at the age of 14 where would I be today? I can hazard a guess and it clearly wouldn't be in academic circles! Go back to 1939. Obviously I didn't see myself as a teacher. The bright pupils went off to Mackie. Everything was programmed steadily. I couldn't see the larger picture, the vista, the possibilities within the vista. I just moved along with it all. Even when I went to university I didn't have a clue what to study. But I had two brilliant women who took me over, literally took me over. They were extraordinarily kind to me – Ethel Jack for German and Ethel Mitchell for French.

I couldn't say whether there was anything special about my education, by virtue of being Scots, of living in the North-East. I had nothing to compare it with. I didn't even know of the existence of Robert Gordon's or Albyn. There was no talk of them in the village. I was the only one in my class who went to university.

All my education has been a source of wonder to me. There were no books at home at all. *The Sunday Post* was there and is still read, much to my astonishment. My mother took in *My Weekly,* and the *Red Letter Weekly*. These were things that my mother bought herself – but, I tell a lie, there was one book – there was Annie Swann, Annie S. Swann. I did read comics; my favourite was *Champion*. It had good sport. There was also *Adventure, Rover*, that kind of thing. One other thing: Mackie didn't have a library. All I remember, every week, there came from the local library an ammunition box of books from which I was allowed to take one a month. None of the schools had a library then. 1939-45, no chance!

We had the radio. It was driven by a wet battery; it was my job to keep it charged up. I listened voraciously – the Home Service, the war time stuff, music. Far better than the rubbish that's on today! Don't forget Lord Reith was a Stonehaven man – Lord Reith of Stonehaven!

Sport. There was little from outside the world of Scotland. We got the daily *P&J* (*Aberdeen Press and Journal*), which I read voraciously. I supported Aberdeen. My grandson supports Aberdeen despite all my best kindness! I played cricket and football for the school. There was nothing else in those days. No hockey – or rather that was for the girls. That was the extent of it. Oh, the children played tennis on the municipal courts, and we swam in Stonehaven pool.

I look back with gratitude on that small community of Auchenblae. I've written something on it, my memories. It gives a picture of a dynamic little society, living in our own village.

The education I got at Auchenblae was replicated throughout the North-East. Like all human activity, it varies according to the character or the dynamic of those who provided it, of the leading figures. That holds good even today. Take the headmaster. He was Willie West. He died 7 years ago, in Forestgait. He was ascetic, austere – and that was how he wanted to be seen. He was in charge! He set the discipline, the framework in which we operated. He was a public figure and an educational figure. I remember a tremendous set-to; it was with the parents of some youngsters in the advanced divisions and also the boys themselves. The near fourteen year-old wanted awa frae the school! There was no answer to that but, 'You'll just stay at the school till you're fourteen!'

We were all frightened, in awe of the headmaster. We saluted all the teachers in the street – or pretended to be looking in at the shop window… Willie West ran a good school: it was ordered, secure; we felt safe and provided for in the school.

But we haven't talked about the music! Most teachers in those days could play a bit. We learned all the standard Scots songs – 'Nut Brown Maiden', 'Ye Banks and Braes'. But when we came to primary 7, that was a different kettle of fish. I don't know why, but Willie West taught primary 7 music – it was situated next to his class, the 'big class', the Advanced Divisions. The first week we were ushered into the class, a Friday afternoon, just before the sweeties. This may surprise you. The music consisted of the good Mr West going into his waistcoat pocket, pulling out a tuning fork and 'do… !… Ye Banks and Braes… do… !' He had disciplined standards of rendition! All the songs were Scots and we got to sing them eventually. This was Willie West with his turning fork. Now we didn't know what a tuning fork was. I went home and said, 'Mr West went into his waistcoat pocket, he pulled out this thing and "do… !".'

We were short of this and short of that. Again, you've got to be careful. This was the hungry thirties. There was not only impoverishment in individual homes – no instruments – but in the school too.

I passed an exam to go to Mackie. I sat the exam by myself – I was the only one to get in that way. Those who could afford the fees went, whether they passed an exam or not. There was a fatalism, a determinism at work. Some families couldn't see themselves doing this. It was not for them at all. I've been asked why I didn't become a communist or a raging socialist. I'm not doctrinaire at all. I have human, moral principles. I've never been a member of any political party. I have my beliefs and, as you'll gather, they are a little left of centre.

There was a classroom democracy. The only people who sent their children off to private education, or to a public school in England, or Scotland, were the landed class, the lairds. None of us who came from a working class or middle class background would ever have dreamt of going into private education. By far the majority sat on the democratic benches of the local school. There was no difference in the treatment we got. But within the secondary school there was segregation – 1A, 1B, 1C, according to perceived ability or performance. Whether that was fair or not is open to question. Once you got to Mackie, there was no mobility. You certainly couldn't move from one class to another. That was you set.

Let me tell you something now that will give you some indication of how things were. First of all, I've got to say we were all extremely proud to be there. The teachers went out of their way, they did all sorts of things to help, they taught across the board when they had to. But what was interesting – and I only learnt this when I went to Dundee when I had to organise an in-service course – and one of the speakers at this course was Alistair Long who was going to speak about, 'Comprehensive Education and the Burgh School'. The fascinating thing is that, if you want to go into comprehensive education, it means real change in the curriculum, in activity, in philosophy and practice. John Hutcheson of Mackie Academy was there and he said, 'Well, I'll have to take the board off the wall in my study!'. We all sat there transfixed. 'Do you know something?' he said, 'When I got to Mackie, I found this curriculum board on the wall in my room. And on it, for each class, S1 to S5, there was painted on – painted on, mark you – a subject with a teacher's name fixed against it for each year. But the teacher's names were only chalked on!'

This indicates to you what we've learned about secondary education in my time. It used to be as absolute as the Laws of the Medes and the Persians. You knew exactly, in fact, you could look it up on the board, what you would be doing with S5 on the third Friday in November. The only choice you had was this – and again, remember this was war-time – you either took art and science or you took French and German. You couldn't do both, or any combination of the four.

The brighter children did languages. Latin was obligatory for A and B classes. I loved Latin. C and D got technical drawing or domestic science, according to gender. I started off: English, Latin, geography, French, German, mathematics and music and PE – that was it. A pity, because a whole lot of pupils could have done well in science. My lot was English, German, French, Latin, mathematics. Some history, a little geography. That was it… No possibility of anything else. You couldn't take any more.

About my relationships with the staff: because I was linguistically inclined, I was the teacher's pet in German and in French. I excelled at these two subjects. The headmaster then was a former prisoner of war – he suffered at the hands of the Germans in the First World War. He had an almost uninhibited hatred of the Germans. I remember when the Germans bombed Singapore, he was in a frenzy: 'How dare they! How dare they!' He didn't disguise his feelings from us. He was a very hard man, very hard. Whether it was because of the prisoner of war experiences, I don't know. But if you got to the old Mackie Academy, which is a lovely building, you will find a long corridor, and we had to parade along it on our way to the classrooms. He carried a leather harrier which he held between two fingers and if we were committing misdemeanours of any kind he would whip us about the face. It was sore. You just can't imagine that kind of thing today! The parents just wouldn't accept it.

On the other hand, he gave us English. He made sure we got the benefit of *Palgrave's Golden Treasury*. He took us through that and also a lot of Shakespeare – *Midsummer Night's Dream, Julius Caesar, Henry V…* He was a great man for learning by rote. There was the time we had to do 'Ode to a Nightingale' – 'O, for one sip of the blissful Hippocrene, with beaded bubbles winking at the brim…' Bertie Andrew, the minister's son from Kineff, was called on to do the recitation. He was getting on fine till he came to the lines 'O, for one sip'. He got to 'with beaded bubbles winking at the… at the… at the…' He was stuck. I whispered to him, 'surface', and he said out loud, 'with beaded bubbles winking at the surface'. 'Come out here Andrew! Out here! How dare you! How dare you! Mangling beautiful poetry!' Four of the best! And I've never even apologized to Bertie… I tell you this as an insight into the kind of man he was. For him poetry, learning was sacrosanct.

This was all accepted. It was just part of the fabric. We all recognised he was the Boss. He always wore a kilt. He insisted on it. He held Mackie Academy firmly in his grasp. He saw that nothing untoward ever happened. He always grasped the nettle. We all knew where we stood with him. If we stepped over a particular line, that was it! There was never anything really to worry about. But now you'll ask, was there anything wrong with all that he did? Yes, sometimes there was. A certain amount of injustice was done. Like Bertie Andrew getting four of the best.

The Latin man was a one-off. He taught us about everything, bar Latin – until the fifth year, when he just crammed us with what we needed to get through the exam. He taught us all about the outside world. All about everything, except Latin!

Let me put it this way. I think we were very lucky in almost every single respect at Mackie. We came to no harm; the war didn't touch us. In Mackie Academy, we could carry on as if the war was nothing. We did have the odd excitement when a Heinkel came over. Then we ran to houses of safety.

Let me tell you a lovely story. We were at the football; it was a Saturday morning, 11 am. The score was standing nil-nil. We heard a noise overhead. We recognised it – it was a Heinkel bomber. It circled around. We were in the direct line of fire. We lay down, face down, all along the pitch. We thought we were about to be bombed! But he just circled around, then disappeared off. The story ran round the town: the pilot of that aircraft, he and his family used to visit Stonehaven for their holidays back before the war. And here he was just having a fond look at the place before going off to bomb Aberdeen or somewhere!

It is important to know the way things were. I've made some strong statements, some extreme statements. But really you can forgive a lot when you understand the social context in which it all happened.

But there is one note of regret. I don't look back with any anger, none at all. But I do regret that things had to be the way they were. So many of my fellows were short-changed and couldn't achieve what they were capable of…

Alan Morrison: October 2001

I was born ten-five-thirty, at Newcraig Farm in the parish of Daviot. I came from a farming background. My dad was a tenant farmer of 175 acres. Cattle farming and grain. He employed four men at that time-horsemen; everything was done by horses and muscles; everything was moved by muscles. Hands, barrows, neeps hoed and the harvest taken in – horse power and man power! There was no silage at that time – just hay and straw and turnips. We grew turnips and only grew one patch of tatties for our own use. At that time there was a limit on the acreage of potatoes unless you were a registered producer, so we just grew only one acre for our own use – but you could sell the surplus. Not till the coming of the end of the war did things change.

I was born at home. Mum, she was foty-two when I was born. I was the youngest of five of a family and she was the third youngest of a family of fourteen. She was born at Kinellar and at that time all her sisters went into service and her brothers, the five brothers, all went abroad and only one ever came back visiting that I know of – he was the youngest. His daughter was back here a year or two ago and she thought she was the youngest cousin, but I'm the youngest cousin! I'm now seventy-one, so that made a big gap between us.

But in 1901, mum left school and she cleaned her bike and cycled nine miles to Aberdeen to go to Webster's classes. She insisted on going instead of going into service like the rest. She actually refused to do that, virtually refused. She rattled over the Tyrebagger and into Aberdeen. It wasn't a very good road in those days but there were no motor vehicles to watch out for. But once in Aberdeen she got to know a pal or two and got to stay in town during the winter-time. It was only a two-year course at that time. She then went into employment and, of course, got better pay than she would ever have got in service. I can't remember exactly… she was at four different places in Aberdeen in her seventeen years there. At Tinnie Robertson's and at the Central Mart at Kittybrewster. She was junior to the cashier there and handled all the money. At that time everyone paid cash – £20 for a bullock, £10 for a ewe – they just paid it out.

She didn't get married till after the First World War, 1919. She was married in Inverurie and came to Newcraig; she thought she was in for a life of leisure because for the first four years things were good. But then came the collapse of 1923, which halved the price of their stock when they'd only newly got on their feet. And she had two daughters by that time, because my sister was born in 1920 and another one in 1922. So she had no option but to put her hand to it. She had two housemaids when she got married in her own farmhouse. But they had to go. So it was necessary when my older sister left school – she's now eighty-one and lives at Westhill – to stay at home until she got married. You've got to remember that in those days the men who worked on the farm got fed in the farmhouse, they got three square meals a day in the house. So my mother always needed assistance. And, of course, there was no electricity – everything had to be done by hand.

My father belongs to Kintore; his father had an even bigger farm. My grandfather, I believe, was a blacksmith and he was at Oldmeldrum and then went on to run his own smithy at Leylodge. I don't know whether you know where I'm at now, but Leylodge is on the back road to the dual carriageway at Kintore. You go down through the Lyne of Skene, down to Kintore. He was schooled there at a wee school called Lauchentilly – I saw the signpost for it just last week when I came through that way – the signpost is still there but the school isn't! My mum went to Glasgow Forest School which was obsolete a long time ago. These were small one-teacher schools. My dad was called up to the army but apparently was then sent home – my brother verified that not very long ago. It was because there was a shortage of manpower on the land. So they didn't get married till after the war in 1919, which made them thirty-one and thirty-three respectively.

The five of us were born in the space of ten years. I'm the youngest, my brother's five years older and my sister in Edinburgh just now is 74. I haven't spoken to her since she came back but she was across in Canada not long ago. My second sister was a nurse; my brother was a farmer all his life, and the older sister was a domestic science teacher and taught in Edinburgh, funnily enough at Mid Calder. She was married to a banker but is now a widow. I speak to her now and again.

We all went to Daviot, the local school but, except for the oldest sister, the other three all went to Inverurie Academy, but I didn't go. They did this at the end of primary, which at that time was Division 5 but is now Primary 7. They did this at the age of eleven or twelve.

We were a mile and a half from the school so we just walked it. Till I got a bike, a wee bike. We walked through all weathers, including the snow, to it. Most of Daviot School, half of Daviot School, came from Westerton because there were 22 houses in Westerton; they were workers' houses so you can imagine how many came from that direction. There were always about 100 pupils: quite big. There were four teachers, you see. Three women teachers and one male, the headteacher. Miss Emslie was the infant teacher I started with. My brother just took me up to the door on the back of his bike and he just pushed me into the room and said, 'Stand there till the teacher comes!'. That was my first day! He just pushed me into the infant room, which was on the right as you come through the door, and said, 'Stand there until you're taken away!'

There were three seats on each desk and I was sat between two girls – Jessie Presley and Maureen Connor. They were two clever girls. I did well the first years at school – two years with her and then two years with Miss Will, who was the Guide captain. You had to go up to another room for that. She cycled three to four miles to school up the hill. All weathers, all weathers! I didn't think much about it when I was at school but when I left, well the road, you see, went through the farm and I used to see her in some very windy days. Just battling on, battling on!

Then you were moved on to another teacher. My biggest problem at school was the boys who were kept back. They were at least one and a half years older than me and they were virtual dunderheads, but they were the big boys in the class. 'Oh, you're in the same class as so and so'. That was all right when it came to football but they were a nuisance in that class as far as I was concerned. You were inclined to look upon them as leaders. I never got on well at school after that. The teacher, I don't know, a Miss S—, just through being blamed for talking, never marked my decimal work – on slates, by the way. She didn't mark the decimal sums on my slate because I'd been bad in the morning. That should have been forgotten about. After all, I'd already got eleven of the strap for being bad in the morning! She didn't mark my slates for the decimal sums. That didn't do me any good at all. You sort of began to resent her. She put me to one side along with all these other boys and then you're inclined to think that they were right at that time, because your young mind at nine or ten is taken up with, 'Hey, look at the big boys. I'll run on with them!' They were a disturbance in the class, absolutely. The teacher couldn't handle them in the class. She couldn't handle the big lads.

Then we went into the headmaster for the 'qualifying' which is now primary 7. But I'm afraid he was more taken up with the Home Guard. He was the Home Guard! You know this, sometimes we didn't write in our jotters at all, didn't write the whole day. Just, we had no idea what we were meant to be doing; all the damned we could think of, drawing tractors, cars, horses on our books. We never were checked. Never checked at all.

Till in the next year we got percentages. So he was giving us our percentages and he got our scale as to what we had been supposed to be doing. He looked back at the jotters and, of course, I hadn't been doing anything. So he took me out to the floor; he put out a sum for me to do it on the blackboard. Well, I couldn't, I just couldn't. So I very nearly got the strap, but then he must have thought – he picked another boy, took him out and he couldn't do it either. None of us could do it. So we got the whole afternoon on percentages and I can do it to this day. He really did what he should have done in the beginning. A whole afternoon on it, the subject never changed, the whole afternoon, and I never forgot it, that 'one percent' was one of a hundred. I didn't known till then!

But, I think, my mother always said that I should have gone to Inverurie but I didn't want to go. I was always bent on the farming and that was the problem. I was already at it when I was 11. Out at the threshing mills, planting the tatties. In those days I just wanted to be out of the school and onto the farm.

No, I never skipped the school. There was too much discipline at home: you couldn't go home and say that you did such and such because then you would have got another dose. The only time I skipped school was very interesting. There was a farm next to the school playground; a man was ploughing there with the horses; the farmer himself was in Aberdeen – it was a Friday. But his son's wife came up and said to the man who was ploughing that he had to take the sheep to a neighbour's for dipping. 'Oh, could you come, boys, and help out? It'll only take 20 minutes!' We all set sail; we got the sheep put in the field and took them up to the neighbour's. We didn't get back to the school at all!

There were two girls there from my area; my mother knew what had happened on the Friday night. The other two didn't known about it till the Monday. On the Monday at school we were taken out to the floor and after the headmaster had heard a description of what had happened, he said, 'Right, you'll write an essay on what you did!' So I wrote in detail all that had happened that afternoon, all about collecting the sheep, taking them to the farm, putting them in the tank and putting them through the dipper and explaining how some of the sheep ran away and all that. I got the whole detail! And by Wednesday we had the essays back. The other three boys got six of the strap but I got off because it was a good essay. I was interested in it.

By the end of the schooling, you had the garden to do, the school garden. There was a lack of boys in the headmaster's classes: he got me onto the digging and we were all given our own wee plot. I was never so surprised, I got the gardening prize! By the time I left school I got into the headmaster's garden. I did the school garden in school time and the headmaster's after. His wife gave me tea. He had a fine steel spade. I'd get home by 7 o'clock.

For my parents things were bleak at that time. They didn't know what was going to happen. I left school in '44; the war was still on. So, I mean most of my schooling was done in war-time. Of course, it was interrupted by gasmasks and air-raid training; it was all interrupted. If the local hospital siren went, we all had to go into what was the air-raid shelter, you see. The shelter was in the school playground, if you like to call it that. It was just the dungeon under the school, actually, but that's where we all had to go.

And I suppose my dad was so pleased to be getting somebody to do the farm work – I don't think mum was, I don't think she was. I have no hesitation in saying that if I had stuck in after I was a nine-year-old there would have been no problem for me, no problem.

I'm sorry about it now. But then I thought it was great; the tractors were coming in, and I didn't regret it till later life when I felt the need for more education: for some of the modern things going on now, for all the paperwork in farming. Farming wasn't complicated then, not as far as paperwork was concerned. Unless you had more than 200 acres you didn't even keep books till 1948. You just did it. Just farmed, and all you had was a bank account, that's all. So that education, things like ordering the seed, selling the livestock, they all just came naturally to you on the farm at that time. You had to have a wee bit in front, you had to be thinking about next year's crops etc. And there were lots of reps from all the companies. They were a nuisance, when I came here thirty years ago – selling fertilizer, selling tractors, gear, implements. So you more or less dealt with the ones you always dealt with.

Education might have made a difference. Financially, I've been inclined to go in with a blind eye and say I'll easy manage when, really, some sums should have been done. I'd say that latterly I lacked an education. I can't do algebra to this day; geometry is double Dutch to me – I could draw some things, but, no, I could not do that. There was no French at Daviot – reading, writing, maybe time at the joiner's bench on a Wednesday when you got bigger. And there were the 'Heritage' books – English reader books, I think. The trouble was, you see, unless you were checked up on every day you didn't do it. You thought you were the big man! 'I'm not doing my lessons today!' And that was quite wrong.

All the brains went to Inverurie. There was a scarcity of boys in the senior classes. There were only the 11 year-olds and only two in the higher classes. Eleven of us were in the 'qualifying' and about six or seven went to Inverurie. That meant that nearly all the farmers' sons went to Inverurie. As you'll understand, most of the pupils left were the farmworkers' children. They were expected to go back into the farm work; there was no other outlook for them. I was just speaking to the tractor driver there, the other day, and he was saying, 'When we were boys, there was nothing else facing us', and he's got two daughters – sixteen and eighteen – he said, 'What a different life they've got. There were seven of us living on a farm wage. We just had to go out to work. There was nothing else; we couldn't afford anything'.

We got some history and geography. I was fairly good at the dates at one time but I've forgotten them now. I learned a lot of dates – 1603, Union of the Crowns, 1314, Bannockburn. You see that sort of thing I was quite good at. But then again, I should have been paying attention! I should have been checked as to what I was doing. I mean that's what happens nowadays, I'm sure. I mean, be checked and double-checked.

The headmaster was good. He was hard – he wasn't like what I've heard at other schools. He could keep control. Mr Kaye he was called. He was an Orcadian. Miss S— was a good teacher but she took something to me and that was that. It's a silly story, but this boy was talking and she said, 'Horne, if you keep talking you'll get six of the strap'. Fordyce said,

'Oh, ho! Six of the strap, eh!', and he was taken out and given eleven. I was across the passage and called out, 'Was it sore?' and I was hauled out and given six. Just for that! I mean, that was ridiculous.

The strap was common – you weren't happy unless you got it once a week! You thought something was missing if you didn't get it once a week. I have seen a girl get it but not often. I'm afraid it didn't have any effect on me. I still agree with modern day thinking that the strap does not deter you. I wasn't scared of it. I suppose we used to say, 'I was pulling neeps yesterday, my hands are nice and hard… ' No, I don't think it deterred you at all. No, I think detention, having to write something, stand in the corner, are more effective. You see, my daughter, when she was beginning teaching, she told a boy to do something and he turned round and spat at her, 'Do I have to?!' Within six weeks, she says, 'I broke him but it took six weeks'. But that was the first thing that happened between them, 'Do I have to?!' And she said, 'I just stared him'. She says you can stare them out. When she started she was just doing half time on a job share and the other girl couldn't handle them. She was out of the picture. She had to go with them, otherwise they would just play up. My daughter's still there – she had primary 7 when she started again but she's now got primary 4 and likes them. She always dreads it after the holidays, a new class, you see. You have to break them in.

My school was very formal. We stood in line in the mornings before we went in. I was fairly informal with the headmaster at the end but that was mainly doing his garden for the last few months. But no, oh no – it was formal. The headmaster used our last names: 'Horne, Morrison' and so on. No, it was always last names with him.

One other teacher went with the bus to Rothienorman. She belonged to Aberdeen, I think. The infant teacher stayed in a schoolhouse. The headteacher was married and stayed in the school-house. The others were unmarried: 'Miss' and so on. I liked them but I didn't care for Miss S— at the end because we had friction. The headmaster, you kept away from him rather than… you couldn't go and tell him a tale, say if anything was bothering you, he just wasn't interested, no!

He was the First Elder at the church. He and the laird had cars. He had a BSA car. But he didn't have a phone, nor the school either. The school had no electricity either. It was heated with coal fires and lit by tilly lamps. If it was a dark day the teacher lit them and, the day before, the cleaner filled them. As for the fires, the Mitchell twins' mother cleaned them and the school as a whole. It was a job, the fires and the toilets; they all required a lot of cleaning. There was sanitation, not dry toilets. There was soup made in the iron shed in the winter by the soup kitchen lady. We got soup in the winter; in the summer we brought pieces ourselves. So we had to carry the soup; four boys went round with the soup at lunchtime.

We had some art and music. But not as much as we should have done. But there again, I wouldn't sing because the boy next to me wouldn't sing. My mother could play the piano; we had an organ in the house. My sister went to piano lessons. My dad sang in the church every Sunday without fail because he was the Head Elder. But me again, I remember being chosen to sing something but I wouldn't because I was so stood up. That's wrong, that's wrong… As for art I just made a mess with the paint brush; you did get an art period, but no… we did hand-copying; there was a great emphasis on good handwriting, copper plate! We didn't do enough actual writing in my opinion. The best essay I ever wrote was the one on the sheep. That was because I knew what I was doing, I knew what it was about. We didn't get enough of that.

It was hard going, the school. A lot of strictness. The stage from 9 to 11 was boring but I got over it. I was very interested to begin but then it all fell away – but then at the end it grew interesting again as I was nearly the head boy, sort of style. But I feel today that I didn't do enough at the school.

In our day you always had to hold your hand up before you could speak and that was just to answer the question. You had to stand up to answer the question. Nobody was allowed to speak, even to your next neighbour: oh no, that was the strap. The strap would be going then, even if you whispered something… The two girls that sat alongside me at the beginning were very clever girls and I suppose that did me more good than anything. A pity it hadn't stayed that way! They're still around – one lives out at Glenbuchat. She was the daughter of the original Connor, of 'Connor Contractors'.

You had to speak differently in the classroom from the playground. It was no problem – you just did it. We spoke as properly as we knew how to at that time.

We played football. You know what we played the most? We played horses. You got a piece of rope, tied it to one boy, tied it to another boy, and then got them going in front and you were behind at the plough. Playground games. Then there were cowboys and indians. That often got us into problems because it meant that half of us went out of the playground to escape. And if you were in the wrong place when the time came to go back in, then that was another strapping. But mainly we played football. There was no school team. Not big enough – and it was war-time and there was very little recreation of any kind. There was a shortage of male teachers and of transport of all kinds. I mean, to get on the bus you had to walk a mile down to the main road; the teacher had to walk that mile down the road to get on the bus to go further north. As for cars, petrol was rationed. My dad didn't have a car till 1949. I was 19 when I started driving. I passed the test for the tractor when I was sixteen – but I'd been driving it before then. May '49 for the car – and I've held a licence ever since.

When we went to dances we did it by cycling there. That was a great time in my young life, when all the girls were there for the dancing. There were forty nurses employed at the Daviot Hospital for a start. I enjoyed that bit! A dancing teacher came up from Inverurie, him and his wife; they trained us and it was fortunate that I had enough music in my head that I could do the waltzes, the eightsome reels, and the modern stuff too. I enjoyed all that – no question about it. We cycled as much as twelve miles out for the dances. We were talking at the piggery the other day, 'I don't see the hall at Barthol Chapel any more'. 'Oh, but that's a house now'. I said, 'I was there at a dance on the 5th January 1948'. It was a leap year, you see, and the dance was called Ladies Dance for leap year and every second dance was a lady's choice. I was never off the floor! Oh God, it was great! I enjoyed myself, I mean there was no evil or anything in anyone's mind. You got tea in the middle of it; benches were put up in the middle and you got your couple cakes.

The lady that's got the farm there now called me in to see something. She'd discovered writing on the boards, the old boards they were ripping out when the new steading was being built. She said, 'There's some writing we've discovered and I want you to come and see it'. It was my writing! 'Started sowing 9th April 1947 and finished 10th May! And the next board showed we had started sowing the 5th of March – there was no snow that year. There had been a hell of a storm in '47 but no snow in '48 and we started sowing more than one month earlier.

There were local sports for charity. There was the Daviot Sports. I cycled as far out as Arnage for their games. Ellon Games was one of the biggest. There were the games at Haddo House and at Oldmeldrum – that's going yet. They were all on the go at that time. But, by the time I got older, I couldn't go to everything. I remember even for the Meldrum Sports staying at home and hoeing the neeps till night fall because I couldn't afford to go. But I went to the dance at night – the dancing came first! No money, you see. I was just getting pocket money from my dad; it was a real struggle.

Usually, people stayed in the community. Quite a lot of boys did move away but I don't know what happened to them. I suppose in their own steer, they did well enough; it all depends on what they followed up. Another family – the dad was at Westerton and the boy did the farming – but he had a heart attack and he's gone as well. I think, what I say at this time and moment, is this: 'I don't care, I'm still getting free air to breathe!' I hope never to be a nuisance to anybody. I'd hate to lose my memory. Who was I hearing of who's away with the fairies now? Oh yes, a far-off relation, something to do with my mother, he's six years older than me and away with the fairies! The last time I spoke to him was away back in '95 and he said, 'You know Alan, working on the farm, we don't know of anything else'. And now he's completely lost his memory!

I don't regret anything. I've been very lucky. I worked with my dad for eleven years, but then, through marriage and family and no house and what have you, I branched out and I was nine years working for other people. I never regretted it. I came down to Muchalls on a Sunday and knocked at 'The Lomonds' door to enquire where Stranathro was situated. Mr Keith came to the door, and he told me he didn't know where Stranathro was! He just didn't want to tell me! I went around the village and was back the next day and got the farm.

I had a happy life when I was young. Good pals. I've never been unhappy. I had a good wife, a good person. She qualified as a nurse; she was interested in farming but not the nitty-gritty of it, if you see what I mean. But you can't do everything: you can't have the food on the table and be outside in welly-boots at the same time. A lot of farmers' wives – it's 'Look what they do!' – but don't you go into their houses!

I think to myself, you've only got one pair of limbs, one set! I've always tried to tell the boys, the best guard is your head. Think before you leap!

And now I'm giving up Greenheads here. I'm a 1930 model, seventy-one! But you know what I think I'll do next year? I'll get hold of a dormobile and drive down to Hampshire in June and help with harvest there. Then I'll work my way north, helping at the harvest as I go – and maybe end up in Caithness in October!

David Eric Brown: 5 December 2001

A story to begin with. At secondary school [Mackie] there was this English and maths teacher. He was a Mr M— and he came from Banchory. He'd been all through the war and had had shell shock. He used to twitch all the time. We didn't get on very well at all. So, I went through the school with him and then I left school, and many years later – it was maybe eight years ago – I used to sell cars, and I had sold him a car when I worked at Mitchell's Garage, a new car. Then years later, when I was working on my own, he phoned me up from Banchory and said, 'I've got to give up driving. Would you be interested in buying the car?' It had just done 13,000 miles, he said. 'Oh,' I said, 'I'd be very interested. I'll come over and see it'. So, I did, but it was just an old rust bucket.

However, after I'd seen it, he took me into the house and he started up about his war-time experiences, and what he'd been when he was young. He'd been brought up on a farm, same as I had. He'd driven the horse and binder and he'd ploughed with the horse. And I'm thinking to myself, 'If only you'd just told us this when I was at the school!' He'd said nothing about it then, and if only he had told me about this when I'd been his pupil at the school, I'd have had a different attitude towards his teaching altogether. He was very, very interesting. In fact, he spoke in the Doric. I was amazed at what had come flowing out. And I was thinking, if only you'd been like that in school we'd have appreciated him so much better. He'd been completely different in the school. There, he was pretty hard, a hard man. He had kept his distance from us.

I was born at Burnorrachie [Muchalls] on the 1st March 1935. I canna mind much about it! I came from farming folks. My father was a tenant farmer at that time. Mum was just a farmer's wife. I was the youngest of seven. They were hard times. The thirties were the Depression years; times were very hard then. And by the time I was in my teens, it was war-time. I got hand-downs, never any new clothes, just hand-downs. But the poverty I'm speaking of wasn't the kind where you starved or had no shoes for your feet. We were well enough fed. In fact, they reckon that the diet during the war was the best ever, for health. My mum could make a plate of soup out of nothing. Hares and rabbits used to be an important part of our diet. We'd catch them with the dog. Mother would make soup with the flesh through it – lovely. In fact, if we hadn't had the rabbits we would have starved sometimes. It was a simple diet. For our tea, have you heard of saps? That was our tea, often enough. Just stale bread with boiling water over it and milk on top of that. It was fine. And brose and sometimes, for supper, milk porridge. They'd turn up their nose at any of that nowadays! I never saw a banana till I was ten or twelve.

But I did get sweeties now and then. My father used to go to the auction mart on a Friday and on his way home, he used to buy some pan-drops or some pear-mints. I only ever had one toy of my own: it was a little wooden engine. It was the only toy that was ever bought for me. A bus used to come and take my father to Aberdeen to the mart at Kittybrewster. You'd go and stand up at the top of the road at 9 o'clock and the bus took you in. Then you'd get a tramcar and the tramcar took you to the mart. I went with my father once or twice and I remember that at the mart you got a bite to eat.

I didn't stay off school for it. No, no, you couldn't stay off the school! You never got off for snow – oh, no, the snow wasn't allowed to make a difference. You just had to walk to the school [Muchalls] in all weathers. It was about a mile. In 1942, we had this really bad winter – you know the road up there with the really wide, big dykes, the consumption dykes, on either side of the road? We were little and had to walk to school on top of those dykes. And the school was always open. Sometimes if the snow was really hard you got home at lunchtime but the next day, scarf round the mouth, and away you went again! No excuses – and there were no in-service days then! Oh no, you just had to go to the school!

I come from a very local family. I've traced the family tree back to the 1680s. How many grandfathers would that be…? They were farming folk, all the way through, and all stayed within a thirty mile radius – from Cookney, Kineff, Riccarton, Elsick – all that area. My own father had 48 acres, all arable with two acres of rough. The land fell down to the burn and some of it was pretty steep. We all had to help out. It was hard work in the morning before I went to school, because then I'd have to muck out the byre. Then, after I came home, I had to muck it out again. And then, on Saturday, I used to take in the neeps with the horse. In fact, when I left school as fifteen, I worked on the family farm for a year; I worked the horse for that year at home.

It was hard work – but all I ever thought about at the school was getting out and getting on with work. My brother, Ian, was in farming all his life; Dorothy the oldest sister, she went to Craibstone, but she was married when I was twelve; Mary, she's down in London now; George, he died a couple of years ago – he'd had his own engineering business down in Fife and did very well for himself; and the other sister, she's in Brechin. So, apart from London, we've only spread out a wee bitty! Must have been contented, you see! I've never had any notion of going anywhere else – the way of life here must have suited me!

When I left school, I had a year at home, then I went to work on a farm south of Stonehaven, on two farms down there. I worked on farms till I was twenty-six. Then I went into a garage in Stonehaven; then another commercial garage in Aberdeen, I got onto repairing washing machines with Hotpoint. I was five years with them and then I had a bit of a nervous breakdown. It was quite a hectic job. They put a lot of pressure on you. You did your own area; I was quite a conscientious chap so no matter how many jobs came into my area, I'd do them all before I went home. That worked all right until there was any slack time: with me doing so much in the one day, there would be other days when there wasn't much to do. So then, Hotpoint started saying, 'There's not much doing in your area, we want you to go over to Oban and lend a hand there'. So I'd leave at 5 o'clock in the morning, drive over to Oban and then do a day's work and end up working there all week; and then, the next week, my own area would have filled up with jobs again.

I did it for so long and then I found it all too much. In fact, I took a labouring job for a year after that just to sort myself out. Then I started selling cars at Mitchell's. I did that for fourteen years; I was the salesman there for fourteen years. Then I started up on my own; I did eleven years on my own. I should have done that twenty years earlier; it was the best thing I ever did. You just make money for other people, working for someone else.

1935 was when I was born. I left school in 1950; I was at school from 1940 till then. I do remember the first day. My sister Mary, I can remember her taking me to the school. I wasn't crying, but there were a lot of kids crying. A lot of them cried when they first went to school at that time. It was because they hadn't done any mixing till then. Before you were five, you never really left your mother's apron strings. Some didn't even go to school till they were six. Oh, they'd be really scared, wet themselves with it. But then after, when the young ones came in the next year, you felt quite big compared to them. Oh, it was a very big wrench to go to school in those days.

The school was not a welcoming place either. You just had to get on with it. You see, the teacher had about four or five different classes in the one room. I suppose there would have been about twenty of assorted ages in the one room up to the age of twelve. You went to Mackie at twelve. We just had one teacher for all of us, but for a while another one did come in – Miss Smith. But when I went, there was just Betty Geddes. I think she'd been there a year by then. Her twin sister, Mary, she just did the housework in the schoolhouse and she used to make soup for our lunch, thick soup – different from my mother's! It would have been good enough soup but your mother's cooking's always the best, isn't it?!

Mary did join in with the teaching later on. She was crippled. I don't know whether Betty was ever a graduate or not; Mary was the cleverer one. I never had her as a teacher, but I do know she had the better personality for it. Betty was very strict, oh yes… very strict! You just had to do what you were told. Everything came from her; she was the boss. If you didn't do what you were told, it was the belt. Boys and girls got it. I'll tell you what one lassie got it for. She came from Muchalls village and she had to cross the main road to get to the school at the Bridge of Muchalls. She crossed the road in front of a car and the car had to brake and she got a belting for that. You could get belted for things you did outside the school as well as in it.

135

But you just accepted it. In fact, it would be better nowadays if they got a bit of that. It's a completely different world now… but not a better one. No, then you just knew how far you could go and that was that. In fact, I'd rather have had the belt than some punishment exercise. It was just a sting! At Mackie you got the belt as well. The Rector gave it out. If you misbehaved in the class, you would be put outside the door to stand in the corridor and then the Rector would come along and you had to explain yourself to him. He was always on his round, you see. He was fairly savage as well. I remember one boy – he'd been pestering the Girl Guides, and he was taken to the Rector's room. He came out with his wrists all swollen; you could see every weal. In fact, his skin had been broken. But it did make you behave yourself.

That was Knox, Rector Knox. It was Hutcheson who had a thing about running in the corridors. Knox got scarlet fever and was off for a good while and then Hutcheson came. Then we had to walk down one side of the stairs and walk up the other side and we weren't allowed to run in the corridor. He was strict as well. There was discipline! It's what you expected from teachers. The Benchwork teacher would hit you with a four-by-two stick. In fact, one of the science teachers, Mr –, he used to – you know these metre sticks, sticks a metre long – he used to hit you over the head with them. Side on, end on – not the flat bit! And if you'd gone home to your parents and complained to them about it, you'd have simply got another one. If you'd gone home and said, 'the teacher did this, the teacher did that,' your parents would have given you some more!

. But it was all punishment in those days. Your parents were like that too. I can remember when I was about seven or eight, my sister and I were up in the loft one Friday – my father was away in Aberdeen at the mart and we were up in the loft picking the sprouts off the tatties. There was a skylight and one of its panes of glass was broken. So, young lad, I started to ping the little tatties out through this broken pane. Well, what happened? I hit the other pane and broke that one! O, God, it was the end of the world! I decided I would go and tell my father as soon as I could. So, I went down the road and met him and told him. He just flew off the handle, completely. 'Right, after that, you'll get your bloody licks!' But you didn't get them right away! He'd make you wait till the rest of the family was there. And then he'd make a great thing of it. 'Right!' He took the razor strap that used to hang outside the door; that would come down, and so would your breeks, right there in front of all your brothers and sisters. And you got it on your backside. The fact that your breeks had come down was a bigger punishment than the belt itself. Humiliation! That was the kind of punishment you got.

My father was not unusually cruel. It wasn't in a rage that he did it. It was just the done thing then. He used to make you wait; that was the worst bit. But you didn't often need it. It was a deterrent, no question about it. I never forgot it! It wouldn't have been so very hard; it was the humiliation, the pants coming down like that in front of them all. George Mitchell, he was brought up at Montgatehead, the neighbouring farm to us. Well, just as we'd be walking back from the school, George's uncle Willy, he'd be working in the fields and he would turn his head and cry out, 'Well, loons, did ye get yer licks the day?!'

We respected our elders. I had a good upbringing. There was discipline in it. You knew your place. If anyone came in and was speaking to my father, you weren't allowed to speak. Little boys should be seen and not heard! He had a Doric expression, he'd be speaking to somebody and he'd say, 'Och, haud yer tongue!' I used to think, 'What a cheeky thing to say'. But mind you, he'd be agreeing with them. 'No need to say any more', that's what he meant. But whenever I heard this expression, I'd think, 'What a thing to say to anybody!'

There wasn't any of the rough stuff you get now. Vandalism, oh no! You respected people, you respected things, property. Our games in the playground were simple affairs. We used to play in the woods at the back of the school, but what I really remember is the sand in the playground, because we used to take a stick and scratch out furrow lines in it. We were pretending it was a field back at the farm, you see.

We might have had bikes, but no cars. There were dances in the hall at Cookney. There was never any trouble. New Year's Day, you went round with a half-bottle in your pocket, but the rest of times, it would be lemonade. At the dances that's what they sold: lemonade. You didn't need to drink then to have a good time. And the pubs closed at 9.30.

The church was important. The roads would be black with folk going up to the church at Cookney on a Sunday. The decline was just starting in my age. But you had to go to the Sunday school. I went to the kirk for a while, but then Miss Geddes opened a Sunday School at the school. It was just learning out of the Bible. Boring, it was all so boring. She was just as strict on the Sunday as she was the rest of the week. You wouldn't have done anything on the Sunday that you wouldn't do the rest of the week. If you met her in the road, you would cross to the other side to avoid actually meeting her. You would never have had a conversation with her. In fact, the first conversation I ever really had with her was when I was working for Hotpoint and I had to go to the house to see to her vacuum cleaner. I got on fine with her then. It was probably the first time I'd been aware of her as a human being.

I didn't like school, not really. I was always happier working. In school you felt imprisoned. I remember the relief when you got your holidays in the summer – woo, two whole months of freedom! And then, the week before you were due to go back, you had this funny feeling that something was not quite right with your world.

The schoolwork was very uninteresting. It was just learning, learning. Learning this, learning that. Things like history and geography, it was just learning up the dates of battles and the capitals of the countries and what they made there. None of it was about where I lived; there was no local geography, no local history.

We wrote essays; spelling was important. I can't remember very much grammar work. But it was all boring stuff. No stories, just straight reading books. Arithmetic was the twelve times tables; a lot of time was taken up with that. We just learned it off by heart, just like a rhyme. The day began with a hymn, accompanied by the piano. Then you'd get your sums, then in the afternoon, you had geography and history, stuff like that. You sometimes got poetry to learn off and you often had to read out loud. There was no nature study. I can remember that later, when I was bigger, three of us were put out to do her garden. Oh, what a treat that was! We were really chuffed, just to be out in the open air… it was a great relief. Apart from that, you never got out; you spent the day, feeling closed in.

We got on okay with each other. We were all from the same kind of life. Some folk were from the village itself and one father worked on the station at Muchalls, but the rest of us were from the farms. There were never any minister's children – the one at Bourtreebush had a son who went to the Cubs at Cookney and when I was eight or nine, I got quite pally with him. The doctor was at Portlethen, so his children would have gone there, I suppose. At the castle, there were the McIntoshes: Mrs McIntosh and her man used to come down and do the prize-giving at the school. For the concerts, Mr Haston and his wife came; she used to play the piano and he would play the fiddle

I can let you see some photos of the concerts, I've got them in this album… You see the size of the school – and they managed to put the stage into it! Skinner, the joiner, and Jimmy Ogg, the blacksmith, and Willy Beattie, up at Blackbutts, they put in this stage and then you had to get in at one door onto the stage and all the audience would come in at the back door, the boy's entrance. The school-room couldn't have been much bigger than this [sitting room]. It would be packed. It was the biggest event of the year! It was on for a whole week. Tuesday to Friday, and a finish on the Saturday afternoon.

The school is the same building yet, that you can see from the road. We had desks, about 4 foot long, and 3 sat at each one, with a lid that folded down. There were inkwells along the front. We had slates the first year I was there, but they were doing away with them. The walls were bare; the only time they weren't bare would be Christmas; they used to put up decorations for Christmas. There was a coal-burning stove, bare boards. There were also radiators. It was warm enough; in fact, it was quite cosy. You would hang up your coats just as you went in, in the little porch place just inside.

Of course, these were the war years. We were quite aware of it; a lot of mines went off along the coast and when the air raid siren went off at Stonehaven, we heard it and then we'd all go into the schoolhouse, under the stairs – there was a cupboard under the stairs for us to shelter in. We used to sing songs. It was a funny thing – whenever we came to 'John Brown's body', the all-clear would go. We had gas-masks – not the Mickey Mouse ones – they were for the infants only. We had to put them on every day to try them out. We used to sit there and if you blew into it, you could make it fart; the rubber would just go…

School was relevant to me in the sense that it gave me what was needed. The ability to count, to read, to write – the three Rs. It gave us the basics. But that's all. Now, my wife at Fetteresso, she got more than I did. She got a lot more poetry and English than I did at Muchalls. Her education was better than mine. In a one-teacher school so much depends upon the one particular teacher. But the basics was there. We all left the school able to read and write, every one of us. At the age of twelve, we could handle ourselves in that way. But a lot had been missed out because of these concerts – they took up three months of every year, with every pupil in them and having to learn up their parts.

At Mackie, I got by okay. But in English and geography I was behind; I had missed out. But the three Rs were all right – there, I was as good as anyone else. I managed to settle in no bother. We went on the bus that picked you up at the top of the road. I did find the timetable more interesting – we got metalwork and woodwork, which I enjoyed. I used to look forward to that. But the English and the maths we got were not very interesting. No, Mr M— did not put it across very well. He put it across better in later life when I met him that time.

But I do feel I had lost out on English. At Muchalls, we had reading and writing, but we didn't get poetry or stories or things like that. The books we got were just there to teach you reading – 'Appleseed Ann' and stuff like that. Not very interesting! At Mackie, I didn't get French but I did get some algebra and technical drawing. We also played football once a week; we walked up to Mineralwell for that. We also got physical training every week.

I would have said that I was an average pupil. In this photo you're looking at, all of us came from similar backgrounds and went on to do much the same as myself. All I ever wanted to do when I left school was to work on the farm, but the countryside has changed out of all recognition. When I went to school in the mornings, you'd see the smoke going up from every cottar's fire. Always at the same time. If you didn't see the smoke rising, you'd know that something was wrong. The countryside was thick with activity. It's dead now, empty. The first time I realised how quiet the countryside had become, there was this chap at Catterline who'd bought a car from me, and he couldn't get in to pick it up. So, I said, 'I'll tell you what I'll do. I'll take the car to your house and then I'll walk back to Stonehaven. It'll be a fine, interesting walk for me'.

So I went out, delivered the car and walked back from Catterline. Four/five miles. You know this, I never saw a soul in any of the fields! In my young day, you'd have seen somebody in any of the fields and you could have greeted them, talked with them. And now, if you do happen to see anyone in a field, he'll be stuck inside a tractor and you can't speak at all. The countryside used to be such an interesting place to go into and now it's dead, just dead.

The schooling is a lot different now. I think it's definitely better – if only they had more discipline. There's better equipment now. But, you know, I think we've had the best of it. I wouldn't want to be a teenager now. It's entirely different. TV and computers have changed their lives. My biggest worry about the young people is obesity. Young people, they never walk anywhere! CDs, TV, computers, whatever – they never build up their muscles. Every day I still do my five miles. I'm out before breakfast, out at 6.30, right up past Mineralwell and then back down to the beach and round. Then at 10.30 back out again. Every day: five miles.

Do you know what I was thinking on just this morning? At the school, we used to take in sixpence a week for the savings. Interest in those days was at two-and-a-half percent, and that is what it was for years and years. And now just look at the *P&J* here. It's just gone up to 37 pence. That's 7/6d for your daily newspaper! Three half crowns! If you'd said that to my parents that, one day, the paper would cost that, they would have thought the world had gone mad. My first job on the farm was for £2 a week. This was at Nethercraig when I was sixteen, in 1951. He said he would raise it to £2.10s if I was any good. I got it.

I remember when I was first married, in my 20s. I bought a flat in Barclay Street, a two-room flat and it was all of £200. And now the old school and house at Muchalls has just been sold for more than £110,000…

Norman Harper: 5 November 2001

I consider myself to be a Donsider. My total Deeside experience amounts to five days in the Kincardine O'Neil Memorial Hospital. So I'm a Donsider and went to Alford Primary School for seven years, from April 1962 to May 1969, and then on to Inverurie Academy from August 1969 to May 1975, and then on to Aberdeen University from October 1975. So I'm pretty well steeped in North-East education.

That difference between Donside and Deeside is an important one – at least to Donsiders and Deesiders. The Deesiders, have, quite erroneously, from my perspective, acquired the reputation of being a wee bit uppity; the Donsiders are more down to earth. But, to be quite honest, I don't see any of it – you're brought up with these prejudices. But there you go, you believe it for a long time – and then you learn better!

My grandparents were all farmworkers or farmers, but my mother's father became a haulage contractor and he ran lorries all over the North-East, over Scotland and England as well. He hired a new lorry-driver who'd just been demobbed from the army in '52, and that driver fell in love with the boss's daughter. So that's how I happen to be here; I came along in '57! And I've lived in Alford all my life, forty-five years, quite happily.

I can remember my first day at Alford Primary School – indeed, I can remember before the first day. My first memory of education is refusing to go to the toilet on the morning of my first day at school in case they started without me. I was desperate to get to school because I had heard so many good things about it. It was mostly propaganda, I'm sure, from my parents and older cousins and, especially, my grandparents. So I was desperate to get there, and, unlike for many people, once I got there, wasn't disappointed; it wasn't an anti-climax; I found it absolutely fascinating.

The teacher who taught me for the first two years was Miss McDonald. She fascinated me. I had never come across anyone quite like her before. I have strong memories of her catching me gazing at her; I was just mesmerised by this figure who was standing there, up before the blackboard. I can remember the overall that she wore, the shoes that she had on, the lipstick that she wore, the colour of her shoes, the colour of hair. She was – I was speaking to her just on Friday there – so I guess, she would have been in her mid to late twenties, maybe. She'd been born and brought up in Alford, but you wouldn't know it from her accent because it was Received English: it was all English pronunciation, no Doric cadences at all. So I suppose it was from Miss McDonald that I learned English, because for the five years before that, at home, there was only the Doric.

I met her once outside the classroom, because my uncle had a grocery in the village and he ran a travelling shop and, when my aunt looked after the store, he would come out in his van and go round all the farms. One Saturday, he offered to take me in the van; one of the stops was the farm where Miss McDonald lived with her parents – she was a farmer's daughter. She hopped into the back of the van, and I, being sat in the front seat, wasn't sure whether I should turn round and have a look. I wouldn't say I was frightened but I was apprehensive at meeting a teacher outside the school. I have a vivid memory of listening to my uncle using her first name, which was Lil. It had never occurred to me that she had a first name! It has now passed into history – it's still talked about in the family – that on the Monday afterwards, I'd hovered about after the bell had gone at 11 o'clock for playtime until Miss McDonald asked, 'Yes, Norman, what is it?' 'Please, Miss, my uncle called you Lil!' She just laughed and said, 'Well that might be because that's my first name. But don't tell anyone else!' And I did keep the secret – you always did what the teacher told you to…

The great thing about Miss McDonald's was that her classroom was an old, old classroom and we still used the slates. I know it's usually pensioners who talk about using the slates, but we certainly used them as well. We used Aberdeenshire County Council jotters as well, and round about the classroom, the lower part, the classroom was filled with blackboards, small blackboards, on an angle for scribbling, and below the blackboards, were rows and rows of books. I remember going up to Miss McDonald and asking whether I could use those books. She said, 'Absolutely! Any time I'm not teaching and you've done your work, you must go and use the books'. I did so, frequently, and I think that's what started me off on the written word. Certainly on a love of books, a love of reading. I was always perfectly happy, sitting there, reading.

She was extremely sensitive towards individual needs and differences. My whole primary career was built around four very happy teachers. I know you've had interviews with people with terrible memories of their primary school and, yes, there were moments when I was apprehensive. But I've got nothing but praise for the education I got at primary school. I can see that because I had four teachers in seven years and there were ten teachers on the staff, I can guess that if the permutations had fallen in any other way, it could have been a disaster, because there were some pretty sharp teachers on the books. But I was handed on from one to two to three to four, and each of them brought something different, and I just adored them, all four of them. Well, not so much one of them – she was a bit sharp.

She was of the old school – she's dead now – but the great thing about her was that as she was one of the old school and she force-fed me the rules of grammar, spelling, punctuation. The others would have done too, but in a much more gentle way. But because, I suppose, I was frightened of her, I did learn these things thoroughly. So from that point of view, she was good for me, I suppose.

But she was a strict disciplinarian. I didn't much care for her at the time. To be honest, when I knew I was going into her class, for the last four months or so of primary 2, I suppose I became a bit withdrawn. I knew then where I was going, and she had a reputation throughout the school. In fact, I remember the first day of primary 3 and going into Miss McDonald's class and sitting in my old desk. I remember having to be prised from it: 'I'm sorry Norman, but you're not in here any more.' I don't know whether I burst into tears or not…

The reality wasn't quite as bad as I feared it was going to be, but I remember she got extremely irritated with me when I once asked a question: 'Please, Miss, are there tatties and mince in heaven?' She just looked… you know how Captain Mainwaring used to give that look – and said, 'Stupid boy!' So I never asked her any more abstract questions. It all made me feel rather small and I realised that it had been a stupid question. So I never asked anything like that again.

She had these very small pince-nez glasses and piercing blue, blue eyes. Just a look from her would have set your hair on fire. I'm told that in social circles she was a delight. But then you didn't mix with teachers socially. In fact, as far as I was concerned, they probably didn't even go home on a Friday but just sat in the cupboards all weekend. You wouldn't see them, speak to them; you only saw them in the classroom, from 9 a.m. to half past three. I know her first name now, it was Frances, but then, we only knew her as Miss A—. And a fiesty old dame she was.

She was excellent for me, I can't fault her. But several of my colleagues got severe leatherings from her in front of the class. You know some people will tell you that they sat there terrified. I have a conscious recollection that most of us sat there raging at the injustice of it all. It was punishment way beyond what the original offence merited – for chatting in class, things like that. One time it was for an incident in the handwork class when one chap to the left had wanted a ball of wool of a particular colour, and the chap who had it flung it across the room, and she spotted this and gave him a severe beating. It wasn't so much the fact that the strap had been used but, in those days, you were put across the knee and, although it wasn't bare bottom stuff, it was bare back of the leg stuff – the boys wore short trousers then.

I know one parent went raging up to the headmaster and demanded to know what had happened. From my perspective as a seven year-old, I didn't find out what the outcome was but my parents told me that this mother had gone up to demand to know what had happened exactly – and we all thought that this was what should have happened. I guess that most were 'fairly handled'. So, of the four teachers I had, she was the one I liked least. But I can't fault what she taught me.

The next one was a delight, Miss Stewart, Jessie Stewart, for primary 4 and 5. The thing I liked about her, I could tell, even as an eight year-old, she had a wee bit twinkle in her eye and had this sort of eternal grin. You felt you could relax with her. She was still a teacher of the old school and was a stickler for grammar, for spelling and punctuation. For instance, when we had English composition, she wasn't averse to seeing a few Doric words and that was very unusual for the '60s because Doric was regarded as slang, definitely not to be used in English compositions!

In my experience, if we used Doric in class, the teacher would pretend that nothing had happened. There wouldn't be a punishment, no verbal reprimand, but a frown or a glare – a silent 'We don't tolerate that kind of thing here!' Anyway, I remember writing this exercise for Miss Stewart in Primary 4/5, in which I used the word 'galluses' for braces and I remember the exercise being handed back and, as she did so, she said something like, 'Well, that was an interesting word you used there, Norman, so I'm going to give you an extra mark for being so enterprising – but I'm going to take it away again because you've misspelt it!' And I remember, years later, oh, I must have been in my late thirties by that time, and she was retired for twenty/twenty-five years, and was almost bent double with osteoporosis, and she was walking past the front of my parents' house. And my father said, 'Now, Miss Stewart, here's somebody you'll recognise!' And then, from this immense stoop, she looked up at me and she said, 'I'll always remember you as a small boy,' and then just walked on. And that was the last I ever saw of her: 'I'll always remember you as a small boy... '

No, I cannot recall having any real feelings about all this classroom control of language, none at all. It didn't occur to me till years later that, in some ways, I had become bilingual. It was a natural switch, made the moment you went into school uniform – you just switched. I never thought about it, you weren't aware of doing it, nobody taught us to do it, you just did it. It was just the way it was. Nobody spoke English to me before I went to school; nobody spoke the Doric to me at the school, and, within months, weeks even, at school, I was speaking 'proper' English at the school, and speaking the Doric at home. The switch seemed perfectly natural and it never occurred to me to do anything different, or that Doric was regarded as inferior at school, or English as superior at home. They were just two equal languages being spoken for different purposes, in different situations. I had no feeling of deprivation about any of this; we spoke Doric freely at home, English freely at school, and it never occurred to me that there was any distinction to be made between the two. Not until years later, when I was speaking in a professional capacity at a school, and it suddenly flashed into my mind – these people are bilingual, which means I must be bilingual too! It had always seemed natural to move from the one to the other, without any consciousness being involved, without thinking about it.

How Scottish was the curriculum? I don't think it was particularly Scottish. There were huge gaps in my knowledge of Scottish history until I made a conscious effort as an adult to put that right. We learned more about the Rump Parliament, Cromwell's period, and English sea-shanties and that kind of stuff. It was as if the curriculum had been prescribed in London, not Edinburgh. And it didn't occur to me till years later, that I was deficient in Scottish history. However, there were, I must say, a few seditious teachers in my primary school; in fact there must have been a little nest of sedition at Alford Primary School because some of the teachers did teach us bits of Scottish history that – I learned later – were not on the curriculum. We also got some modern languages – all sorts of things we didn't know at the time we weren't supposed to be getting. But... English sea-shanties! 'Bobby Shaftoe', which didn't mean a thing to any of us, and yet around the coast, thirty/forty miles away, there was a huge oral tradition and a musical tradition from the fishing industry, and there were bothy ballads – but we didn't do any of that. It might not have done us much good, but at least it would have been our own North-East heritage, not some sea song from Bristol. But we didn't know, we didn't have any perspective; we just accepted that this was history, that this was music.

There was no use made of the environment, no field trips, next to nothing of that kind of thing. I can recall only one, and that we were so mesmerised in being out of the classroom, that we just wandered about in a daze. It was a botany trip, or something, to two fields outside the school, where we played anyway, and because it hadn't been explained to us that this was something called a botany trip, we didn't know what was going on. We didn't go into the village, go through the bakery shop, or any of the kind of things they do nowadays. It was all quite classroom-bound, using prescribed texts, which came from Aberdeen, Edinburgh, or even London.

Geography consisted of the capitals of the world. I have vivid memories of the map of Scotland. I can quote you now all the colours of all the thirty-three counties of Scotland on that map. I remember Miss Stewart would catch me gazing at that map and say, 'For goodness sake Norman, if you don't stop staring at that map, I'm going to turn it to the wall!' Years after, I'd written a column about that map in the *P&J* and then got a letter from a former teacher, in which she had told that she had actually taken that map, which had by then served its purpose, and put it in the loft, and only thrown it out just weeks before. She told me, if only she had known, she would have given it to me. 'Aberdeenshire-pink, Invernesshire-yellow, Perthshire-brown… '

Most of our learning was by rote, the learning up of facts. History, too, was like that: '1066, 1314… ' but I took to it all; I loved it!

Some of the pupils were slow, but I know for a fact that when we got into primary 7 everyone of us could parse, everyone was literate, everyone was numerate, our spelling was good, and we had a store of general knowledge. I could tell you what the capital of Uruguay is to this very day! It wasn't very detailed stuff, it was superficial, perhaps, but it served you well in the future. Rather than a detailed knowledge of specific subjects, we had been given a good broad general knowledge.

We had tests every day. We had a daily mental arithmetic test, from the 'Seven a Day' book. The form was: the teacher would call out sums, we weren't allowed any pen or paper, there were to be no workings out, except to jot down the answer, and the person who got all seven right stood up and got a round of applause from the rest of the class, a willing round of applause. I was top of the class in primary 5 and can well recall the rest of the guys in the class coming up and slapping me on the back for beating the girls. It was normally a girl, and it was very important for male pride to get a boy at the top of the class.

I know this is sounding rather idealistic… I would say we were fairly diligent. There was no backchat. As your older interviewees will tell you, parents, especially in the country, still saw value in education. Consequently, you had the impression that they were more on the side of the teacher than on the pupil, the child. It never occurred to me not to work hard at school because the teachers made the atmosphere for learning so congenial. It was enjoyable, fun to do, even in Miss A—'s, because she clearly knew her stuff and we listened to her because she was the teacher.

The school sat in the middle of the community. We all respected it. I have a memory of the deputy head – I was being sent to the butcher on a Saturday morning, and the deputy head was being served in the queue, ahead of me. He said, 'Good morning, Norman', then he turned to the butcher, and said, 'This is Norman, who likes school so much, he wishes he would open it up on Saturday and Sundays! 'And I thought, 'ooh?' I remember walking home and wondering whether he was joking or not.

He was a local. I never encountered a non-Alford teacher till I went to secondary school. They were figures in the community, though I wasn't aware of it at the time. They played a part in the church, the social clubs, they were very active in the theatre club, which ran in Alford in the '60s, and all of them were members of that.

143

It was a real community, partly because it sits in the middle of its howe. The Vale of Alford is surrounded by hills and that gives you a feeling, not of being cut off, but of being quite separate from the rest of Aberdeenshire. It was quite an introspective place. The village itself then had about 700 people, but it was in its dying days as a real centre, as a railway terminus – that ended in 1965. It had a thriving mart, four garages, two shoe shops, three hotels, three bakeries, four hairdressers. I remember the cricket pavilion and the pitch.

It was a real farming community. A good place to grow up in, I would say so. I can never understand nowadays when young people complain of being so bored, that they've nothing to do, because we didn't have play-stations, video recorders, computers in the '60s. But I've no recollection of anyone being bored or depressed. I know this is the phrase that every old sod pumps out, but we made our own entertainment! We just wandered the highways and the byways. And we felt perfectly safe – though my mother did give me a dark warning to be wary of people who might stop their cars and ask the way. 'Don't give them directions, because they'll take you away to Africa!' So, whenever I was out as a kid on the bike, I was worried about the traffic behind me, because in those days a car was a rarity – my parents didn't have one till I was sixteen. Yes, it was a good place to grow up in; everyone seemed to rub along together.

I would imagine that this quality is replicated elsewhere in the North-East, though maybe not to the same extent, because not everywhere else would have this sense of being cut off. But I imagine Torphins and Tarland, or Foggieloan and Rothienorman, for example, would be much the same.

I can recall one of my fellow pupils, who is now an orthopaedic surgeon at the ARI [Aberdeen Royal Infirmary], coming to the school with a piece of scandal on the Monday morning. He told us that one of our teachers had been to his house for dinner that Saturday night! We all crowded round, 'What did she eat? What did she say? Did she go to the toilet?' There was this feeling that they didn't have an existence beyond the classroom; there was a mystique about them. That might apply to others in the community – the minister, the doctor, the banker – the traditional professional class of the rural community. Most of the rest were artisans, farmworkers, people serving the community. Very few commuted to Aberdeen then, although my own mother went on the train every day to work for Aberdeenshire County Council in Union Terrace. But most of the population worked there: it was an agricultural community, and most of the children would have been expected to grow up to go into agriculture.

Certainly, from my point of view, it was a conscious aim of my parents that I was to go on, get out and go to university. I was the first from my family to do so. Not that my parents were stupid by any means, certainly not, but I suppose the opportunities and the finance didn't exist for them in their day. But for me, it was a mark of prestige, as it would have been in any community in the North-East. I still bear the scar, even though I'm forty-four, that I didn't complete my university course. I still feel a sense of failure that I didn't fulfil that destiny.

I was down to be a doctor, but I just couldn't stand the university. I left before the second year exams because I couldn't stand university life. It wasn't so much the course, but the life that went with it. It didn't sit well with a young man from the country; the two lifestyles were so disparate that I couldn't adjust to the university, to the social life, to the regime. There was no personal support, though I do remember some people pleading with me to give up medicine and switch to an arts course, and I had to explain that it wasn't the medicine that was the problem, it was the university that was the problem. But probably I was the problem, not the university!

I remember learning to read and to write, the shape of the letters, the syllables. We were all given tests at the end of primary 1, when we were asked to read a passage and write a prescribed passage, to copy it. Based on the results, we were then divided into five streams and Miss McDonald, the teacher, then put all her efforts into the strugglers, trying to help them catch up, and just a little less effort into us, though still plenty of effort for the top stream, as it were. But I was conscious of her spending more time on the strugglers and trying to bring them up.

One of the chaps in that category – I was actually speaking to him on Saturday night, we were talking about education, and I told him I was coming here today. He still says that, as far as he is concerned, the primary school was the best thing that happened to him, because even though he was a struggler, and he had to work really hard – this was the same guy whose mother tramped up to the school to demand justice when he was strapped that time – he now runs his own business and he says that compared to the staff he's getting now, our grammar, our spelling, our punctuation, were really hot. We were just expected to reach the required standards.

If there were new arrivals, they just got sorted out. You know, people coming in. There was one from Aberdeen who decided we were a bunch of hicks and she had to show us; but the girls put her right, and she toed the line and became a hick herself, a local. I remember one young Englishman, whose father had been born in the Howe – but he'd been born in England and his father then returned to the Howe – and this chap came up, and was telling us all how things should be – but we sorted him out. Not physically – we just encouraged him to see things from a different point of view! He responded well; he still lives in the Howe, and a finer chap you couldn't come across.

Then in primary 6/7, we went to Miss Walker. There had been this children's programme on BBC about some kids who ran their own newspaper. I thought this was fascinating and went up to Miss Walker to ask if there was any chance I could run a class newspaper. She's actually written the foreword for my latest book, and she said, 'okay, but in your own time; I can't help you because I know nothing about newspapers.' So, we ran a newspaper and produced all this voluntary work. It must have been mesmerising for the teachers to see the boys, particularly the boys, willingly producing all this written work. There were news stories, jokes, cartoon strips, fiction – and I was the editor, of course! It had been my idea. I remember Miss Walker telling me that I had gone up to her and said, 'We could quite like to run a competition, but what can we do for prizes?' And I remember her, dipping into her own purse and handing over half-a-crown. So, we bought ten packets of crisps, at three pence each, and every week we handed one out as a prize.

In the April of my final year at primary school, I think, I sat the eleven-plus and passed. Alford was not a six-year secondary school in those days, and the theory was that the best way to handle the switch to Inverurie Academy for those pupils who were going to go on to a fifth and sixth, was to switch them early, at the beginning of the first year, and leave those who were probably going to finish after the fourth year at Alford, and then, if any of them wanted to go on, they could make the switch then.

So the six of us were sent to Inverurie Academy and I remember feeling extremely depressed and unhappy and apprehensive at switching to a place I'd only ever been to two or three times before. I remember my parents having to talk me into it, tell me that this was the best thing to do. And I did it, not because I was looking forward to it, or saw the sense in it, but because it obviously meant a great deal to my parents.

Inverurie was an excellent school, but, socially, it ruined me. It made me awkward socially because – it wasn't the people or the teachers there, there was nothing wrong with them – but, if you have someone from twenty miles away, he is neither the one thing, nor the other. I was now regarded as a different beast by the people I'd left behind at Alford, but I was never quite one of the crowd at Inverurie, because, obviously, I went home on the bus at ten to four each day, so I could never stay behind for any social activity. I had a sense – I'm talking personally here – I had a sense that it wasn't that I was no longer welcome but that there was now an awkwardness with the people I'd grown up with. So I was left in a social limbo, and the five others felt the same. So, on balance, if I'd been able to carry on and get the same type of schooling at my old school, I would rather have done that. It probably wouldn't have been such a rounded education but I wouldn't have been left…

We were separated for life, more or less, at the age of eleven. I still see – I was talking to one of them the other day, and there was an unconscious, an unspoken realisation that for each of us our life experiences had been different. I trace that back to 11th August 1969 and I wish, in some ways, I wish, it hadn't happened. But then, what would I have been denied if it hadn't happened? What have I gained because it did happen?

August '69 to May '75. I have vivid memories of being lined up in the playground and being absolutely terrified because, from a school of, maybe, 250 pupils – that's both the primary and the secondary – I'd been moved to a school of 1,200, at the age of eleven. I felt very small and insignificant. So, we were lined up, and the six of us from Alford were almost clinging to each other. It must have been quite pathetic to look at. But they didn't separate us, because we'd all been placed in the top stream, all six of us. And we were sent to our register teacher, virtually dumbfounded; we didn't know what to do, what to say; we were terrified every time the door opened, because we didn't know what was going to come through it. It was like living in a horror film.

I settled down quite quickly, but there was this sense of the new, and it unsettled us. I hated it for the first couple of months, at least. I used to go home very unhappy because I no longer felt an Alford person. I suppose I came from a fairly working class background and of the five others, one was the minister's son, one was the deputy head's son, one was the banker's daughter, one was the doctor's daughter, one was the MP's daughter – James Davidson, the MP for West Aberdeenshire. The five of them and me! And if you know anything about social dynamics at all, when somebody from a working-class background moves into a middle-class milieu, that compounds the social problem of moving into a new experience. I felt that I got on perfectly well with the five others; we were friends of seven years, boys and girls, but I was conscious that parents – not my parents but other parents – in the village, thought the family was getting above itself. The parents of the other five were perfectly civil, if you met them in the street, but there was no sense of any mingling beyond that. They would chat in the street but that was that. I imagine that there was a sort of social determinism at work, yes.

On the whole, the first few months at Inverurie were not happy ones! Once I got settled, I did get used to it, but the fact that I had to leave every day at ten past four did mean I missed six years of social life, and that didn't set me up very well for university life later on. I have vivid memories of being sent out of the classroom – not as a punishment or anything like that – but I was sent down to the office for something; this was within about two weeks of beginning there, and I was feeling very small and insignificant, I must say. Inverurie is set up in such a way that the school offices are at the end of a very long corridor, about 100 metres long, and this classroom was right at the other end of it. This was during school time, so the public areas of the school were completely empty and, as I stepped out of the room, so the headmaster left his office and came walking towards me; it seemed as if we were the only two people in the whole school and there I was, an eleven year-old from Alford, already feeling very small, and thinking, 'What on earth is going to happen here?' He's walking towards me, and I'm walking towards him, and I can feel the sweat pricking out and the red face coming, and he's walking towards me, and I'm walking towards him, and I'm thinking, 'What can I say? What is he going to say to me?' And, as we met in the middle of that corridor, he just passed me and said, 'Good morning, Norman!' I remember being very impressed that here was this man who must have had to learn hundreds of names, all within a fortnight or so, and he knew who I was! That probably was the beginning of the end of my feeling of complete isolation at Inverurie.

This was the great Dr Dixon. He had this great trick of being able to memorise all the pupils' names – no, not a trick, a facility. There's a revisionist theory abroad that he didn't think so much of the non-academic pupils, and he was certainly the one who told me I was going to be a doctor, and who pushed and pushed for it. I know it shows a lack of will in me, but I thought, well, if that's what he sees in me, that's what I've got to be. Whereas, what I really wanted to do was to work in the media; but to express an ambition like that would have made me seem stupid, I felt. If I'd said to my parents, 'I don't want to be a doctor, I want to go into TV', they would have said, 'Don't be ridiculous! What do you think you're doing? You're going to be a doctor, a doctor!'

This was the philosophy of the school in general: good pupils went to university and became a doctor, a teacher, a lawyer. Bankers, even, were regarded as rather 'modern'. The professions were regarded as the thing; I felt I was selected from the third year for one of them. All my curriculum was designed, not because it was to be found enjoyable or rewarding, but to act out the assumption that I was to go on and do medicine at Aberdeen. The curriculum was probably the standard one that you would find in any other secondary school. English and maths were the core, modern languages, history, geography, sciences, with an opt-out and an opt-in at the end of the second year, and then at the end of O grades.

The teaching style was much more belligerent, I'd say, than at Alford. I had a class teacher who seemed to regard it as his life's work to humiliate me as frequently as possible for the amusement of the rest of the class. To their credit, they didn't seem to find it especially amusing – probably because they feared one of them might be next in line for the treatment. Then there was a French teacher who used to bounce me off the blackboard, for something fairly inconsequential; I wouldn't say I had a great natural facility for modern languages, but I can't say she was picking on me, especially as several others got the same. But if you meet any of us nowadays, and the subject comes round to Miss C—, we all say at some point, 'Well, she might have been a holy terror, but she certainly taught us our French!'

I'm not sure, however, being taught by fear works, to be honest. I think my primary teachers were far ahead of their time, and if their ways could have been applied to the secondary school, I feel that would have been much better. There might be reasons I'm not aware of in educational science why they can't be applied but I felt at the time, that if they had used the same approach, it would have been so much more productive.

I wrote her a letter, you know, the French teacher. I'd been on a business trip to France with the *P&J* and all this French came pouring out of me – from where, I had no idea. I was extremely impressed, not with myself, but that she had taught me so well. So I wrote her a letter and thanked her very much for all she'd done for me, and told her that, although it hadn't been a class I had particularly enjoyed, I couldn't fault her for what she had achieved. But there was no reply for five months, and then I got a Christmas card, and, in the same feathery hand, it said that she was always delighted to hear when her work had been of benefit to anyone. Yes, she did remember me and, no, I shouldn't be so hard on myself for thinking I was a struggler, but she thanked me very much for writing to her. Then two months later, her death notice appeared in the *P&J*. I was sad about that, but so glad that I'd written that letter.

Then and now? I, obviously, have no detailed knowledge of how education is carried out now, but I can tell you what the results are, because I'm in charge, not of training itself at the *P&J*, but I do play a heavy role in training the new journalists. And I look at the test papers we set for trainee journalists, and I despair at how they are using the language, just the mechanics of the language – the grammar, spelling, and punctuation – and I get the impression that, with aspiring journalists, they don't see the personal need for grammar, spelling, and punctuation, because that's what sub-editors are for, to take care of such things. But that's taking no pride in your own work. You wouldn't hire a mechanic who didn't know one end of an engine from another, so why have a journalist who doesn't know about grammar, punctuation, and spelling? It's a question of attitude towards work, of having a philosophy of what an educated person is.

It's a seamless generalisation, I know, but the philosophy now seems to be, 'I have made this life decision, I will do the best I can, as far as I am able to do the best I can. But, if I fall short in any particular, it's not incumbent on me to do anything to improve it, because other people are coming along behind me to clear up my mess.' I see this time and again, and it annoys me. It annoys me that people are prepared to accept this as the standards for the new century. We should be explaining the practice and the principle of being a journalist, and of the basics of a good education. I don't mean to be disparaging about those who were teaching in the '70s/'80s, because I know this policy was handed down from on high, and they were just as frustrated about it as the rest, but I think it's fairly clear that the results of this education mean that the people who had their education in the '70s/'80s, even '90s – I don't know – haven't had the same basic grounding my generation had.

The compensation is that they are much freer and more at ease in social situations; they can relate to people a lot more. That's why we hire journalists who don't have the mechanics of the language but who are brilliant at interviewing people, who relate to people, who can draw people out. So they make excellent journalists in that respect, but not in the other. So where do you draw the line? Not sure… it's more of a *me* culture now…

Oh dear! I would never have dreamed that I'd be sitting in Muchalls in the year 2001 and be speaking like some old fuddy-duddy! Isn't it awful! I once spoke to a lecturer from Glasgow and he said, he took everything that people told him about dropping standards with a pinch of salt, because he found that what everyone claimed was that it was the year after they had finished, which was the year when standards began to drop. That's what the people who finished in '75 said about those who came later, and what people in '65 said about the generation of '75, and so on. It's all relative. So I suppose I'm guilty of that. I suppose if I was training someone whose education had finished in '85, he would claim that the rot set in '86… I don't know.

There's a certain integrity in values about the North-East. The education reflects those values – I can't be certain how unique these values are, because the North-East is the only place I've ever lived in, but I'd be prepared to put a lot of money that just about everyone of my vintage, or slightly younger, would be prepared to tell you that that's just the way we are. Not just in education, but in most things that matter. There's this work ethic; if you can't afford something then you just can't have it. HP and credit are anathema to most people out in the country. I wouldn't dream of entering into an HP agreement. If you can't afford something, don't get it! Wait till you've saved up! I still operate on that basis. No short cuts, no loans. This springs from the morality of the North-East; I can't imagine that this applies to the same extent elsewhere, not in Aberdeen. But by the time you go to Dunecht, going out towards Alford, most people would have this mindset.

We are talking about the past. Now, social mobility is such that the Alford I knew is not the Alford of today. I'm not saying this as a matter of regret, but the people I was born and brought up with in Alford, feel, I know, the same way. You barely get any Doric nowadays from school pupils; you never really hear people using Doric words in the playground at Alford. I'm very conscious of that, because I sometimes walk down to the village at lunchtime, and I listen to what they are saying, and it bears no resemblance to what we talked about thirty/forty years ago. If I used Doric words to them nowadays, they wouldn't even think I was just being quaint – they'd think I was some kind of a pervert! They would think I was just an old mannie and very strange. They'd probably listen intently, then go into a huddle, and burst out laughing as I walked away.

I sometimes wonder if primary teachers realise two things: that they have an immense formative influence, not just on the seven years of primary education, but on their pupils' whole lives; and secondly, if they are aware that their pupils are much more alert, even the slow ones, at picking up signals all the time and modifying their behaviour accordingly. If the students who are training to be primary teachers knew the immense influence they are going to have over whole lives, seventy years or whatever, they'd be petrified! Certainly, that's what's happened to me: scarcely an hour goes by of my waking existence that doesn't refer back to what I learned at Alford Primary School – even more than Inverurie Academy. The skills I use, the social skills, the intelligence – or lack of it – the life experience, the way I behave in treating other people, in working hard, in simple things like that – abstract things, moral values, all sorts of things. Everything, in some way, I can trace back to those four teachers at Alford Primary School. It's an extraordinary responsibility to have and, if you hit a bad one, if the primary pupil hits a teacher he hates, I hate to think of the effect that will have. Far more than the educational psychologists realise.

I was lucky, I hit four excellent ones and in the right sequence. They had an enormous effect, far more responsibility than a doctor; a doctor does not shape your entire existence; the banker doesn't; a teacher certainly does. A huge responsibility. A frightening thought.

North-East Education: Interview Schedule (given in advance to interviewees)

Individual details

Own background
Primary School
Secondary School
Later involvement personal; parental; professional

General memories

Early days: initiation; contrast with home world; family attitudes; fellow pupils; classroom layout and routines; pains and pleasures; travel to school; playground activities.
Later: transference to secondary; as above.

Features

Curriculum – range, academic character, role of arts and games; role of exams; child or subject centred.
Ethos – role of rewards and punishments; discipline; attitudes towards learning difficulties; relationships with teachers and among pupils (of all backgrounds); work ethic.
Teacher – status in community; status in your eyes; teaching styles; age and gender.
Language and Culture – attitudes towards the language and experiences of the home; how North-East (or Scottish) the curriculum was.

Retrospect

Then and now – profit and loss; how much change has there been?
How typical do you think your experiences were?
What has happened to your classmates since?
How well did your school serve you – and them?
Standing of education, teacher and school in your/the community – then and now.
How 'North-East' and how 'Scottish' do you judge your education to have been?

Anything else?

NB: the above is intended as a series of suggestions only – please feel free to select or to elaborate. It is not the intention to hold anything but a relatively informal interview/ conversation. It is your memories and your opinions that count.

Appendix Two

In and Out the Classroom: That's the Way the Doric Goes

David Northcroft

Example 1

How long is the Scottish dialect to last? When will it be put on the shelf with other specimens of antiquity? At what epoch of the world will controversies occur as to the meaning of its words, and be referred to the decision of the learned, not the vulgar? Judging from what passes around us, we should say the period is not far distant. Within our own day a very sensible change has taken place; and in the classes of society where, in our youth, the broadest Doric prevailed, we find few remains of it but the kindly tone and accent we should be sorry to part with. As for the higher classes, there it is lost altogether. Inquiring lately of an old Scotchwoman as to the individuality of a lady who, she said, had called on her, we asked whether her visitor was English. 'Oh, that I dinna ken,' was the reply; 'they a' speak sae *proper* noo – there's nae telling the differ.'

'Ballantine's Poems', *Chambers' Edinburgh Journal*, 5 (1855), 350.

Example 2

She could certainly handle a strap. Somebody or other would get it daily. Probably for backchat or for inattention or for going outside without permission – you always had to be properly excused for that, however desperate you were to get to the toilet. But things have changed completely now. And I think this is where I get my great chip on my shoulder from – the treatment meted out to our own Doric language. It was literally drummed out of us. When we were speaking in the playground it was one thing, but as soon as we entered that classroom door it had to change completely. The only concession was, I remember, one poem by Robert Burns and another by Charles Murray – two poems in the whole of that time. I don't remember any Doric prose at all. Not in my whole time there. So it was standardised English for us right from the start. That was the rule.

I remember one lady who came in and played hymns with us. We would be singing 'The Lord's my shepherd' and she would cry out, 'No, no! Not the Lord – *theee* Lord…' She had the whole lot of us going from 'the' to 'theeee' and it just didn't sound right. She was overemphasizing in order to drum our own 'tha' out of us, and ended up with something that was neither Doric nor English!

> Retired accountant and present-day broadcaster (Robbie Shepherd); schooled at Dunecht and Robert Gordon's College, 1940s.

Example 3

School was completely separate from your home life. Whenever you got home and out of the school door, in the playground it was all Doric, ye ken. Your teacher spoke English, you see. The two were separate; it was a different language. You couldn't go up to the teacher and speak Doric, not even outside. The teachers kept it up all the time. That was your education. If you were educated, you spoke English! It was the mark of being educated. That was the attitude, and is still the attitude!…

That's why we have this reputation for being dour and quiet because we're not sure what we're supposed to say. I made mistakes, I affronted myself with the wrong words. I mean, I'm now going on sixty and only recently have I got more confidence. Only recently, if I've been saying something in Doric and the other person doesn't understand, I don't feel obliged to translate because they live here too and it's up to them to understand. Especially if they've been living here a long time. Whereas, you always felt you had to accommodate the stranger, the person who didn't speak our language here. You always felt you had to adapt to them because that's what you were expected to do…

A friend of ours, —, he was second dux at [a north Aberdeenshire school] and he was seventeen. He was asked a question in a science class and he said, 'Aye!' – it was a yes/no question. And he was sent home! But now, there are so many English teachers in the schools and they don't even understand what the children are saying.

> Barbara Denoon, daughter of Violet Cassie (see Example 4), schooled at Strichen and Mackie Academy, 1940s/50s.

Example 4

We didn't speak Doric in the classroom. If you did, you got a scolding and if you insisted on doing it deliberately, you got smacked. No, no it was very confusing when you went new to the school. It was very hard for all the kids, with the

Buchan dialect and all that. The first week or two when you got to school, you'd be learning to read out loud – it was like a foreign language – it had to be Standard English, and ye couldna spik it! In the family or on the farm it was all Doric. You had to learn two languages – and you hadn't much time, you had to learn it pretty fast. I was speaking about Miss Taylor, who had all the little ones; she used to go to the WRI and tell jokes and things about some of the things the little kids said. And this boy, —, his father was a shepherd, and he went to school, you see, and he had on this suit and a little waistcoat and some men at the farm gave him this watch, and he said, 'Gad a' michty, Miss Taylor, is it nae near lowsin time yet?' She got great fun – but she explained the right way to say it to him, you see. That was fun – you went to school and it was completely different. You couldn't understand the way you had to change your tongue, you see. You just learned it, just learned it!…

It doesn't bother me, it's just my language. I can understand it in a way, not being allowed to use it because you're going to go away because not everybody's going to bide in the little bit they were brought up in, in Strichen or around the Mormond Hill. You're going to be travelling and you've got to have a universal language they can speak, and that would have to be English, I think. The only time you got to use Doric, or a Scots word, was in the singing lessons when you had a Burns song or something like that. Then you were allowed to use it. But for just speaking, oh no!

> Violet Cassie, 82 year-old farming widow, various schools in Strichen area, 1920s/30s.

Example 5

We didn't speak Doric in the classroom. We did in the playground but, whenever you went in, you switched. It was a problem to start with. I can remember one boy who was reading and came to the word 'bull' and he said 'bull' ['u' as in 'umbrella']. 'No, no! It's not "bull", it's 'bool'. Now say it properly, "bool, bool!"' There were a lot of things like that, with various words. When you went home, your father and mother would be speaking Doric and they would be talking about 'the bull' right enough. But when you got to school you suddenly had to change it to 'bool'. I think that was all wrong. It was something we had to worry about that we shouldn't have had. Yet my Doric was as broad when I left school as it was when I had entered it. In fact, I'm as broad now as ever I was. What made me go back to it was 'Scotland the What'. I just loved all that. They had the right Doric.

But one advantage we had was that we could change when we had to. I did learn proper English as well as my own language, and I could use it when I went out into the world. But we could have used them both in the school and we didn't. The Doric was treated as dirty, as something low and foul. 'Not nice!' But if Doric is spoken properly, it is nice to listen to. That Mr —, when I met him in later life, my old teacher, he was good to listen to then. He spoke nice Doric then.

> Eric Brown, retired farmworker and car salesman, schooled at Muchalls and Mackie Academy, 1940s.

Example 6

In the classroom you had to speak proper English, Standard English. I didn't find that too difficult. When you're reading, Scots is just counted out, anyway. So we'd use English in the classroom and then just slip back into Scots afterwards. After all, the books were all in English, but in the playground we could just get back into our everyday language. It's only now that they are trying to bring the Doric back; now it's going, they're getting worried that it'll disappear altogether. And when you communicate in the street you hardly hear real Scots now. It's all Standard English now.

Of course, there's Robbie Shepherd in the paper… Now Robbie Shepherd, his father was a soutar over at Dunecht. He keeps the Doric going with his column in the paper each Monday, but, really, it's not so easy to read as English. You're just not used to it, not in writing, you see. And a lot depends on the district you come from, too. Some of the words he uses are new to me – I reckon he makes some of them up! But at school we didn't find it difficult to switch from one to the other. After all, your reading, the books you read, and the papers too, are all in English. You just associate English with your reading, with the books at school and elsewhere. English was the school language – and that was that.

> James Edwards, 76 year-old retired farmer, schooled at various places in the Mearns, 1930s.

Example 7

We were not allowed when we read out in the classroom to read in our own dialect. I must say – and here I must be careful – a lot of people give a superficial impression of what was going on; you see, some people write with venom that we Scots were not allowed to use our own Doric, Lallans, or whatever, that that was all suppressed. The fact of the matter was, the medium of teaching was English. That was accepted by the parents, by everybody. Perhaps it was a great pity that more attention wasn't given to poetry in the Doric, although we did get some. But I think the fact of the matter is that English was universal for teaching and that it has become the universal language for human life. English has become the lingua franca because dialect, the Doric, is no longer understood even locally, far less nationally and internationally. When we have a world language like English, it opens the world up for you, then regrettably the local working language is dying out. That is happening quite notably during my lifetime.

James Michie, retired educationist, schooled in the Mearns, 1930s/ 40s.

Example 8

No, I cannot recall having any real feelings about all this classroom control of language, none at all. It didn't occur to me till years later, that in some ways, I had become bilingual. It was a natural switch, made the moment you put on the school uniform – you just switched. I never thought about it, you weren't aware of doing it, you just did it. It was just the way it was. Nobody spoke English to me before I went to school; nobody spoke Doric to me at the school, and within months, weeks even, at school. I was speaking 'proper English', and speaking Doric at home. The switch seemed entirely natural and it never occurred to me to do anything different, or that Doric was regarded as inferior at school, or English superior at home. They were just two equal languages being spoken for different purposes, in two different situations. I had no feeling of deprivation about any of this; we spoke Doric freely at home, English freely at school, and it never occurred to me that there was any distinction to be made between the two. Not until years later, when I was speaking in a professional capacity at a school, and it suddenly flashed into my mind, these people are bilingual, which means I must be bilingual too! It had always seemed so natural to move from one to the other, without any consciousness being involved, without thinking about it at all.

Norman Harper, journalist, schooled Alford and Inverurie, 1950s/ 60s.

Example 9

But some schools, they do have Doric classes now. (Speaker 3 interjects: 'But that's a terrible admission, to have to have Doric lessons! It's a terrible admission concerning our self-regard'). But we've all got into the habit of using English because folk don't understand us if you don't. We've all got into the habit of using English! I've lost all the words of my father's and Uncle Tam's. All the words they used, the real auld Scots words, because nobody would understand what you was saying and so you gradually stopped using them.

Speaker 4 (Violet Cassie).

Example 10

However, I do have some optimism for the future. At least about our local culture. The work being done by Leslie Wheeler and Sheena Blackhall is a great work. But there again, the work that Leslie does for example, is of his own free will. There was a time in the '60s and '70s when a musician friend of mine was going around the schools and getting paid for it. But now they've cut back on that and also on the provision of instruments for youngsters. That's a real deprivation. But they are now getting a greater chance to study the local culture – the Elphinstone Institute is so important for that. The university is now holding out its hand to the rural community. Yet, you get people saying that Doric is doomed, that we no longer use the old farming terms, that the rural way of life that gave it its vocabulary and its texture has gone. That there's no Doric word for 'helicopter' or for 'computer' and so on. But the same thing could be applied to Gaelic and look at the money that's being poured into that! I counter the arguments against that by saying, 'Well, the Gaelic lobby have come up with bilingual programmes, they run a national Mod, so it's right they should get the support!' It's up to us to do the same; we're only on the first rung of the ladder.

I recognise the problems; the life of the land is ebbing away, I know. But that makes it a cause worth fighting for. I was doing an interview the other day with an 'enterprise' lad out at the Brig o' Don and we were talking about rural depopulation and the fact that at present we're not using our natural resources in the way we should. We've overfished, we've overfarmed, we've cut down trees; the land's been overworked and as a result the rural community has fallen away. If we want to reverse that – and we surely must – then we've got to bring the people back into it. And if it's accepted that the rural community has to survive, then the tongue has to be part of it, the living Doric.

Speaker 2 (Robbie Shepherd).

Commentary

The question posed by the anonymous reviewer in the April edition, 1855, of *Chambers' Journal* (Example 1, above) is still very much with us. So, too, are the issues which are listed as surrounding it: the problem of definition – dialect, speech variant, subset of English, or a language in its own right; the pace and force of the social changes that assail it; the perception that 'nowadays' it is only the older generation which uses it; the relationship within a community between local oral patterns and social class; the diluting effect of immigration (i.e. by the 'English'); the popular association of Standard English with 'proper' speaking.

What has shifted, perhaps, is the extent to which these various influences have had the opportunity to work their further pressures on, or rather against, the Doric – or, indeed, any strongly marked form of regional language. Yet, given that we are now 150 further years down the line of decay, and in the midst of a range of forces which our early Victorian ancestors could not have clearly envisaged – television, radio, the oil industry, a clamant youth culture, the rise of popular consumerism, and the globalization of the media, and of the market place among them – the very fact that we can still ask, 'How long is the Scottish dialect to last?', must point to some degree of survival, however unlikely that would have appeared in 1855.

In the experience of many, the most powerful agent of all is the one that is not mentioned in *Chambers'* – the national school system. The piece was written sixteen years before the Act of 1872 brought in a state-controlled scheme of universal education; although at its time of writing, the legislation which gave Scotland its celebrated 'school in every parish' had been in force for some two centuries, its operation had been entrusted to the local presence of laird and minister; school attendance for the 'peasant' and the 'labouring' classes tended to be a patchy, short-term and voluntary affair. Within a generation, that was to begin to change: seven to eight unbroken years of school career for everyone; a curriculum controlled centrally by the 'Scotch Education Department' and its mechanisms of standards, tests, and code; the prestigious target of the 'Highers'; the ubiquitous vigilance of Her Majesty's Inspectors; the growth in secondary education, slow and cautious at first, but later accelerating to the point where, today, all pupils have come to be nationally examined, and the majority of them expected to proceed to some form of higher or further education.

The testimony offered by the accounts quoted above would confirm the common perception that the highly efficient and organising Scottish education system is one that has, historically, set out to give each of its charges a standardised form of English as his or her educated speech; and that, frequently, this has been achieved as an imposition, backed by punitive measures and a repressive approach to the individual child's home language.

Not all of the speakers, however, would wish to have been able to resist the process. Doric, they have accepted, might be the speech of the hearthside and of the playground, but 'English' is the medium of education, and that is the way it just has to be. It is, moreover, the one widely accepted form of our written language – because of this, it is the Doric which, when translated into print (Example 6), can seem the artificial and difficult proposition. More personally, some (Examples 4, 6, 7, 8) explain that what has been at work is a properly educative procedure which has given them an important resource – the ability to cope linguistically with the full range of social and vocational situations of their time and of their place. They see themselves, most usefully, as having become bilingual.

While none of the witnesses would appear to question the validity, or practicality, of an approach that places the goal of standardised English at the centre of the classroom career, others claim that it has been pursued with exclusiveness and an unfeeling zeal which has led to disproportionate loss. For them, their own language has not so much been supplemented as relegated, cast out into the educationally marginal zones of the playground or the after-school home life. The fact that it might be granted the occasional airing as an annual Burns piece or Charles Murray recitation (Example 2) only confirmed the impression that no form of Scots was to be regarded as a normal and wide-ranging medium of pupil-teacher communication.

For these speakers, most of the resulting controversy has centred on the personal impact that this policy of apparent extermination has had. This ranges from phlegmatic acceptance (Examples 6, 7, 8) through a retrospective sense of contradiction and absurdity (Examples 4, 5), to a bitter feeling that the growing child's own identity as a North-East Scot has been under sustained assault (Examples 3, 5).

As these witnesses retrace their school steps – and, along that journey, evaluate the longer-term effectiveness of what their education has given them – there is a realisation among some of them that what has been at work was not merely a form of school discipline, or a practically appropriate induction into the ways of the wider world, but a sustained scheme of cultural remodelling. As Speaker 5, in particular, recognises, the impact on the unformed sensibility is likely to be more than a temporary uncertainty: the consequence can be a sense of pained alienation from the whole academic environment and the frigidly impersonal terms in which its teachers habitually address them. The result for this evidently intelligent and thoughtful individual, at least, was a rejection of all that the teacher had to offer, an early leaving and, half a century later, the revelation that it could have been very different. Even for those who stayed the course (Example 3), the feeling of diminishment and resentment could be lifelong.

As the testimonies cited earlier have indicated, such consciousness of injury does not appear to be universal. It is, however, difficult, half a century on, for either speaker or listener to unpick the entanglement of personal, social and intellectual factors that will be at play in the attempt to account for the contribution of any one aspect of one's schooling towards the life that was to follow. It is, for instance, possible to posit that in the case where an elderly resentment is being lodged, a spread of causes – psychological or economic, perhaps – will also have been at work in generating the alleged outcome. But it is equally plausible to argue that where there has been the claim that a standardised English had to be acquired at the cost of the home language – because that is what the school or the world 'is like' – the linguistic and cultural colonisation has been so insidiously complete as to lead to the obliging assumption that the Doric, as the unrefined utterance of the primitive native, must be expelled.

Observations such as these lead into issues of democracy and of political power. Each of these speakers is reporting, with whatever degree of acceptance or dissent, a conflict between the inherited values of their region and their home, and those imposed, necessarily or no, by the national system of education. And in a region which, historically, has prided itself on being the nation's strongest representative of the traditional claims of the Scottish school to be the local place where all social backgrounds may freely mingle, and where even the most humble lad is equipped to 'get on' in life, the implications are especially challenging. How democratic can a system, where the individual's very own language is so discriminated against, be? How can its teachers practise a welcoming respect for each single child, when the home language and the place he or she comes from is liable to be subjected to daily denigration? And how distinctively 'Scottish' is the vaunted national system when it insists on expelling from its curriculum what has been for many the essence of their Scottishness?

These are questions which are not easily penetrated. Answers to them will be as much a matter of interpretation on the part of the listener as of the speaker. And for both parties, the conclusions are subject to the influence of the individual's own particular life experience and the ideological shaping which it will have received. Here, it can be said that of the overall total of thirty-five interviewees only Speaker 3 appears anxious to shift the account of profit and of loss onto an explicitly political level. And, to repeat, for each view which has pointed to a sense of deprivation, there has been another which has been content to react to the whole process as being part of a wider linguistic and social evolution, which the school was obliged to assist, in the interests of preparation for life 'as it is'. Nevertheless, it is impossible to ascertain the extent to which such 'realism' was as much grounded in the respondents' general acceptance of the prevailing institutional structures, or in a contentment derived from personal success in managing their own way through them, as in any more widely considered view of the matter.

Clearly, to follow the ebb and flow of response in a total of sixty hours or so of biographical testimony is both a complex and a sensitive task. What we are encountering in these mature reminiscences is not only the passage of a region's culture from one age to its next, but a series of individual reports on the effectiveness with which a particular schooling has prepared their speakers for the life to come – as it was then, as it is now, and as it appears to be ever moving onwards. At this point, it may be useful to introduce a ninth witness who is now in a position to look back over sixty-five years of educational experience and to assess how effectively the North-East education he himself received has served his language, and, with it, his personal development.

Example 11

We all spoke the Aberdeen lingo at home and in the playground – that's what I was brought up on. But coming into the school, you changed into the English, into polite language. I call it 'polite' because of its comparison with the Aberdeen lingo, which seemed to be much more racy and less formal – that was the language you associated with using with your friends and in your personal life.

But my language was mixed in with my country connections. As a boy of five or six, I would go out and stay with my Auntie Annie and Uncle George, who stayed at Netherley where they lived on this croft, a proper working croft. There weren't that many of those around Netherley because it wasn't really a crofting area, but theirs was a proper working croft of about five acres and I'd go there for my holidays. I was always delighted to get into the country for the holidays, away into the country. I felt at home there, more so than at Esslemont Avenue back in the town. I enjoyed the atmosphere of being there, of being with the hens and with their one cow that they milked every day and with the sheltie – the light horse that they kept for work about the place. And Uncle George, being a crofter, used a scythe for cutting the corn and I remember him being there of an evening, sharpening his scythe ready for the next day's work.

I've always held that picture in my mind. A bit idyllic no doubt, but so different from being stuck in the back end of the town. And I enjoyed that difference, the fact that I could escape from the two-room tenement and get out into the freedom of the open air. I liked the contrast, liked the contact with the animals; it gave me a freedom so that I always wanted to return to it straightaway, whenever I got back into the town. It all made a very strong impression on me, those sojourns in the country at the ages between five and eight or so. My mother's mother was also staying with them out there – I don't know how old she was, probably only in her sixties – but to all of us she was 'auld granny' in contrast with the other one who lived in Chapel Street. The granny in Chapel Street was very much a town woman, very sociable, liked visiting, the odd game of whist, and so on. Whereas Auld Granny was a girnie old body and a law unto herself, but she still had her function, would do odd jobs about the croft. She's a figure that stood out in my memory. She had only a few ragged old teeth left and had great difficulty in chewing her food. I used to watch fascinated as she was at her eating. I've actually written a poem about it – it's in Scots, in the Doric, needless to say [see below]. That's what they all spoke there, out at Netherley. I've inherited a mixture of the two – if I'm with one group or the other for any length of time, I'll lapse into the appropriate language. You have to get into the patterns; it takes a while to re-enter, but after a bit, I'll pick it up again and away I go.

The speech thing is important to me. I find if I've written any poetry – and I've done this for a long time now, both in English and in Scots – but the only ones that really work are the Scots ones. I haven't yet knocked enough together to make up a collection, but I keep writing away from time to time. Some of them seem to me to be quite good – and they're the Doric ones – conversational, familiar, the intimate, personal ones. They are the ones that link back to the time I was a child. I suppose it all depends on what is natural for you; the formative influence of the language that surrounded you in childhood is very strong. That's where my most personal language has come from, that's the place where my most natural feelings are.

None of this came into the classroom. There, you would never have dreamed of speaking Scots. I've never felt bitter about it; it's what you simply accepted that you had to do as part of your education. But I do think there were difficulties for me. I think I had to struggle with the English a bit, struggled to learn how to express myself in English. It's partly because I was quite a sensitive young guy, maybe had a bit of an inferiority complex. For example, I found it quite difficult speaking in public and, as a boy, speaking out in class. It's a feeling that persisted into adulthood; I don't know why exactly. My father had something of a speech impediment and that might have given me a heightened awareness of the importance of getting it right – of using the right English.

My speech was full of complexes – it's where they all met. It took me a long time to work them out, to resolve them. To confront them, even. My education is bound up with all of that. It takes a long time to work through all those differences – between yourself and your home, the way education can create that difference. Language is at the centre of all of that. If you want to make language more than a simple tool for conversation, if you need it to express ideas and your own feelings too, then the way I was brought up was bound to create problems for me in knowing which was the right language to use – in developing your own voice, in knowing what that voice is. In fact, I've had to master a range of languages. That's obviously included Standard English – I needed that to grapple with complex academic ideas – and that was always a bit of a struggle. Not that I didn't learn to do it… but it's impossible even in my advanced years to leave behind the fundamental questions – they're still part of you. You can't escape.

But all that hasn't necessarily been a bad thing. The effort to overcome the problems, the problems of articulation, that can be a driving force. It's an experience that can help you to sympathise with others, to understand the difficulties they may have had to overcome in trying to express themselves, in finding their own voice.

Peter Murphy, retired teacher and current county councillor (author of the paper on R. F. MacKenzie)

The speaker is a seventy year-old man who grew up in a working-class tenement in Aberdeen during the decade before the Second World War. He attended first, Mile End Primary School and then, being judged to be academically bright, went on to the city's Grammar School. University and an English honours degree followed, before his entry into that most respectable of professional destinations for one of his background, a career in teaching. Here, the progress was, on the face of it, straightforward and assured: by the '70s, he was headmaster of a large secondary school; on his way to that eminence, he had returned to Aberdeen Grammar School, there to spend several successful sessions as a member of staff.

It is a career which testifies to a completely successful assimilation into the culture of Standard English, of national examinations, and of academic discipline – the traditional hallmarks of the Scottish way. Yet, as the words reveal, the match achieved between individual and linguistic environment, between formal role and personal needs, never did become a fully mutual one. Something has been left over, a sense of emotional satisfaction and communal identity that can only be grappled with by a recourse to the intimacies and the sense of belonging that must, forever, it would now seem, be rooted in the first language of the home and of the neighbourhood.

What this witness is really talking about is linguistic diversity, as it has come to be in society at large, and as it has, or has not, been developed within the individual. His account tells us that if any one of us is to lead a life of wholeness and of easeful self-expression, then we must be allowed the verbal resources to do so. Our education must engender within us the ability not only to play a range of parts but to be able to work out just where, for the particular self, the root of the matter really lies.

Here, it has to be pointed out that as many as one-third of the witnesses – all native to the North-East as well as educated within its public schools – would recognise their home language to be 'English', albeit spoken with the accents and the cadences of the area. For them, the challenge of linguistic accommodation was that much easier to meet, the possibility of personal fracture correspondingly remote. But for those who have been brought up within its structures and amidst its most common reference points, the Doric can never be regarded as just another register, one whose survival may be ensured by granting it the occasional set-piece airing against a near-monopoly of standardised discourse. And even for those 'English' others, a full participation in the life of the people among whom they lead their daily lives would, likewise, demand a greater involvement than that.

Above all, the interview catches someone in the act of articulation – of attempting to understand where his language(s) have come from, where they have given him strength and where they have created uncertainty. The abrupt immersion at the age of five into the formalities of 'English' was, he realises, fundamental to establishing the schism he quickly suffered between home and the world of education, one that was exacerbated by the fact that here was a labourer's son thrown, by his own native cleverness, into the west-end environment of Mile End Primary School and the Grammar School. The long-drawn-out struggle to cross that gap has involved more than the mere acquisition of an extra facility with language: for him, a set of personal allegiances, his earliest sense of self, were also being redefined and, to an extent, set at a distance from what he was now to become. And although the new skill was to act as an immensely important part of his ability to move through an academic career and to manage his profession, it never did, on its own, become sufficient to reach into his most intimate self, to discover his 'own voice'.

Yet, it would be wrong to see this process as predominately negative. Growing away has also meant growing up. The effort to master the language forms, standard to our society's intellectual negotiations, has extended not only the range of his own words but that of his human sympathies as well, has given him the expressive insights to be able to engage with the complex rigours of modern existence.

What is notable in all this is the speaker's recognition that a language is an expression of a community, of a way of living. In that conclusion lies both a justification for the present day school's adoption of Doric, and a caution against it. The life on the croft at Netherley in the 1930s was even then something of a marginal pursuit. Sixty years later, it is not even that. Almost certainly, Uncle George's place will have been converted into either a commuter's residence or be a professional consultant's tele-cottage.

We are separated from *Chambers' Journal,* and the anxieties of its 1855 edition, by more than simply the passage of time. The whole nature of our North-East life has changed, and changed utterly. One of the pervasive themes of these witnesses' recollections is the immeasurable distance between then and now. Sitting in their comfortably furnished and centrally heated rooms, the fitted carpet beneath their feet, the TV and video-player in the corner, a car or two in the drive-way outside, they lose themselves for a while in the memory of a Buchan or a Mearns of bustling little rural communities, of village streets full of local stores and craftsmen's workshops, of passers-by who would always stop and speak, of permanently unlocked doors, of clubs and societies and a kirk to which most families still walked out at the end of each shared week. And just beyond the last corner shop, the intricately patterned land of farmtouns and of smallholdings that stretched away towards an Aberdeen made remote by the hour-long bus ride and the self-sufficiency of their own entirely local satisfactions. To listen to Speaker 5's interview (see Appendix 1, pp. 138–39) is to join him in knowing that a whole countryside has died away, and with it the very sources of his old language's communal points of meaning.

Against such an emptiness, the current drive to rehabilitate Doric by utilising the very academic means that once worked towards its dying can seem no other than a painful – and at this late date wholly artificial – admission of past dereliction (Example 9). Certainly, any attempt to introduce its rhythms and its textures into the contemporary classroom must be guided by a frank recognition of what, in the 21st century, the Doric can, for its younger citizens, possibly be. And yet to listen to each of these witnesses is also to be reminded of the importance of the personal voice, and of the speech that is rooted in the communities of childhood, to make any sense of what our own lives have meant to us. And for that sustaining power, only a language which has been enriched by the fullest available range of human experiences, inherited as well as contemporaneous, will serve. In the ecology of 2003, more than ever before, there are choices to be made. And that, as Robbie Shepherd suggests (Example 10), is a matter of resource, of having regard for what we have inherited, for what we wish to conserve, for what we need to set growing once more.

Example 12

Auld Grannie

Auld grannie's mou aye held me in its thrall,
  Or so it seemed, at meals, the chawin', grindin', ritual
Scunnert me. But she wid hae her full,

162

Afore gyaun awa oot tae dae her chores
(On the craftie on the hull, wi' its chappit doors.)
Cairyin watter frae the wallie, bakin' scones,
Pokin' up the fire, burnishin' the bronze,
Peelin' tatties, sweepin' the flair o' steer,
And noo and than, milkin' Bessie the coo.

Airms akimbo she staunds in an auld snap
Side on tae the camera, glarin' at it, daunder up,
'Dinna fash yersel', she'd say, 'I'm ill-taen
Wi a thae new-fangled ferlies, the wheen
O' them. Amph'. She'd say nae mair.

That nicht in her neukie at the fire she'd bear
Witness tae the winters tholled, dykes fill'd wi' snaw,
Blin' drift on the roadie, hands frozen raw,
Milk and water solid, beasts roarin' for their feed,
The wood ahint the craftie silent as the deid –
Nocht but the real coorse widder, nae plooin', grun ower weet
Spring feart tae mak a showin', enough tae gar ye greet!

The tully lamp's hiss-hissin', wind howulin' in the lum,
Connachs a' her caiklin', as she sinks intil a dwam.

Peter Murphy – 'Written on and off during the 1990s'.

Note on Research Background

With the exception of Example 1, each of the above speaker extracts, used or referred to in this paper, is taken from a series of audio-taped interviews carried out by the author, working in association with the Elphinstone Institute of the University of Aberdeen, during the twelve months beginning October 2001. They are part of a research project, the overall aim of which is to build up an oral history archive that will be made up of individual accounts of the experience of going to school in the North-East of Scotland.

Examples 2–10 consist of extracts taken from one-to-one interviews, each of which runs to some eighty to ninety minutes, recorded in a secluded, informal setting (in nearly all cases the interviewee's own home). For this purpose, the subjects were invited to 'tell the story' of their own schooling in approximate chronological order, and to do so with sufficient flexibility to set it in the context of the respective environments of time, place and social circumstances. The interviewer (the editor of this volume) also raised a number of generic issues at appropriate moments in the interview, such as 'discipline', 'relevance', 'teaching methods'. One of them was 'language' – the discourse used in the classroom as compared to that of the home and of the neighbourhood. The selection set out here, above, is taken from their responses to that specific question.

The subsequent procedure has been to write out a complete transcript of the interview and then to send a copy to the speakers so that they may make any amendments that they judge to be necessary. The accompanying advice is to confine these to points of fact: any additional, or 'second thoughts', comment to be forwarded as supplementary, or 'follow up', material. An agreed record is then arrived at and a final copy sent to the speaker.

To date, thirty-five 'older' (ages 48 to 99, 16 male, 19 female) subjects, all of whom have received the whole of their schooling at establishments in the North-East (i.e. present-day Moray, Aberdeen, Aberdeenshire, and Kincardineshire), have had their experiences recorded. In addition, six 'younger' subjects (ages 21 to 29) have also been interviewed. It should be noted that while nine different speakers are represented in this paper, and three of them through two separated extracts, the more general aspects of the commentary have been informed by knowledge of what the sample as a whole has reported. It should be clear from the text where this has occurred.

Selection for interview has been made on a networking and opportunistic basis. The initial subjects came from the author's own circle of acquaintants: subsequent word-of-mouth recommendation has extended the circle. The essential criteria have been North-East schooling and a span of available memory sufficient to reach back over more than one generation. Because of the nature of the author's own previous career (in education) and of his home location (Muchalls), two occupational backgrounds have so far predominated – farming and teaching. It should also be noted that all but two of the interviewees (see Example 8) are either completely retired or are no longer in their original mode of employment (Examples 2 and 10).

The author is aware that the interview itself may be categorised as a particular species of language encounter and that however 'natural' and open it may have appeared to be, a certain degree of construction is inevitable, as in all linguistic situations. Responses will be shaped, in part, according to the speaker's implicit (or explicit) consciousness of the specific situation, which will, of course, include the interviewer and his inferred purposes. Here, it should be noted that the latter is an exciseman's son who went on to a 32-year-long career, first in an Aberdeen school, then in teacher education at the local College of Education. It must further be recorded that he lived and went to school in a number of localities south of the border until the age of fourteen, at which time his family settled in Banffshire and he spent four years at Aberlour High School, followed by degree study at Aberdeen, then Cambridge University. Given this background, no claim on his part to speak the Doric 'naturally' would be credible. However, he is fully accustomed to its usages, having been immersed in a broad range of North-East speech patterns for some forty-seven years, and he would certainly claim to understand and to be able to respond to them. As far as he was aware, none of his interviewees modified their normal informal speech for his benefit, beyond what would be expected in dealing with a lengthy personal interview. Nor did the recording apparatus – a simple and unobtrusive pocket-sized machine – appear to generate inhibition, or even, after the opening minute, be noticed.

Memory, its vagaries and its constructions, will also have played a shaping role. Here, it may be said that not only is this an inescapable influence in any act of distanced recall but that, in terms of 'inherited' belief and tradition, it is the *perception* of what has been experienced that will make up the legacy to be passed on, whether to be cherished, conserved, modernised, or rejected. Any considered account of what has constituted the 'North-East school' experience will naturally resolve itself into a mixture of what is reconstructed as the 'typical' flow of events, punctuated by an occasional and personally significant piece of drama – an unjust punishment, a daunting test, a favourite teacher's praise, the painful repression visited by some feared authoritarian figure, and so on. These are the highlights that will settle in the memory, there to be transmuted into a shared folk knowledge and, as such, become the basis for opinion and appraisal.

Although all thirty-five 'older' speakers were speaking in the accents and tones of the North-East, only eight could be said to be employing a medium which would customarily be recognised as 'Doric' – and in each case they came from an agricultural background. Of these, five would be typified as 'broad' in the sense that an outsider might experience some uncertainty in picking up more than, say, 80% of the delivery. They include, here, Speakers 4 and 6, but not 3, the daughter of 4. Not one of the 'younger' six could be said to fall into this category. All of the 9 Speakers represented in this paper would, however, describe their own original language as 'Doric' but in the case of Speakers 3, 7, 8, and 12 English would appear to have become their habitual form of speech, and the Doric a secondary resource to be reverted to, and, with some self-consciousness, according to the situation. It is also worth noting that of the total thirty-five, twelve would claim that their natural 'home' language was not Doric but English, and as such was close to what the school demanded of them. Seven of these came from a professional (teacher) background, but there were five of farming/working-class origin who reported that their parents took pains to ensure that, even at home, it was English that was used by their offspring.

Reviewing all of these factors, it must be concluded that the project that is the basis of this paper cannot be said to constitute a scientifically controlled programme of investigation. It does, however, present a sample of a growing range of detailed case studies, each of which has the depth and the commitment, by both speaker and interviewer, to offer authentic evidence of what the experience of going to school in the North-East of Scotland has been for a number of its representative inhabitants, both as lived encounter and as considered retrospect.

Select Bibliography

Basic Documentation

The Statistical Account of Scotland, drawn up from the Communications of the Ministers of the Different Parishes, ed. by Sir John Sinclair, 21 vols (Creech: Edinburgh, 1791-99).

The New Statistical Account of Scotland by the Ministers of the Respective Parishes, 15 vols (Edinburgh: Blackwood, 1845).

The Third Statistical Account of Scotland: Volume 7, *The County of Aberdeen*, ed. by Henry Hamilton (Glasgow: Collins, 1960); Volume 10, *The County of Banff*, ed. by Henry Hamilton (Glasgow: Collins, 1961); Volume 17, *The Counties of Moray and Nairn*, ed. by Henry Hamilton (Glasgow: Collins, 1965); Volume 29, *The County of Kincardine*, edited by Dennis Smith (Edinburgh: Scottish Academic Press, 1988).

Education Enquiry: Abstract of answers and returns made pursuant to an Address of the House of Commons, dated 9 July 1834, Parliament: House of Commons Papers, 133 (London: 1837).

Education Commission (Scotland), [The Argyll Commission], *Report on the State of Education in the Country Districts of Scotland* (Edinburgh: Constable for HMSO, 1866).

Education Commission (Scotland), *Third Report of Her Majesty's Commissioners...Burgh and Middle-Class Schools* (Edinburgh: Constable for HMSO, 1868).

[Menzies, Allan], *Report to the Trustees of the Dick Bequest for the benefit of the parochial schoolmasters and schools in the counties of Aberdeen, Banff, and Moray, after ten years' experience of its application* (Edinburgh: Blackwood, 1844).

Menzies, Allan, *Report of twenty-one years' experience of the Dick Bequest for Elevating the Character and Position of the Parochial Schools and Schoolmasters in the Counties of Aberdeen, Banff, and Moray, embracing an exposition of the design and operation of the parish school* (Aberdeen: William Blackwood; Edinburgh & London: Brown, 1854).

Laurie, Simon S., *Report on education in the parochial schools of the counties of Aberdeen, Banff and Moray, addressed to the Trustees of the Dick Bequest* (Edinburgh: Constable, 1865).

Laurie, S. S., *Report to the Trustees of the Dick Bequest on the rural public (formerly parochial) schools of Aberdeen, Banff and Moray, with special reference to higher instruction in them* (Edinburgh: Constable, 1890).

Laurie, S. S., *Dick Bequest Trust: General Report to the Governors, 1890-1904* (Edinburgh: Constable, 1904).

Wheeler, Les, and Sheena Blackhall, *The Elphinstone Kist: The Official Doric Site* (Aberdeen: Elphinstone Institute, University of Aberdeen, 2002), <*http://www.abdn.ac.uk/elphinstone/kist/* > [accessed 1 August 2004].

General Educational Histories

Anderson, R. D., *Education and Opportunity in Victorian Scotland: Schools and Universities* (Oxford: Clarendon Press, 1983).

Anderson, Robert, 'Education and Society in Modern Scotland: A Comparative Perspective', *History of Education Quarterly*, 25 (1985), 459-81.

Anderson, Robert, 'In search of the "Lad of Parts": The Mythical History of Scottish Education', *History Workshop Journal*, 19 (1985), 82-104.

Anderson, R. D., *Education and the Scottish People, 1750-1918* (Oxford: Clarendon Press; New York: Oxford University Press, 1995).

Northcroft, David, *Scots at School* (Edinburgh: Edinburgh University Press, 2003)

Scotland, James, *The History of Scottish Education*, 2 vols (London: University of London Press, 1969).

Periodical and Pamphlet Literature

Aberdeen Censor, 'A Chapter on Schoolmasters', 1 (Aberdeen: Smith, 1825), 223-28

Aberdeen Censor , 'The Autobiography of Caleb Concord', in several parts (Aberdeen: Smith, 1825).

Aberdeen Magazine, 'The Autobiography of Rory McFigh', [Ogilvie, John], in several parts (Aberdeen: Davidson, 1831).

Aberdeen Magazine, 'The State of Education in Scotland, 1 and 2 (4 parts) (Aberdeen: Davidson, 1831/32), 61; 250; 343.

Aberdeen Magazine, 'Remarks on Parochial Education in Scotland', 2 (Aberdeen: Davidson, 1831/32), 395-406.

Northern Iris, 'Bye-gane Days', April 1826 (Aberdeen), pp. 94-97.

Bulloch, J. M., 'Billy Dey', *Aberdeen University Review*, 3 (1916), 103-14.

Donaldson, William, *Popular Literature in Victorian Scotland: Language, Fiction and the Press* (Aberdeen: Aberdeen University Press, 1986).

Donaldson, William, *The Language of the People: Scots Prose from the Victorian Revival* (Aberdeen: Aberdeen University Press, 1989).

School and Teacher Histories

Barclay, William, *The Schools and Schoolmasters of Banffshire* (Banff: Banffshire Journal, 1925).

Bennett, Richard, *Elgin Academy 1801-2001* (Elgin: Moravian Press, 2001).

Chambers's Journal, 'The Parish School of Kemnay', 9 (1841), 412-13.

Cormack, Alexander A., *William Cramond, M.A., LL.D., 1844-1907: Schoolmaster at Cullen, Researcher in History* (Peterculter: the author, 1964).

Dixon, Norman, 'Comprehensive Education and the Small Burgh School ', in *Education in the North* (Aberdeen: Aberdeen College of Education, 1965), pp. 19-22.

Downie, Duncan A., Donald M. Morrison and Anna M. Muirhead, *Tales o' the Maisters: A History of Kemnay School, 1820-1948* (Kemnay: Time Pieces, 1995).

Duff, John, 'Ait up yer Pizzers Laddie', [Schooldays at Midmar], *Leopard* (September 1999), pp. 6-9.

McLean, Douglas G., *The History of Fordyce Academy: Life at a Banffshire School, 1592-1935* (Banff: Banffshire Journal, 1936).

[MacGillivray, William] *Rob Lindsay and his School: A Reminiscence of Seventy Five Years Ago, 'by one of his old pupils'* (Edinburgh: Hay, 1905).

Michie, Mary, 1988, 'Strichen Schooldays', *Heirskip* (1988), 13-15.

Murphy, Peter A., *The Life of R. F. MacKenzie: A Prophet without Honour* (Edinburgh: John Donald, 1999).

Nicol, Alisoun S., *Tak Tent o Lear: A History of Dunnottar School, Stonehaven* (Stonehaven: Dunnottar School, 1990)

Nicol, Peter L., *Ramblins o' a Dominie: 'Peter Nicol Looks Back'* (Inverurie: Nicol, 1995).

O'Dochartaigh, C., A. Jaffray and M. E. Sutherland, *Esslemont School Centenary, 1881-1981* (Aberdeen: Schools Resources Service, 1981).

Shanks, Alastair, 'The Changing Village School ' [Strichen], in *Education in the North* (Aberdeen: Aberdeen College of Education, 1965), pp. 55-60.

Simpson, Ian J., *Education in Aberdeenshire before 1872*, Publications of the Scottish Council for Research in Education, 25 (London: University of London Press, 1947).

Simpson, Mary, 'Education around the Foot of Bennachie 100 years ago', in *Bennachie Again*, ed. by Archie W. M. Whitely ([Aberdeenshire]: Bailies of Bennachie, 1983).

Smith, Graine, 'The Crofter who Dedicated his Life to Teaching', *Leopard* (July 2000), pp. 4-5.

Smith, Robert Harvey, *An Aberdeenshire Village Propaganda Forty Years Ago* (Edinburgh: Douglas, 1889).

Thomson, Charles W., *Scottish School Humour* (Glasgow: Gibson, 1936).

Wood, Sydney, 'Education in Nineteenth Century Rural Scotland: An Aberdeenshire Case Study', *Review of Scottish Culture*, 7 (1991), 25-33.

Young, Alexander, 'Education ', in *The Book of Bennachie*, ed. by Archie W. M. Whitely ([Aberdeenshire]: Bailies of Bennachie, 1976).

Youngson, Flora, *Dominie's Daughter* (Aberdeen: Centre for Scottish Studies, University of Aberdeen, 1991).

Local History

Bridges, Roy, *People and Places in Newmacher Past and Present* (Newmacher: Newmachar Community Council, 2001).

Buchan, Jim, *From Parish School to Academy: The Story of Education in the Parish of Peterculter* (Aberdeen: Aberdeen County Council, 1967).

Buchan, Jim, *In Schoolboard Days 1872-1919* (Aberdeen: Aberdeen County Council, [1972]).

Cameron, Archibald Cowie, *The History of Fettercairn: A Parish in the County of Kincardine* (Paisley: Parlane, 1899).

Callander, Robert, *History in Birse*, no. 3 (Finzean, Aberdeenshire: the author, 1983).

Carter, Ian, *Farm Life in Northeast Scotland 1840-1914: The Poor Man's Country* (Edinburgh: Donald, 1979).

Cranna, John, *Fraserburgh: Past and Present* (Aberdeen: Rosemount, 1914).

Duffus, H. G. and Stanley H., *A History of Monquhitter* ([Galashiels]: [the author], 1985).

Fraser, William Ruxton, *History of the Parish and Burgh of Laurencekirk* (Edinburgh: Blackwood, 1880).

Gilbert, Heather, *As a Tale that is Told: a Church of Scotland Parish, 1913-1954* [Lumphanan] (Aberdeen: Aberdeen University Press, 1983).

Godsman, James, *Glass, Aberdeenshire: The Story of a Parish* (Aberdeen: Reid, 1970).

Imlach, James, *History of Banff and Familiar Account of its Inhabitants and Belongings* (Banff: Leask, 1868).

Jamieson, Agnes C., *Education in Fraserburgh* ([Fraserburgh]: [the author], 1992).

Kinnear, George H., *The History of Glenbervie* (Montrose: Montrose Standard, 1895).

McLeman, Janet, *Rosehearty As It Was* ([Rosehearty]: [Living Archives Project], [1991]).

Mollyson, Charles A., *The Parish of Fordoun, Chapters in its History; or, Reminiscences of Place and Character* (Aberdeen: Smith/Wyllie, 1893).

Penny, Cecilia, ed., *Stuartfield: Our Place* (Stuartfield: Stuartfield Millennium Group, 2000).

Pirie, James, *The Parish of Cairnie and its Early Connection with Strathbogie* (Banff: Banffshire Journal, 1906).

Porter, William A., *Tarves Lang Syne: The Story of a Scottish Parish* (York: Maxiprint, 1996).

Sinclair, George H., *The History of the Parish of Daviot* (Aberdeen: [the author], [1980]).

Smith, Alexander, *A New History of Aberdeenshire*, 2 vols (Aberdeen: Smith/Blackwood, 1875).

Smith, W., *A Buckie Loon Remembers: Growing up in the Thirties* ([Buckie]: the author, [1998]).

Thomson, James, *Recollections of a Speyside Parish Fifty Years Ago, and Miscellaneous Poems* [Aberlour] (Elgin: Moray & Nairn Newspaper, 1887).

Reminiscence and Comment

Allan, John R., *Summer in Scotland* (London: Methuen, [1938]).

Allan, John R., *North-East Lowlands of Scotland* (1952), 2nd edn (London: Hale, 1974).

Allardyce, John, *Byegone Days in Aberdeenshire: Being a History of the County from a Standpoint Different from that of Previously Published Works* (Aberdeen: Central Press/Milne, 1913).

Beaton, Helen, *At the Back o' Benachie; or, Life in the Garioch in the Nineteenth Century* (Aberdeen: Central Press, 1915; 2nd edn, Milne, 1923).

Brown, Ivor, *Summer in Scotland* (London: Collins, 1952).

Bruce, W. S., *Reminiscences of Men and Manners during the Past Seventy Years* (Aberdeen: Bisset, 1929).

Buchan, David S. C., *St Combs: My Buchan* (Edinburgh: Pentland, 1993).

Cameron, David Kerr, *The Ballad and the Plough: A Portrait of the Life of the Old Scottish Farmtouns* (London: Gollancz, 1978).

Cameron, David Kerr, *Willie Gavin, Crofter Man: Portrait of a Vanished Lifestyle* (London: Gollancz, 1980).

Carnegie, Winnie, *Ugie Pearls: And Other Stories* ([Peterhead]: [Scrogie], [1980])

Carnegie, Winnie, *Gently Flows the Ugie* ([Peterhead]: [Scrogie], [198-]).

Gibson, Chrissie, *Memories of Finzean: Schooldays 1925-1933* ([Aberdeen]: Braw/Grampian, 1997).

Gregor, Walter, *An Echo of the Olden Times from the North of Scotland* (Edinburgh: Menzies, 1874).

Kerr, John, *Memories Grave and Gay: Forty Years of School Inspection* (Edinburgh: Blackwood, 1902).

Lawrence, W. Gordon, ed., *Roots in a Northern Landscape: Celebrations of Childhood in the North East of Scotland* (Edinburgh: Scottish Cultural Press, 1996).

Low, William Leslie, *Vignettes from a Parson's Album* (Dumfries: Mann, 1904).

MacKenzie, R. F., *A Search for Scotland* (London: Collins, 1989).

Ogston, David D., *White Stone Country: Growing up in Buchan* (Edinburgh: Ramsay Head, 1986).

Ogston, David D., *Dry Stone Days* (Edinburgh: Ramsay Head, 1988).

Paul, William, *Past and Present of Aberdeenshire; or, Reminiscences of Seventy Years* (Aberdeen: Smith, 1881).

Rae, Elsie S., *A Waff o' Win' fae Benachie: Country Cameos in Prose and Verse* (Aberdeen: Bisset, 1930).

Stewart, Jean Cantlie, *Pine Trees and the Sky* (Edinburgh: Scottish Cultural Press, 1998).

Thomson, Peter, *A Scotch Student: Memorials of Peter Thomson, Minister of the Free Church, St Fergus* (Edinburgh: MacNiven & Wallace, 1881).

Watson, William, *Glimpses o' Auld Lang Syne* (Aberdeen: Aberdeen University Press, 1905).

Biography

Allan, James Baxter, *Rev. John Duncan, D. D.: Trinity Congregational Church, Aberdeen: A Memoir and a Tribute* (London: Hodder & Stoughton, 1909).

Allan, John R, *Farmer's Boy* (London: Methuen, 1935).

Black, John Sutherland, and George William Chrystal, *The Life of William Robertson Smith* (London: Black, 1912).

Diack, Hunter, *Boy in a Village* (Nottingham: Palmer, 1962).

Fordyce, T. T., *Memoirs of a Provost 1896-1980* (St Andrews: [n.p.], 1981).

Fraser, Amy Stewart, *The Hills of Home* (London, Boston: Routledge & Kegan Paul, 1973).

Fraser, David, ed., *The Christian Watt Papers*, 2nd edn (Collieston, Aberdeenshire: Caledonia, 1988).

Gilbert, Heather, *Awakening Continent: The Life of Lord Mount Stephen*, Volume 1, 1829-91 (Aberdeen: Aberdeen University Press, 1965).

Glennie, Evelyn, *Good Vibrations: My Autobiography* (London: Hutchinson, 1990).

Grant, James, *Alexander Craib, M A: An Appreciation*, reprinted from *Dufftown News*, 8 July 1905 ([Banff]: [1905]).

Jolly, William, *The Life of John Duncan, Scotch Weaver and Botanist* (London: Paul, Trench, 1883).

MacKay, Adam, *Distinguished Sons of Cruden: General Patrick Gordon, Bishop Robert Kilgour, Hon. Thomas Smith, Sir Hugh Gilzean-Reid, Dr. Alexander Bruce* (Peterhead: Scrogie, *Buchan Observer*, 1922).

McBey, James, *The Early Life of James McBey: An Autobiography*, ed. by Nicolas Barker (Oxford: Oxford University Press, 1977).

Mackie, Maitland, *A Lucky Chap: From Orra Loon to Lord Lieutenant: Autobiography of Sir Maitland Mackie* (Methlick: Ardo, 1992).

MacDonald, J. Ramsay, *Wanderings and Excursions* (London: Cape, 1925).

Murison, F. Alexander, *Memoirs of 88 Years, 1847-1934* (Aberdeen: Aberdeen University Press, 1935).

Murray, Isobel, *Jessie Kesson: Writing her Life: A Biography* (Edinburgh: Canongate, 2000).

Nicoll, W. Robertson, *James Macdonnell, Journalist*, new edn (London: Hodder & Stoughton, 1900).

Peter, Tom, *Salthousehead Remembered: An Early Autobiography* (Peterhead: the author, [1994?]).

Smith, Alexander, *Forty Years in Kincardineshire, 1911-1951: A Bothy Loon's Life Story*, 2nd imp. corrected (Collieston, Aberdeenshire: Caledonian, 1990).

Smith, Alice Thiele, *Children of the Manse, Growing up in Rural Aberdeenshire* (Edinburgh: Bellfield, 2004)

Strahan, James, *Andrew Bruce Davidson* (London: Hodder & Stoughton, 1917).

Webster, Jack, *A Grain of Truth: A Scottish Journalist Remembers* (Edinburgh: Harris, 1981).

Wilson, Robert Franklin, 'Life in Banffshire in the Nineteenth Century', *Aberdeen Daily Journal*, 12 March 1902; rpt (Auckland: [n.p.], 1989).

Fiction

Alexander, William, *Johnny Gibb of Gushetneuk: In the Parish of Pyketillim*, 2nd edn (Aberdeen: Walker/Smith, 1871).

Alexander, William (1826-1894), *Rural Life in Victorian Aberdeenshire*, ed. by Ian Carter (Edinburgh: Mercat, 1992).

Alexander, William, *The Laird of Drammochdyle and his Contemporaries; or, Random Sketches Done in Outline with a Burnt Stick* (1865), rpt edn, intro. by William Donaldson (Aberdeen: Aberdeen University Press, 1986).

Cameron, David Kerr, *A Kist of Sorrows* (London: Gollancz, 1987).

Gibbon, Lewis Grassic, *'A Scots Quair'* [a trilogy]: *Sunset Song; Cloud Howe; Grey Granite* (London: Jarrold, 1932-1934).

Gibbon, Lewis, Grassic, *The Thirteenth Disciple: Being Portrait and Saga of Malcolm Maudsley in his Adventure through the Dark Corridor* (London: Jarrold, 1931).

Gibbon, Lewis Grassic, *The Speak of the Mearns: With Selected Short Stories and Essays*, [unfinished] (1931); Edinburgh: Polygon, [1994]).

Kesson, Jessie, *The White Bird Passes* (London: Chatto & Windus, 1958).

Kesson, Jessie, *Glitter of Mica* (London: Chatto & Windus, 1963).

MacDonald, George, *David Elginbrod*, 3 vols (London: Hurst & Blackett, 1863).

MacDonald, George, *Alec Forbes of Howglen*, 3 vols (London: Hurst & Blackett, 1865).

MacDonald, George, *Robert Falconer*, 3 vols (London: Hurst & Blackett, 1868).

Maclean, Neil N., 1874, *Life at a Northern University* [Aberdeen University] (Glasgow: Marr, 1874).

Macpherson, I., 1931, *Shepherds' Calendar* (London: Cape, 1931).

Shepherd, Nan, *The Quarry Wood* (London: Constable, 1928).

Shepherd, Nan, *A Pass in the Grampians* (London: Constable, 1933).

Poetry

Abel, George, 'The Dominie', in *Wylans fae my Wallet*, 2nd edn (Paisley: Gardner, 1916).

Blackhall, Sheena, various, esp, 'The Dominie', in *The Cyard's Kist* (Aberdeen: Rainbow, 1984); 'Buik-Learning', in *The Nor-East Neuk* ([Aberdeen]: Charles Murray Memorial Trust, 1988).

Caie, J. M., 'The Rector', in *'Twixt Hills and Sea: Verse in Scots and English* (Aberdeen: Wyllie, 1939).

Garry, Flora, 'The School at Cairnorrie', in *Bennygoak and Other Poems* (Preston: Akros, 1974).

Gibson, Alexander, 'Uncle William's Sketch – the Dominie', in *Under the Cruisie; or, Saturday Nights at a Buchan Farm in the Middle of the Last Century* (Aberdeen: Wyllie, 1916).

MacDonald, Angus, 'School Days', in *Naethin else tae dae* (Avoch, Rosshire, 1996).

MacDonald, Frances, 'Mrs. Mearns an her Skweel', in *A Drappie Rayne* ([Inverurie]: the author, 1995).

MacKenzie, W. A., 'Shon Campbell' [1894], in *Poetry of North East Scotland,* ed. by James N. Alison (London & Edinburgh: Heinemann, 1976), pp. 84-85.

Mackie, Alastair, 'Primary Teachers, in *Twelve More Scots Poets*, ed. by Charles King & Iain Crichton Smith (London: Stodder & Houghton, 1986).

Milne, Gladys, 'Country School', in *Country Road* (Peterhead: Scrogie, 1984).

Milne, John C., *Poems* (Aberdeen, 1963); new edn (Aberdeen: Aberdeen University Press, 1976).

Morrice, Ken, 'Culture', in *Twal Mile Roon* (Dyce, Aberdeen: Rainbow, 1985).

Murray, Charles, 'It wasna his Wyte' [1929], in *Hamewith: The Complete Poems of Charles Murray* (Aberdeen: Aberdeen University Press for the Charles Murray Memorial Trust, 1979).

Rich, Lillianne Grant, 'The Empty Playground', in *Gweed Gear, Sma' Buik: An Anthology of North East Poetry, Songs and Prose,* ed. by Alistair Taylor & Les Wheeler (Aberdeen: Grampian Regional Council, 1989), pp. 124.

Ritchie, John W., 'George Tough's Squeel', Aberdeen City Libraries Collection (Kinross, 1881).

Symon, Mary, 'The Glen's Muster Roll' [1916], *Deveron Days* (Aberdeen: Wyllie, 1933).

Thom, William [Inverury], *Rhymes and Recollections of a Hand-loom Weaver* (London: Smith, Elder, 1844), new edn (Paisley: Gardner, 1880).

Notes on Contributors

Robert Anderson is Professor of History at the University of Edinburgh. He has written extensively on Scottish education, most notably in *Education and Opportunity in Victorian Scotland, Education and the Scottish People, 1750-1918* and *The Student Community at Aberdeen, 1860-1939.*

Gordon Booth was for many years Educational Psychologist to the Grampian Region. He has recently completed a doctoral thesis on William Robertson Smith and, with Smith's great-great grandniece, Astrid Hess, has prepared an edition of the life of Alice Thiele Smith (a sister) from a recently discovered manuscript: 'Growing Up in Victorian Aberdeenshire'.

Ian Campbell is Professor of Scottish and Victorian Literature at the University of Edinburgh. He has written widely on Scottish literature, especially that of the North-East. His studies include Lewis Grassic Gibbon, Thomas Carlyle, and the Kailyard group.

Derrick McClure is Senior Lecturer in the Department of English at the University of Aberdeen, specialising in Scots literature and language. He has published numerous articles on these topics as well as book length studies of North-East Doric and of Scots in modern poetry.

Peter Murphy was once Head of English at Summerhill Academy, Aberdeen, and is author of the biography of its famous headteacher, R. F. MacKenzie, *A Prophet without Honour.* He is currently serving as Carnoustie's first ever Labour councillor.

David Northcroft was for many years at the Northern College of Education. He is currently carrying out research into the experience of 'growing up and going to school in Scotland'. He is author of *Scots at School.*

Robbie Robertson worked for the Scottish Consultative Council on the Curriculum. In the years leading up to his recent death he was concerned with the areas of Information Technology and 'human rights'.

Douglas Young was for many years at Northern College of Education. He researches the literature of the North-East and is author of a study of Lewis Grassic Gibbon, *Beyond the Sunset,* and also of Ian Macpherson, *Highland Search.*

Index